SHEMHAZAI'S GAME

A Novel

Harry Ringel

www.auctuspublishers.com

Copyright 2020 Harry Ringel
Book and cover design by Sarah Eldridge

Published by Auctus Publishers
606 Merion Avenue, First Floor
Havertown, PA 19083
Printed in the United States of America

Shemhazai's Game is a work of fiction. It is a novel of fantasy, many of whose characters are drawn from Jewish myth, legend, and mysticism. The situations in which these figures are placed are purely the result of the author's creative fiction. Similarly, all other characters and events in the novel are products of the author's imagination. Any resemblance to real events, specific locations, or persons, living or dead, is coincidental.

All rights reserved. Scanning, uploading, and distribution of this book via the internet or via any other means without permission in writing from its publisher, Auctus Publishers, is illegal and punishable by law. Please purchase only authorized electronic edition.

ISBN 978-1-7327882-8-2 (electronic)
ISBN 978-1-7327882-7-5 (print)

Library of Congress Control Number: 2019957502

Foreword

One of the many Kabbalah-related terms that appear in *Shemhazai's Game* is *"Chitzonim."* On a person-to-person level, this Hebrew word may be used to mean "outsiders"—ones who stand apart from others in a negative way. It is a term I know well. In my Yeshiva school of study, we would speak of a type of student who wears the cleanest of white shirts but who never actually learns. Such a student may look good to his teacher, but his laziness and lack of true diligence were well known to his fellow students. "He's a real *Chitzon*," we would say.

There is a higher level of meaning to the word, one to be found in a variety of Kabbalistic sources. Here it refers to forces within ourselves that entrap us in the negative aspects of this world. We become "externalities"—exiled not only to others, but to G-d. And to ourselves. Like parasites, these *Chitzonim* feed on our very life force. They stand as obstacles to every avenue to goodness, even to holiness, accessible to us in our lives on this earth. Great or small, extensive or trivial, each negative act strengthens the *Chitzonim* within us. Once created, their hold is powerful and profound.

We all wage battle with the *Chitzonim* daily. Sometimes we prevail, sometimes not. But the more the negative "wins," the more forces of *Chitzonim* we spawn in ourselves. They separate us from unity with G-d, from harmony with each other. We truly become externalities—outsiders to our own world.

Similarly, *Shemhazai's Game* offers meanings on two levels. On one level, its plot chronicles the animosity between two middle-aged characters: a bitter, frustrated woman and the mentally handicapped brother for whom she has had to care for decades. Yet the book also dramatizes this ongoing war that each and every one of us carries on against the forces of the *Chitzonim*. The arena for this struggle is depicted in the fantasy framework of *Shemhazai's Game*.

Shemhazai's Game has other goals. Yes, it is a novel, and yes, its story does involve characters who progress through what is fundamentally a Jewish fantasy. As a "good read," replete with character conflicts and surprises in plot development, it does succeed as fiction. Yet author Harry Ringel has another purpose in mind. He wants the reader to become aware of what he terms "the Other Judaism"—a path through Jewish faith that parallels, without eclipsing or denying, the importance of traditional Jewish knowledge and practice. The novel is enriched throughout by comments and quotes taken, both directly and indirectly, from key sources in Jewish mysticism. In this capacity, it serves as a road map for any individual, Jewish or non-Jewish, who seeks to launch his or her journey along this less known, but no less vital, avenue of spirit.

Shemhazai's Game also carries a message that may not have been so obvious to its author. As a rabbi, my duties involve me in the community in various ways. I have counseled drug addicts, people in prisons. I have met with teenagers alienated from their families, couples considering divorce. In many of these situations, I have thought to myself, "Perhaps they should read *Shemhazai's Game*. Maybe somewhere in its story, they will find a path that leads to some oasis of peace, of truth for themselves." The book mirrors the conflicts we all face in our human relationships, our struggles with the material, our groping for the spiritual.

Reflected in its fantasy, I too have glimpsed reality. I have glimpsed truth. *Shemhazai's Game* addresses the *Chitzon* in us all.

Rabbi Shaya Deitsch, Lubavitch of Montgomery County, Fort Washington, Pennsylvania

Preface

The Other Judaism

The door to the Other Judaism opened for me through the Book of Numbers, Chapter 11, to be precise. It was a Saturday morning. I was participating in a study group that was discussing *Beha'alotecha*, the weekly Torah portion in which this chapter is found. The Jewish people have begun their 40 years of wandering in the wilderness. Jethro, Moses' father-in-law, has warned Moses that tending the needs of the 600,000 or so people who have left Egypt is too much for any individual, even one of Moses' stature. Seventy elders are appointed. God descends in a cloud and bestows upon them the spirit of prophecy. Some of this spirit spills over into the main camp where two of the elders, Eldad and Medad, have remained. Much to their surprise, they start spouting God-inspired prophesies. When Moses is told what's happening, he's happy about it. Everyone should have such power to channel the word of the Lord, he tells the messenger.

Most in the study group focused their questions on other elements in *Beha'alotecha*—the Tabernacle's candelabrum, the Levites' service, Passover observance in the desert.

Me, I wanted to know more about Eldad and Medad.

The parting of the Red Sea, the giving of the Ten Commandments—these were already as much a part of me as dreidels on Chanukah and groggers on Purim. My Jewish upbringing had taught me to look upon these Divine interventions into human existence as near-folklorish islands in the ocean of historical, ethical, and worship-related values that was the Judaism of my childhood. Mine was a Judaism built on rational thought derived from the stories of the patriarchs and matriarchs, the redemption from slavery in Egypt, the entering of the Promised Land, and beyond. Even now, this Judaism remains a vital part of me. But only a part.

Then along come Eldad and Medad. Along comes the Other Judaism, as I have come to call it—a realm of Judaism that is the domain not of analytical thought but of intuition; not of logic but its opposite, whatever that may be. The secular world has placed many names upon this dichotomy within human consciousness—Jung's synchronicity vs. cause-and-effect concept and Jaynes' bicameralism theory, to name but two. Put simply, it is the belief that this dichotomy expresses itself in two manifestations: sequenced/conscious thought and random/subconscious thought. For *Shemhazai's Game*'s purposes, let me label its presence within Jewish belief and behavior as Left-Brain Judaism ("tradition"-based) and Right-Brain ("mysticism"-based) Judaism—this latter, the Other Judaism.

Where does the Other Judaism find its beginnings? With the Oral Law, given side by side with the written Torah at Sinai? With the works of the *Pseudepigrapha* (so called because their "authors" are Biblical personages, or surrogates for same), of which *I Enoch* was a prime source for *Shemhazai's Game*? It is a literature that swarms, collectively, with angels, saintly or fallen; demons, gullible or crafty; visions of apocalyptic confrontations of good and evil; tours of the Seven Heavens and *Sheol/Gehenna*; Messianic visions of the End Times. And so much more.

Does one move from there to the *Zohar* and *Sefer Yetzirah*? Both are key Kabbalistic writings. Both are not cozy reads, the type of books one can cart to the beach and simply enjoy. The pathways of learning in these texts are not often traveled by minds seeking rational explanations; it requires no small amount of mental gymnastics to position oneself correctly to their teachings. Daniel Matt's twelve-volume Pritzer edition of the *Zohar* provides not only Professor Matt's carefully researched translation but also his extensive and lucid annotations at the bottom of each page. The *Sefer Yetzirah* is available with translation and commentary by Rabbi Aryeh Kaplan, whose own advocacy of Right-Brain Judaism is articulated throughout his many works, including *Jewish Meditation*, from which the following quote is taken:

> The ostensible goal of the Enlightenment [the Age of Reason]...was to raise the intellectual level of Judaism, and positive as this may have been, it was often done at the expense of other Jewish values. The first values to fall by the wayside were Jewish mysticism in general and meditation in particular. (page 40)

Rabbi Kaplan's analysis is quite at home in a modern cultural context more inclined to accept exploration of mysticism, meditation, and the like. Yet a century earlier, in his landmark work *History of the Jews*, Heinrich Graetz expressed this opinion of the Other Judaism:

> ...there insinuated into the general life of the Jews a false doctrine which, although new, styled itself a primitive inspiration; although un-Jewish, called itself a genuine teaching of Israel; and although springing from error, entitled itself the only truth. The rise of this secret lore... was called *Kabbala* (tradition).... Discord was the mother of this monstrosity, which has ever been the cause of schism. (vol. III, page 457)

Graetz may have had other, perhaps even justifiable, axes to grind—the continued prevalence among Jewish people of superstitious practices, the misplaced hope in false messiahs that had gone on for centuries. Regardless, by the turn of the nineteenth century to the twentieth, the Other Judaism lay buried under years of Left-Brain Judaic thought. In ensuing decades, it has been uncovered, cleaned up, read and studied and even revered—not at the expense of Left-Brain Judaism, but often in addition to it, and in many cases as an amplification of it.

In the post-1960's world of my adulthood, it has not been too far a stretch to view human consciousness in general, and Jewish consciousness in particular, as flowing from two disparate streams only too prone, on given occasions, for reasons that may or may not be explainable, to spill into each other. Say what one will of the limitations of the counterculture of the sixties or of the New Age Judaism that at least in part sprang from it, both have widened the doors to further acceptance of the Other Judaism within the collective Jewish mindset.

My primary contemporary sources in researching *Shemhazai's Game* included *The Encyclopedia of Jewish Myth, Magic, and Mysticism*, by Rabbi Geoffrey Dennis; *Tree of Souls: The Mythology* of Judaism, by Howard Schwartz; and, earlier, *The Legends of the Jews*, by Louis Ginzberg. Gershom Scholem's scholarly writings are a Left-Brain voyage into the philosophical and spiritual landscapes of Right-Brain Judaism, guided by an impassioned and informed master. In his work, Rabbi Adin Steinsaltz manages to link the spiritual struggles of twenty-first-century humankind to various texts of Kabbalistic tradition. He doesn't talk down to you. He talks into you.

Chabad Judaism values observance of the 613 *mitzvot* that characterize traditional Jewish practice. Yet its Judaism also hears and heeds the voice of Jewish mysticism. Without the guidance of Lubavitch of Montgomery County's Rabbi Shaya Deitsch, I never would have found my way to Rabbi Schneur Zalman of Liadi's seminal *Tanya*, Jacob Immanuel Schochet's *Mystical Concepts in Chassidism*, or Lubavitcher Rebbe Menachem M. Schneerson's Torah commentaries.

I would be remiss were I not to add—well, confess—that *Shemhazai's Game* falls woefully short in two ways. First of all, it barely scratches the surface of the depth of thought given by rabbis, scholars, and others to numerous Jewish concepts and figures included in the novel. Lilith legends abound—the tales would fill several bookshelves. *Shekhinah* lore would stock an entire store. The same holds true of Azazel, Asmodeus, Tubal-Cain, Naamah, and other characters found in Part II. All are composites, to a greater or lesser extent; all are grounded responsibly (I hope) in the various sources.

Secondly, *Shemhazai's Game* scarcely touches, if at all, on many other topics that fall within the province of the Other Judaism. Reincarnation, alchemy, *gematria*, interpretation of planetary movements, spirit possession, astral projection—all and more are present in one corner of Judaism or another. To borrow a phrase from the Christian Bible (John 14:2, to be precise): "In my Father's house there are many mansions." Judaism is, indeed, a faith of many mansions.

The Other Judaism isn't simply an eccentric offshoot of traditional Judaism. It has its own set of branches that have grown, and continue to grow, from the same trunk that collectively forms Judaism. At times, the branches of Left-Brain and Right-Brain Judaism expand in separate directions; at times, they intersect and intertwine. When we speak of them as two Judaisms, we are analyzing realms of belief and tradition that are not mutually exclusive. In Talmud alone, one can find precise examinations of what makes a *sukkah* kosher or not kosher, side by side with equally detailed comments on the functions of demons. Many within the religion have seen Left-Brain and Right-Brain Judaism as joining hands, not raising fists.

Shemhazai's Game is at most a beginning. For me, it has been one of infinite value. There is so much more to read and absorb, to experience, by which to be illuminated. It is my hope that this novel provides the reader with a few steps in that direction.

Harry Ringel

GLOSSARY NOTE TO THE READER

Every effort has been made to explain Judaic/Kabbalistic terms in the flow of the narrative. A glossary of key terms is also available for readers in the final pages of this book.

THE KABBALISTIC TREE OF LIFE

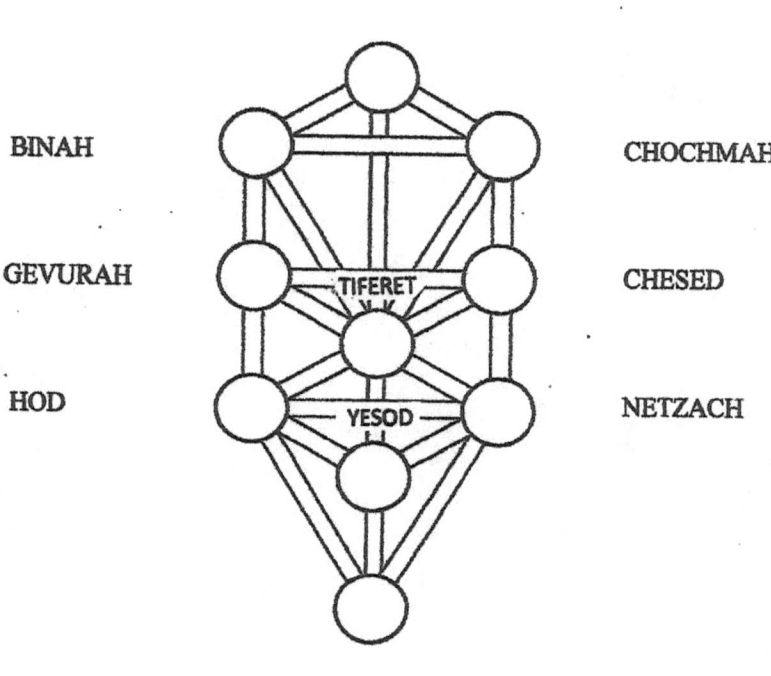

"When men began to increase on earth and daughters were born to them, the sons of God saw how beautiful the daughters of men were and took wives from among those that pleased them.... It was then, and later too, that the *Nephilim* appeared on earth—when the divine beings cohabited with the daughters of men, who bore them offspring."

—Genesis 6, 1-4

"Man's two urges or drives, for good and for evil, are implanted within him as possibilities of action, just as the qualities of love and severity are present in God Himself....We learn here that evil is nothing other than that which isolates and removes things from their unity.... Severity, as a restrictive quality, tends to seek independent existence.... So long as man absorbs this separation into his being..., he creates inauthentic, false systems of reality...."

—*On the Mystical Shape of the Godhead*, Gershom Scholem

Part I

CHAPTER 1

The screaming follows Debbie as she leaves Lowery Middle School. It has stalked the corridors of her awareness long after the boy whose eye had been kicked out was taken away by the paramedics. Her secret gnaws at her insides, its fangs still in her as she drives away.

She was the sole witness. It happened at the far end of the corridor she is assigned to watch as hall monitor. Most violence in this "Turnaround School," as Lowery has been rather optimistically labeled, unfolds in too much haste to be prevented. Not so today. Tall and muscular, sealed in quiet, eighth-grade Korean football player Josh Kim falls into conflict with Derek Winslow, whose conspicuous smallness has always been compensated for, at least in Derek's mind, by a sneering voice of accusation heard by many yet tolerated by few.

No one likes Derek. No one knows Josh, though he is on the football team. All issues of social hierarchy vanish under Derek's cries after Josh finally responds to Derek's unceasing taunts at their lockers by pushing him to the floor. Derek lies, spewing protests, on his left side. Josh stands over him. In one well-trained move (learned, it later becomes clear, in the karate class he attends on Saturdays), he rises from the ground and, with a high-pitched squealing release of power, drives the point of his cocked boot straight into the eye of the fallen boy.

While Debbie watched. She stood there, halfway down the hall, locked in place by the voice within her that says, watch death, watch misfortune unfold. Just watch.

Later she sits with Josh in the principal's office. She takes in the narrative that Josh supplies, his voice soft and precise, his account halting as the words exit his accustomed quiet. "He is always after me at my locker. He jacks me up from behind with his knee. He spills my books when I turn around. For months, he goads me to fight him then runs off. I try to ignore him. Today I lost it." His great shoulders heave, sealing the inevitable. And shaming Debbie further for her silence.

Now problems await her at the other end of the day. She must rush home. To baby brother Jacob, who has spent the day entirely alone.

She pulls into the Kroger parking lot and hurries into the supermarket. Derek's bleats of agony follow her down the wine aisle. She cannot stop seeing the bright red blood that dribbled through Derek's cupped hand, then down his cheek as his sneakers spun him round and round on the hallway floor. She tries to replace the image with the red of the bottle of kosher wine she now carries to Kroger's bread aisle. The separation of focus does not distance her from what she has done. Or not done. Nor does she find distraction in rummaging among the store-packaged challah rolls for a bag with one of several kosher emblems for which Rabbi Seth Hartman, the young leader of Broadview Chabad, has told her to search.

Friday night. She will try her first Jewish Sabbath. Maybe it will help. Maybe. "The glow of the candles will absorb the cares of the week." Rabbi Hartman's wife, Rebecca, has smiled this encouragement to Debbie. She is a woman of imposing largeness, Rebecca Hartman, taller than her diminutive weed of a boy-man husband, wide enough to contain two of him. Softened by the spirit of uplift in her gentle brown eyes, her size serves not to intimidate but to reassure.

Debbie doubts that today's events will absorb to anywhere. Her shame recedes only as she is rushing her bagged items through the main door of her apartment building. Rather, it is shoved to the background by cries of a different order. Howls of delight these are, of bloodthirsty relish. Her brother Jacob's cries. Over some moment in some violence-drenched DVD that Mrs. Benederet, Jacob's paid companion until yesterday, must have smuggled into their home before Debbie let her go.

Debbie instantly recognizes the signals. First, Jacob's laugh escalates to a donkey's bray, hee-haw snorts that more than once have brought down the wrath of their high-strung female neighbor upstairs. It is a good thing that this neighbor works all day. Otherwise, she would be down here right now, hands on her Mallomars-fed hips, threatening yet again to contact the landlord, to pursue eviction, "if your inconsiderate racket does not cease." Such are her exact words, delivered with ritualistic slowness each time she appears, a ceremony completed by Debbie's contriteness, her promise that it will not happen again. Which of course it does.

Then comes the silence. Jacob has heard the noisy clap of the building's main door, the slap of his sister's flats along the common hallway. When Debbie enters, Jacob will be sitting on the living room floor, before the television, dutifully watching one of the "appropriate" discs on which they have agreed for the day. The behavior is a relic from the days when Debbie was beginning to lose her trust for Mrs. Benederet as a daytime companion for Debbie's savant syndrome brother. Returned from work, Debbie would find Mrs. Benederet seated in the kitchen, her purse just closing to hide evidence of the latest violence-gorged DVD with which she has "liberated" Jacob from Debbie the Warden, Jacob's tyrant sister. *I let him breathe*, Mrs. Benederet's timed blinks would say.

"And I let you go," Debbie had finally responded, late yesterday afternoon, when she discovered, beneath Jacob's kitchen-table chair, a luridly illustrated comic book entitled *Sisters of Nightfall*. "It has its own morality," was Mrs. Benederet's sole justification for the purchase. For Debbie it was the last straw. She paid the woman her final full week's salary and told her not to return.

Yesterday had been too late to phone for a last-minute Friday replacement. This once, she had to leave Jacob home by himself. The arrangement cannot last; the problems will quickly worsen. On Monday, Debbie will call a different caregiver service. She will stay home, sealed inside, this entire weekend. With Jacob. Her 37 year-old idiot savant brother. It is the term for his condition which, in her bitterness of heart, Debbie prefers to savant syndrome.

####

The living room floor radiates neatness: oppressive, tyrannical, Jacob's one control in a home otherwise run, at least on its surface, by Debbie. It is all Jacob's things: the "safe" DVD movies Debbie has purchased for him, the 45 rpm records (all oldies), the video games (mostly *Star Wars*). She steps gingerly among the carefully ordered stacks. Toppling one of them would catapult Jacob into a frenzy of reorganization, coupled with recriminations screeched at his clumsy sister. The floor is criss-crossed by a defiant cluster of wires and cables connecting her younger brother's devices to the television across from which he sits.

The only sign of mess is the lunch she made this morning. In the refrigerator, she left for Jacob a tuna salad sandwich, shorn free of crusts, encased in plastic wrap. The half-finished sandwich now lies not on the plate but on the floor, its gummy residue intermingling with the shag carpet. His glass of grape juice has spilled to a stain. It does not matter. Debbie will be paying to replace the carpet when the axe falls, as it no doubt soon will, and they vacate this latest of their parade of dwellings. The building superintendent has warned her as much during one of his landlord-mandated drop-ins to register the upstairs neighbor's complaint about Jacob's racket. He is a simple man, tall and gaunt with weary eyes, sun-leathered skin, and a nose that hawks over sorrow-thinned lips; a human being of working-class origins, one exhausted by the demands of his own chaotic family life, to which he has alluded; a person given neither by his nature nor by his age (closer to sixty than fifty, Debbie has figured) to delivering ultimatums.

"What she *really* needs is—" once he had tried to leaven the warning he bore by hinting at the reason he would suggest for the upstairs neighbor's obsessive focus on Jacob's noise. He had stopped himself, recognizing the impropriety of such a remark. He'd had no need to finish; too well, Debbie had understood.

At the center of the living room floor sits Jacob. He has taken off the pants and long-sleeve shirt in which Debbie dressed him this morning. He wears only a white tank shirt and jet-black boxer shorts checkered with green faces of Yoda from *Star Wars*. He is watching *The Three Stooges*.

Jacob is Debbie's younger brother by three years. Though 37, he remains, still and always, baby brother Jacob. His short height no doubt has fed his identification with Yoda, as has his wish, however opaque, that his savant side transcend his idiot side and merge into full fusion with Yoda. Miss Nancy, a nurse at Jacob's pill-prescribing psychiatrist's office, once commented that he has the face of a "dark cherub," by which she must have meant the combination of his five-feet-four-inch height, his sparkling black eyes, his rounded cheeks, and his lips pursed in perpetual wonder at what parades before him, which usually is nothing. Of that Debbie feels quite certain.

Jacob should not have lived. He surprised his pediatric physician by surviving past two weeks. "He could die anytime," this same woman told the Formans, in an effort to temper the inaccuracy of her prognosis. That was almost four decades ago. Half of which Debbie has spent caring for her brother. "Autistic savant," their father would pronounce, whenever the term slipped into family discussions. Or, in Doc Forman's final years, savant syndrome. Congenital left hemisphere damage with acquired right hemisphere compensation.

"An idiot savant is what you really mean," teenaged Debbie once blurted when their father had asked her for the thousandth time to "man the crow's nest" for baby brother Jacob while he put in extra hours at the hospital—"to keep the wolf from the door," he would say, but in actuality, Debbie had always suspected, to avoid spending time at a house permanently dimmed by the demands of Jacob's handicap and the premature passing of their mother from breast cancer. For the crow's nest's sake, Debbie had earned her bachelor's degree at nearby Emory University. She had always assumed her caring for Jacob to be temporary, even after their father had persuaded her, despite her high grades, strong recommendations, and acceptance to two Ivy League law schools, to return to Emory for her Doctor of Juridical Science degree. Naturally given to the enclosures of study and research, Debbie had constructed her days around preparing for her dissertation and looking after Jacob.

After law school, the temporary morphed into the permanent. What could Debbie say? Was it their mother's fault that she had shown the courage to give birth to Jacob even after tests revealed his health issues? Could Elise Forman be criticized that breast cancer had passed the burden of tending Jacob into their egghead daughter's hands? Doc Forman (as he preferred to be called, though his days were spent isolated in medical research, not in contact with the ill) had tried a parade of in-home caregivers but dismissed them all. Slowly, the hope in Doc Forman's once-spirited gaze had atrophied. More and more he had turned to Debbie, with less pleading and increased expectation that she simply accept her duty. Then a heart attack claimed Doc Forman. And permanent care for Jacob fell into the lap of his dutiful older sister in her twenties; of his routine-bound sister, in her thirties; of his spinster sister, recently turned forty. With no one else to share her store-bought birthday cake except Jacob. Who mashed up his slice instead of simply saying that the icing was too sweet.

####

The 1,000-piece puzzle Debbie bought for Jacob yesterday sits on the card table against the living room wall. Completed, it replicates the pointillism of Monet's *Water Lilies*, the abstract bleeding of its blues into greens having done little to slow the pace at which Jacob assembled it. She should give up. She should recognize that jigsaw puzzles no more fill Jacob's time than the Rubik's Cubes she occasionally brought him. She would marvel at the speed with which he would twist the Cube until its sections aligned. His actions seemed all impulse, devoid of thought. Yet this same Jacob cannot fit a key into a door. He cannot find his way alone around the block. He cannot dress himself. The action of putting a leg through trousers confounds him. The challenge of tying a shoe lace reduces him to bawling paroxysms of defeat. She buys for him slip-ons, which he puts on the wrong feet, but not without first contemplating the slopes and contours of their rubbery shapes. He cannot count change, so he does not make purchases. Yet he has learned to read, albeit without help from any tutor.

He does not notice her entering today. Or better to say, he does not take note of it. The Three Stooges have initiated one of their timed rounds of head bops and hair pulls and finger pokes; the vaudeville-perfected timing of their actions hypnotizes Jacob, enthralls him. His fixed gaze does not so much as flicker as Debbie stoops beside him to gather the remains of his decimated tuna sandwich and toppled juice glass. Different brays burst out of him now. Honks of delight at the Stooges' violence, these lend painful counterpoint to the shrieks of pain she had heard at school. They lash her with what seems distinct purpose: to ridicule her shrinking from what she witnessed. Her resentment flares; with a peremptory shift of the Kroger bag in her arms, she passes between Jacob and the television set. He continues to ignore her, his only concession to her presence a curt angling of the head so that he misses no moment of what Moe is doing to Curly or Curly to Larry.

Her pulse quickens as she enters the kitchen. Fresh hope, a new path, lies before her. It is Friday afternoon. The Hartmans have tutored her on welcoming the Jewish Sabbath, and this is to be Debbie's first.

"Visualize a wall," Rebecca Hartman told her. "Repeat one word. Separation. Make the word live in your mind and heart. It will divide the trials of the week from the peace of the day of rest. Eventually it will become a part of your weekly cycle."

Debbie readies the table as Rebecca instructed. First, she clears away the week's accumulated postal bric-a-brac: bills, mostly, and the avalanche of charity requests. What of the comic books which pacify Jacob as they sit, together yet separate, at dinner? *Donald Duck, Uncle Scrooge, Chip and Dale*—these are his favorites, among the ones Debbie brings home as approved for him to read. Unlike the *Superman* and *Batman* comics of their childhoods, the Disney ones do not seem to have changed. And they do coax Jacob through meals blessed with silence. But what about tonight? One evening a week, can't Jacob do without them? She transfers the stack to the extra kitchen chair by her own seat. Then she wipes down the table with a new sponge. Finished, she stares at the clean surface. A faint voice of renewal whispers through her. It is blunted by the echo of Derek Winslow's screeches, Josh Kim's kung fu pirouette.

From a high cabinet she takes down the box of Sabbath supplies the Hartmans have given her. Sabbath Survival Kit, Rebecca has scrawled on the cardboard lid. Inside the box is a how-to pamphlet. *An Oasis in Time*, it is called. The meaning of the title is easy to discern. It puts a positive spin on every negative she has read of the "burdens" of the Jewish Sabbath as kept by the Orthodox. Thou shalt not tear toilet paper. Or cause a spark to be born in a car's ignition. Or break a sweat. Or turn on a light. Instead, use a timer. Hire a Sabbath *goy*. A repulsive word, that one. *Goy*. Not *Christian*. As her father had taught her never to say "Jew" when referring to a Jewish person. "It's one shade shy of *Yid*, two shy of *kike*." And she had nodded. His parents had been Orthodox. Doc Forman had run to Reform. She to nothing. Until tonight. Until the flimsy walls of her routines had begun to collapse. Until her encroaching mortality had driven her to consider dipping at least a baby toe into the waters of Jewish ritual. Why not make of one day an oasis? Everything else had failed. And she could not accept the position of the nihilists, as she had read them to be called, that we come into a godless world, we do our good acts and our bad ones, then die and go down into dirt or up in cremation. There has to be more. There has to be renewal. She has to believe in that. Otherwise—

From the box she takes out the pair of blue-lacquered candlesticks, the small silver-plated goblet. She moves the candlesticks to the center of the table and stands a candle in each.

Their tallness seems dignified and strong, their whiteness pleasing to behold. Derek's shrieks recede somewhat. The impression of Josh's fatalistic shrug fades. The high-strung neighbor upstairs no longer fills the doorway with the shape of her complaint. The building manager stays distant. The silence spreads to the living room. Has Jacob sensed his sister's intention to make this evening different? Has God recognized Debbie's efforts and intervened? Has He read her intention—*kavanah* is the word Rebecca used—and helped her along? Or has Jacob simply fallen asleep?

She unscrews the kosher wine cap and fills the goblet to its brim. She knows nothing of the significance of drinking wine to greet the Sabbath. The transliterated prayer in *An Oasis in Time* simply blesses God for bringing forth the fruit of the vine. But why bless God? Shouldn't He be blessing us? *An Oasis in Time* offers no explanation, only the blessing itself. She will have to ask the Hartmans. She uses one of her own plates for the two challah rolls. Why two? She will have to ask. She covers the two challah rolls with a paper napkin. It is all she has.

She opens *An Oasis in Time* to its first page, which begins: "The Parental Blessing. Of children by their parents." She hurries on.

The Song of Songs is next. It takes up ten pages in the pamphlet. She skims it, lighting on a few sensuous phrases that surprise her. "O that he would kiss me with his lips... On my bed at night I seek him whom my soul loves." A footnote explains: "On Friday evening God embraces His bride the *Shekhinah*, returned from her exile in the turmoil of *Malchut*."

Debbie is confused. What exile? Who is *Shekhinah*? Where is *Malchut*?

She flips more pages to preview them. Her attention lights on a shorter section entitled, "Welcoming the Sabbath Queen." The *Shekhinah* is mentioned. Again, this *Shekhinah*. "Come meet the Bride, come welcome the Sabbath," it begins. "Come forth from the ruins... the vale of your tears... why are you downcast... God will show you mercy... He will rejoice like a groom for you, His Bride, the Sabbath Queen. Come meet the Bride, come welcome the Sabbath."

Another footnote: "The exiled *Shekhinah*, the Sabbath Queen, unites once more with her Husband the King, her Divine Lover, on Sabbath Eve."

God as a Lover? Debbie understands nothing of such foreign terrain. Yet she cannot prevent images from taking form. Of sexual union at a level far higher than human. Far more ethereal than what most men have in mind. She has tried so hard not to think of men. It has been years, close to a decade, since one even tried. *What you really need is—*

She slaps the pages forward. At last she comes to it:

"There was evening and there was morning—the sixth day."

Here she will begin.

####

At the door to his bedroom Debbie stands, observing her younger brother Jacob, her baby brother, not moving, asleep on his side.

"Jacob," she calls. He does not stir. Again she calls his name, the snap in her speech intended to prod him awake. *We are going to try something a little different tonight,* she thinks to say. *We're going to welcome the Sabbath. Together.* "It's time for dinner," she adds instead.

With a rare grunt of acquiescence, Jacob rouses himself from his bed. Debbie hurries ahead of him to the kitchen. She wants to be in position when he enters. She wants to face him, her encouraging smile providing the shorthand which, on occasion, has allowed his savant side to embrace a truth that his idiot side would reject. He comes in, still bleary from rest. His half-lidded eyes take in the transformed table. For a moment he says nothing. Then he asks:

"Where's my comics?"

Before Debbie can answer, Jacob stomps out of the room. He returns, a comic gripped in one fist. He slaps it down on the kitchen table, seats himself, and sweeps the comic open to the first page.

"Can you put that away? Just for a few minutes? You can read it when we eat."

He closes the comic but remains seated, head down, eyes latched to the cover. *Sisters of Nightfall,* of all comics. Two wing-plumed females perch like birds of prey on a boulder. Side by side, they face the reader but peer down in concern at two words cried by an unseen voice in blood-red letters dripping down the bottom third of the cover: RESCUE ME. Their figures bloom in voluptuous counterpoint to Debbie's tall, lean shape—scrawny, she has been called, though by whom she can't remember. The blonde Sister has ivory skin and vibrant blue eyes; her darker counterpart is more mysterious, more threatening, her severe gaze lent power by her chestnut complexion and flames of red hair. Their faces are alert and vital, free of the creases that worry and age, guardedness and self-denial, have etched into Debbie's features. High boots accent the fullness of their thighs. Debbie owns two pairs of low-heel pumps that wear on their inner edges from her slightly knock-kneed manner of walking. Both Sisters boast elaborate manes of hair that spill over breasts coyly concealed. Debbie's small breasts already give in to the incipient sag of her 40-year-old body. A soup bowl of black hair rims her forehead, the tops of her ears. "Sheepdog chic," an opposing lawyer once called it, in an effort to rattle her concentration before a trial. His ploy had worked.

To Debbie's knowledge, it is Jacob's only copy—the final legacy of Mrs. Benederet's "free poor Jacob" crusade. "The characters in *Sisters of Nightfall* are patterned after Lilith and Naamah from Jewish mythology," Debbie's Internet research informed her last night. "Fallen from grace, they seek redemption by traveling, in each new issue, to a different pocket of Earth where forces of pure evil plan to poison humankind. *Sisters of Nightfall* is often cited as a prime example of all that is prurient in comic book art, in its fetishizing of female anatomy, as well as the gleeful nature of its splatter-driven violence." Last night Debbie tried to confiscate it. Jacob's howls had brought down more neighbors than just the woman upstairs.

She does not try now. Five measured breaths, she takes. From the abdomen. Diaphragmatic breathing, it is called. To control anger. It has helped in the past when Jacob has pushed her too far. It works well enough now for her to gather her thoughts. "Beginnings are always difficult": both Hartmans have quoted this axiom from the Talmud. For Debbie. "Who one day will find her inner Devorah," Rebecca has smiled, adding, "as your Jacob may find his inner Israel. As Jacob becomes Israel in the book of Genesis. But not overnight."

Maybe Debbie can talk to Jacob across the week. Explain the virtue of separation, how he might enjoy his movies and video games and 45rpm records even more if he withdraws from them for 24 hours. Or twelve. Or just overnight. But savants relate to the concrete, one of the cognitive therapy specialists had told their father, before the family had given up on psychologists.
So start with the candles.

She strikes a kitchen match. With no more glances at Jacob, she recites not the transliterated Hebrew but its English translation in the pamphlet.

"Blessed art Thou, O Lord our God, King of the Universe, Who has sanctified us by Thy commandments, and instructed us to kindle the Sabbath lights." She lowers the match. Each wick absorbs the flame and rises, as if awakening to life.

What comes next is the part to which she has looked forward all week. "Circle the candles three times with your hands," Rebecca has instructed. "Cup the palms to your face. Cover your eyes and pray. Anything that comes into your mind. Any longing, any supplication. Any pain that weighs upon your heart."

Hands against her eyes, Debbie prays. For God to reveal Himself in her life. *Our lives. For strength to deal with Jacob. For Derek Winslow's eye, for Josh Kim's shrug.* She prays to know what to say when the building manager appears to evict them. *For strength to face the coming week,* she prays. *For peace. With Jacob. For deliverance. From Jacob. For respite from Jacob. For the wherewithal to shepherd Jacob when—*

Jacob's raucous bray shatters her prayer. It mocks the very moment at which her spiritual self has opened, reached upwards, like the flames on the Sabbath candles, towards the mystical, the ineffable, THE WHATEVER.

Her hands drop into fists.

"Shut up! Shut up! Shut up!"

Already Jacob is up from his chair. A howl bleeds out of him as he flees the kitchen. Debbie waits before following. *Forgive me,* she will say. *Try to understand. After the week I have had, what I have seen today, my nerves are shot, simply shot—*

The television blares, louder than ever. Some action TV show regurgitates explosions, gunshots, screeching wheels. Out of this spew of barbarisms knocks on the door emerge, their increasing loudness drawing Debbie from the kitchen, through the living room to their apartment's front door, which opens, as she knew it would, to the upstairs neighbor, plump and freshly bathed, in silk pajamas and terrycloth bathrobe.

"Tomorrow this ends." She intends to frighten Debbie with her calm. All Debbie can think to do is nod.

The television is off. Jacob is in his room now, his light off as well. Exhausted, Debbie returns to the kitchen. She has no desire to see him, no energy to ponder how to suture the rift in their universe that her rage has created. The comic book, still on the table, leers up at her. Mocks her. She longs to crumple it, trash it. Instead, she mashes the two challah rolls into balls and flings them to the floor. The unsipped wine she empties into the sink. Then she turns off the overhead kitchen light and just sits. Her crushed gaze seeks out the candles. One has wilted in the kitchen's warmth. She watches in the same frozen passivity of earlier today as the wax dribbles, the wick droops, breaks off then falls, is extinguished. The second candle has begun to melt as well. She observes it for a moment. Bending forward, she blows it out.

CHAPTER 2

Saturday morning. The rap on her door comes earlier than expected. She throws on her bathrobe, slips on her tattered bedroom slippers, and pads past Jacob, already seated before the blaring TV, to the door. *Who will be our bearer of bad tidings?* She expects the upstairs neighbor and the building superintendent, allied behind a formal letter from the landlady requesting that they meet first thing Monday. She knows enough about this esoteric nook of law to feel assured that they can't demand immediate eviction. A formal complaint has to go to the police. So maybe that is who it is. A burly policeman, grumpy to have been called to a task as trivial as a complaint about a barking dog. She opens the door and looks up. And up. Debbie is a tall woman, 5`10" at last measurement. But her visitor is much taller.

The man is dressed as an Orthodox Jewish individual of Seth Hartman's Chabad. The belted waist of his long black caftan is level with Debbie's chest. His *yarmulke* skullcap brushes the top of the door sill. He is very thin, with broad shoulders that frame him like wings. He seems at once massive yet ethereal, imposing yet delicate. His black beard tumbles down his face, without the sidelocks of some Orthodox men she has seen. His exposed skin possesses the smooth whiteness of alabaster, as on a statue. Perhaps he spends all day poring over his Jewish texts and never sees the sun.

"The Hartmans sent me." His voice has a processed quality, as if it were a recording of what a human voice should sound like. Or perhaps she has not heard very many accents beyond the softly rounded Atlanta twangs that fill her days. Plenty of non-natives have moved to the city in the past thirty or forty years. They bring with them their own eccentric patterns of speech. From everywhere.

"They told me that you need someone to stay with Jacob while you go to *shul*."

"How do you know my brother's name?"

"The Hartmans told me."

"I don't recall ever saying it to them."

"Maybe I overheard it. Sometimes I sit in their *shul*. I study in back. Nobody notices me."

"I think I'll stay home today."

"Today's portion for the week is *Bereishit*. In the Beginning. The first section of the first book of the Torah. You don't want to miss that, do you? Don't you want to know more about Judaism? Isn't that why you've gone to see them?"

"Just twice," Debbie tries to explain.

"Both times on a weekday afternoon. Both times, after work."

"How do you know when I went?" *Are you stalking me?*

"Seth and Rebecca are very excited that you want to become more, what would be the word, observant. They're hoping your first Sabbath went well."

"It didn't."

"I'm not surprised. You have your hands full with Jacob, don't you?"

"Everything's fine."

"Listen. If you want me to go away, I will. I'll understand. But I am here to help. I can sit with Jacob. I can make him his sandwich. We'll get along fine. You'll see."

"Are you sure that the Hartmans sent you?" It is a stupid question. What would she expect him to answer? That he is trying to lie his way past her in order to kidnap her savant syndrome brother? To hold him as ransom for the nonexistent Forman fortune? Instead he says nothing.

"And if I do go, what would I wear?"

"Skirt below the knee. Sleeves over the elbows. The collar high on your… throat."

Your pretty throat. For a moment she thinks that is what he was going to say. His eyes send forth an odd flash, a certain wanton lunge of the animal within him that he fast harnesses, as she has seen some men do. It plants in her a feeling of having been penetrated, if but slightly, though she is suspicious enough of her own aversion to male agendas to attribute her reaction to her own inner mechanisms, not to his.

"Lemme see him!" Jacob bellows excitedly.

"No, Jacob."

"Ya want me tah stay here all by myself? Ya want real trouble?"

Why is he so interested? Has his savant side picked up something she hasn't seen in this stranger? She tightens her grip on the lapels of her bathrobe and steps aside. Jacob is watching a DVD entitled *The Three Stooges: the Shemp Years.* The visitor stoops by Jacob.

"Which one is Shemp?" he asks, nodding at the screen.

Jacob tries to point. But the Stooges are moving around too fast.

"It's the one with his hair parted down the middle."

"Hey, that's my name!" Settling beside Jacob, this Shemp joins him in following the roughneck antics of the Stooges.

"I thought you weren't supposed to watch TV on the Sabbath," Debbie calls from behind.

"The rabbis say you can do anything if it's for health," Shemp answers. He goes back to enjoying *The Three Stooges* with Jacob. In moments, they are laughing together. And Debbie is forgotten.

####

I shouldn't have gone. The doubt taunts her as she walks through the Buckhead section of Atlanta. What kind of a Jewish man would be named Shemp? The Three Stooges were Jewish. That much she knows. Jacob's savant side had tracked down any number of facts about them. Howard had been Horowitz, Fein was Feinberg. It doesn't matter. Jacob had fallen in so readily with this newcomer. Has his idiot or his savant side determined his choice? Who knows?

A honk, a screech. A white Lexus sedan halts in the crosswalk below the green light Debbie has not noticed. She is not surprised that the driver is male. She is surprised that he is not irate but shaking his head, smirking in masculine chastisement behind glimmering sunglasses. With a slight nod of apology, she retreats to the sidewalk. *You forget where you are,* she tells herself. Buckhead at 10:00 on a Saturday morning. Friday night is done, its collected Dionysian forces at rest until the failing sun of late September allows Buckhead's Saturday night to enter. One unfamiliar with Buckhead might assume from its name that the area is dominated by hillbillies with heads of shotgunned deer mounted in their shacks. But Buckhead is upscale. Buckhead swaggers. Buckhead is everything that Debbie Forman is not. The party bars and dance clubs she passes lie dormant at this hour.

She continues on, scuttling rodent-like, hunched in the wool business suit she bought years ago for court hearings. The black skirt sheathing her calves restricts the speed of her pace yet covers her knees, as the sleeves of the black jacket stretch over her elbows, as the black blouse forms a demure scoop at her throat. She hopes that its blackness will match in both color and spirit the outfits of the room full of Chabad-Lubavitch that she expects to see at this morning's service.

Born into Reform Judaism, she has reached out as far right as traditional Conservative (no choir, no organ) in her fitful, despair-driven excursions from secularism. But not Orthodox. Never Orthodox. Was there not a blessing in the Orthodox prayer book, thanking God for "not making me a woman"? Were there not still synagogues where women had to sit in balconies, a form of second-class separatism she had always likened to the days of Atlanta blacks being exiled to the back of the bus? Then at her school a co-worker, another woman named Debbie, had effulged about Chabad. Yes, the men and women sit separate, but side by side, with a curtained partition between them. "It's the men's weakness, not the women's," that Debbie had explained. "They can't control their want of us. So we are the strong ones. We are the ones in charge. And when I am among them, I am no longer Debbie. I am Devorah. I take on dignity with my name. I ascend on the power of the name." Then, like a courier whose message has been delivered, that Debbie quit her job and vanished.

The Hartmans' Chabad House is neither a house nor a synagogue. It is located in one of the few pockets of Atlanta that development has not yet touched. It is not a pretty section, not an Atlanta to court nostalgia, so much as a wrinkle overlooked in the collective face lift to which the city perpetually treats itself. This wrinkle is a strip mall, half-vacant, half-filled with the detritus of sagging or collapsed business constructs. It is anchored by a moldering K-Mart on one end, a shuttered dollar movie house on the other. Between a Chinese takeout and a Goodwill is the door to the Chabad House. There is no sign over the door. Have the Hartmans chosen such anonymity on purpose? Do they prefer to camouflage themselves in this far-flung corner of the diaspora to which history has exiled them?

The inside looks different from her two weekday visits. One long table has been pushed against the wall by the entrance where she stands. The other stretches before a red-curtained cabinet at the far end of what is now a makeshift sanctuary. Twin sections of folding chairs face this cabinet. They fill the center of this large one-room space. Running between them is the white-curtained partition of which the other Debbie had spoken. It is indeed high enough to prevent men from staring at women during worship. *Mechitzah*, it is called. Division, the Hebrew word means. Debbie has looked it up.

Rebecca Hartman sits up front on the women's side. Debbie recognizes her by the gray scarf that covers her head and droops between the mounds of her shoulders. Next to her sits a young woman, dressed in her own version of Rebecca Hartman's garments. She is as thin as Rebecca is massive. Her black skirt falls to her ankles. Her white blouse lends modest contour to her sylph-like figure. Lithe, she would be called. The sleeves button over her wrists; the throat rises to her collar bones. She wears no scarf. Her hair, a cascade of lustrous black, contradicts the seeming denials of sensuality embedded in her garments. Its ebony curls flow past her shoulders and halfway down her back in a way that seems intentionally glamorous.

Aside from Rabbi Hartman, only one very tall individual, in front on the men's side, wears the Chabad calf-length black robe, sashed at the middle. Two rows behind him, the more secularized males in attendance have laid claim to their own space. Four wear coats and ties. Three others have on polo shirts whose candied colors and animal emblems (alligators, penguins) might fit in more readily at a country club. One older man wears khaki shorts rich in buckles, a black vest open over a white T-shirt, and heavily strapped sandals. He compensates for his bald pink pate with a silver-gray beard of such carefully arranged unkemptness as to echo images of what the wild-man prophets of Biblical Israel must have resembled. His granny glasses bespeak former days spent probing the hinterlands of the counterculture. Now he explores Judaism?

He has heard Debbie enter. His interested glance pins her to the entrance. She thinks to leave, just back out the door. Instead she scurries to the safety of the *Mechitzah*, passes the other six women in attendance, and settles in the row behind Rebecca.

"*Bereishit*," Rebecca whispers. Smiling, she hands Debbie a large hardbound volume. "Genesis. Chapter one, page one."

The Torah reading begins.

The Torah scroll is lifted, dressed, returned to its cabinet. Rabbi Hartman squares himself to deliver his comments on what has just been read. His too-long black robe hangs off his shoulders, which he hikes, as if to extend his height. Again Debbie is struck by the physical contrast between slight Seth Hartman and his plus-sized wife.

What will his subject be? The Garden of Eden? The Tree of Knowledge? Satan as a serpent? Why Cain really murdered Abel?

"*Tohu* and *Bohu*." He lobs the phrase into the group then waits. "Three words from Genesis one, verse two. Three words so easily bypassed," he continues, his faint Atlanta drawl soft, focused. "Does anyone know what they mean?"

"It's slime." The male voice carries insouciance. Debbie assumes it belongs to the aging hippy.

"All right, Saul. I guess you've been reading your *Zohar*. But suppose we stay inside the fence of traditional Judaism, at least for now. 'When the earth was astoundingly desolate' is one rendering of *Tohu* and *Bohu*, 'unformed and void' another. The translations may vary, but they all boil down to one word: chaos. And not just any chaos. Primal chaos. The gunk into which God dips His hands to mash this world together. The six days of Creation follow. Flash forward, and Moses is climbing Mount Sinai to receive the Law. Chaos evolves into the order of Jewish Law. And it works. For centuries, Jewish people steer their lives with the Law as their rudder. 'It is a Tree of Life to those who cling to it,' the book of Proverbs tells us. Or, as that famous Jewish rabbi, Jesus of Nazareth, assured his followers: 'I come to fulfill the Law, not to violate it.'"

Rabbi Hartman pauses to scan the group. He knows he has them. For a Chabad rabbi to quote Christ—it is something that one who has returned to the fundamentals of Jewish observance might do. A *Baal Teshuvanick*. Which is exactly how Seth Hartman characterized himself, not without pride, to Debbie during their first meeting.

"But let's examine *Tohu* and *Bohu* through the lens of another Judaism, one not too many of us know much about. The Other Judaism, let's call it. It's the weird stuff. *Twilight Zone* Judaism. *Outer Limits* Judaism. We are not speaking here of aliens from outer space bringing Torah to Earth. No. We're speaking Kabbalah. We're speaking *Zohar* and *Tanya*, *Bahir* and *Sefer Yetzirah*. We're speaking Abulafia, Cordovero, Luria. And so many others. For the Kabbalists, the primal root of *Tohu* and *Bohu* sprouts in an entirely different direction. It flowers not into Law but into something that has nothing, yet everything, to do with Law. But I get ahead of myself. Tell me, how many of you have heard of *Tikkun Olam*?"

Several raise their hands.

"*Tikkun Olam*. Repairing the World. A very popular concept these days, is it not? And never more vital than in the diaspora exile of today. What more bracing logic could there be than to believe that we are on a mission in this twenty-first century America, this Buckhead, this Anywhere? Seek the fallen shards of Creation where they have dropped, God tells us. Elevate them through our good actions, restore them to Heaven. But where in the Torah will you find *Tikkun Olam*? Is it anywhere in the Five Books of Moses? The prophets? The histories? No. But enter the *Twilight Zone* of the Kabbalists, the *Outer Limits* of Jewish thought, and it's everywhere. And it starts with *Tohu* and *Bohu*. There's this chaos, you see. This astonishing void, this profound emptiness, into which God pours the force of Creation. It's too strong, though, this force. Elements of it burst and scatter in the *Tohu* that precedes Creation's finishing. *Tohu* becomes a dumping ground for all kinds of unpleasant matter. Excretions is a common analogy. Waste matter. These foul remnants congeal in the forms of shells. *Kelipot* is the word the Kabbalists borrow from the *Zohar*. Husks. They contain every atavistic shadow that haunts us. Every demonic force that weakens us. They are constantly falling towards our earth plane. And the lower they descend, the more corrupted they become. The more foul."

Again he pauses.

"Worst of all, we humans have the capacity to help the *Kelipot* along. With every breach of good, we bring down more shells. With every sin—every indulgence of our evil inclination in what we think, what we say, what we do—we weaken the good side and empower the *Chitzonim*. The World of Outsiders. A Mirror World. What is pure in higher worlds becomes impure in this lower one. This Other Side, you might say."

A hand is raised.

"Yes, Saul." Rabbi Hartman blinks at the interruption. Debbie senses pre-existing antagonism between these two men.

"The Dark Side, *Star Wars* lovers call it."

"If you say so, Saul."

"Why would God create something that's imperfect?"

"I don't know, Saul. Maybe, in His perfection, God creates the imperfect so that we have something to perfect? In this Other Judaism, existence becomes something of a cosmic Easter egg hunt. It is, but isn't, the Chaos-to-Order path of the traditional commentators. *Tohu* to *Tikkun*. Chaos to Correction. Which is exactly what *Tikkun* means. Correction."

Again, Saul's hand shoots up. "And how is that to be done, may I ask?"

"Through the *mitzvot*, Saul. All 613 of them. The 248 positive ones are the good Easter eggs. The 365 negatives are the ones to avoid. Ultimately, it's up to us."

Saul straightens, arms folded. "Free will, that's called. So what you're saying is that Jewish Law and this Other Judaism take different roads to the same place. To Route 613."

"That's right, Saul."

"So it isn't two divergent traditions. They don't diverge. Nothing diverges. Not in the long run. Not if you believe your Buddhism. And your Judaism too, I guess." Saul shrugs his bony shoulders. "Boy, I wonder what those Kabbalah guys were smoking."

####

After the service, Debbie does not ask questions. She understands Chaos to Order. Creation makes sense to her in that regard. She does not want to hear of the Other Judaism. Let *Tohu* be *Tohu*, then move on to Adam and Eve, serpents and apples and fig leaves, all the rest of the Sunday School stuff, to which she had never fully listened.

And what had that Saul character been up to? Was he playing Milton's Satan to Rabbi Hartman's God? Better to reign in Hell than to serve in Heaven? Yet at the end, he had backed off. Was he the kind of person who starts to tear you down then pulls back, as if the whole thing is a game? She hides from Saul during the *Kiddush* snack afterwards. She knows he will try to engage her at the food table near the door. So she takes nothing more than a couple of cookies. She carries her plate over to the women's side and sits alone, on the periphery of human interchange. She feels safe in the shelter of the *Mechitzah*. If Saul wants to speak with her, he'll have to make himself conspicuous in chasing after her. In which case he will lose the edge of casualness with which such come-ons, to her limited experience among her old law firm's professionals, were generally perceived, by the men at least, as most effective. But that was how long ago? Ten years, twelve?

Debbie hides from the Hartmans as well. Her lack of understanding of Rabbi Hartman's comments on the Other Judaism has stoked her insecurity. Or was it her lack of receptivity to such ideas? In any case, she will pick a moment, thank them for sending this Shemp, then go.

They find her first. She rises, straightening, like an army private greeting a pair of colonels. She is surprised at the level of authority she invests in two people who have shown her nothing but good cheer and humility.

"So how was your week?" asks Rebecca.

Debbie rolls her eyes. She gives a shorthand version of what had happened yesterday at the school where she works but says nothing of last night's disastrous launch into Sabbath observance.

"Too much *Gevurah*," Rabbi Hartman comments. "It's everywhere in this day and age. It infects everyone around us. And we don't even know it."

"I guess so." Debbie does not know this word, *Gevurah*. She thinks to ask but does not. "By the way, thank you for sending Shemp," she adds instead, in way of preparing to leave.

"Sending Shemp?" Rebecca blinks, her surprise patent.

"The young Lubavitch man. The one you asked to be with Jacob. So that I could come to…."

"We didn't send anyone." The mix of worry and puzzlement in Rabbi Hartman's face requires no polite response from Debbie to slow her exit through the door.

####

She trots home in the heat. To the extent that she can, she hurries, fearing what may have happened, praying that Jacob is there and okay. She would have hailed a cab, except there were none to be hailed, and calling for one would require who knew how long a wait. Besides, she has no money. She left her purse at home. This much she has conceded to Orthodoxy—not to carry on *Shabbat*.

A car pulls up beside her. An old BMW, of a gold now compromised by faded wax and a dented passenger door. "Need a lift?" Saul calls.

"No thank you." It is an automatic response, one she instantly regrets.

He keeps pace with her, having detected the flimsiness of her rejection. "Are you sure?"

Instead of answering, she scurries to the curb where Saul has veered his car. She tugs at the passenger door. It will not open.

"Hold on a minute." Reaching over, he performs a deft unhitching of the latch. The door coughs wide. As Debbie readies herself to climb in, Saul tosses fast food wrappers from the passenger seat into the back. "Sorry," he says. "Where to?"

She points him to his first turn.

"Don't I know you from somewhere a long time ago?"

"I don't think so."

"Wait a minute. Sure. You used to do public defense cases for the city, didn't you?"

He has trapped her into a nod. She hopes he won't pursue that thread of conversation. The last thing she wants is to make small talk of having been let go by her law firm, failing in independent practice, taking occasional work as a public defender, then quitting the profession altogether.

"Sure," he continues. "I used to prosecute. We used to face each other on opposing sides of litigation. It's been how long, ten years? You know, if an old guy like me may be forgiven for making such comments, may I add that you haven't lost your looks?"

She points him to the next turn.

"I'm retired now. Don't know what to do with myself. So I take classes from Seth Hartman. Nice kid. Good Presbyterian upbringing. A lot of Atlanta's Jewish parents got into the habit of sending their kids to a private school instead of Redneck Prep and Cracker High. But that's hearsay, the judge would rule. Are you still practicing?"

"That's my corner." It isn't, but it is close enough. Besides, she doesn't want him to see where she actually lives. She pushes on the door handle. It won't open. Saul leans across her, so suddenly that she thinks he is going to try to steal a kiss. His right shoulder comes so close that she smells the spicy tang of his deodorant. With the same dexterous flick, he pops the door open.

"Thank you." She chatters out the words, then starts walking in the opposite direction from where she lives. When she feels sufficiently certain that he has driven out of sight, she turns on her heels and rushes home.

####

Beyond the door, laughter resounds.

Debbie enters to find both of them seated on the floor, side by side, facing the TV. She knows the movie they are watching: *The Bowery Boys Meet the Monsters*, one of Jacob's favorites. He especially relishes Leo Gorcey's Brooklyn-tinged malapropisms. Letters in algebraic order... I depreciate your kindness... an estimated benefracture of humanity....

"You can go now." The words slip out of her. One side of Debbie wants to cross-examine this Shemp Whoever-He-Is as to how he has really gotten here. The other side just wants him gone.

"He's stayin', okay?"

"Jacob—"

"Nah! Your sister's right. She's probably figured out that the Hartmans don't know me at all."

They are both speaking like Leo Gorcey now. Why? What has happened in Debbie's absence? Shemp stands to leave. Again, his height cows her. His eyes, of a pure and unrestrained violet, take on added brightness as he scans her, just once, fleetingly, but enough for Debbie to fold her arms across her chest.

"How did you find out about us?"

"I was at one of Hartman's *farbrengen* gatherings. He wouldn't remember me. I was sittin' way in the back and didn't say anything. Plenty of people were asking questions and shooting off their mouths anyway. After it was over, I kinda just hung around. I heard Rebecca talkin' to some woman about Debbie Forman needing someone to sit with her brother. To watch him and make sure he didn't get into trouble while she was working. Anyways, the woman wasn't interested. So I kinda, well, just checked their files for your address and showed up. Hey, if you don't want me here—"

"He's okay!" Jacob bellows from behind them.

"Like I said, if you don't want...."

"What's your last name?" Debbie asks.

Shemp hesitates. "Horowitz," he finally says. "Same as Moe and Curly and Shemp in the Stooges. Funny coincidence, right? Except I never changed mine to Howard, like what Jacob says the Stooge brothers did."

"He's comin' back tomorrow!" Jacob again.

"You won't hafta spend money on a daytime person either," adds Shemp.

"How did you know about that, Mr. Horowitz?"

"Jacob told me. And he says you're perspicated about him gettin' his pills."

"Perturbed, you mean." Debbie corrects him.

"Yeah. Perspiring."

Jacob brays his laugh. It is loud enough to bring down the upstairs neighbor. Debbie starts for the door, but Shemp stays her with his hand and opens the door instead. She watches the two of them: this squishy female bundle of neuroses from upstairs, staring up at this male of overbearing yet delicate height. The neighbor's blue eyes soften and enlarge, her fists unclench. No words are exchanged; still, a message is sent and acknowledged. The woman nods once, then backs away. And that is that. Debbie never sees the upstairs neighbor again. At least, not at their door.

CHAPTER 3

The next week, Shemp comes everyday—his appearance timed, with uncanny accuracy, to when Debbie is about to leave for work. She offers to make him a sandwich for lunch, but he never eats, at least not in their presence. "I got stomach issues," he confesses, when Debbie asks.

Jacob dotes on Shemp's company. It is his ritual to select the films they will watch together on the living room floor. His savant side relishes the act of putting his DVD's in order. He groups them by category, stacking them vertically to be shown one right after another. Giant insects go together, as do ghost stories. Alien invaders that look like people. Alien invaders that don't look like people. The date limit (virtually all pre-1960) is not entirely of Jacob's own choosing. Debbie had long ago sensed Jacob's passion for the violence that imbibes so many of the films made after that date. It attracts him almost instinctively, as sharks are stirred by the scent of blood. He has begged Debbie to bring him films like *The Last House on the Left* and *The Texas Chainsaw Massacre*. He knows of them from previews on some of the discs she has purchased. Debbie refuses to allow such films into their home. She is the guardian of the portal. Mrs. Benederet may well have bought some that now lay sequestered in Jacob's off-limits bedroom. However, Jacob cannot make purchases in stores. Without Mrs. Benederet, he has had no choice but to capitulate to his sister's censorial demands if he wants any new movies at all.

Monday belongs to gorilla films. Debbie arrives home from work to find them in the middle of *Robot Monster*, its villain a large man in a gorilla suit, a fish-bowl space helmet over his head. Shemp is devoting serious attention to the film. He seems to be lecturing Jacob, who listens with rapt attention. She thinks she hears the words "some kinda Amorite" but isn't quite sure. She passes through the living room to the kitchen, where Jacob's medications were laid out that morning. He has been given them all.

Tuesday is for dinosaurs. Debbie lingers close enough to overhear Shemp's comments during *Rodan*, a Japanese science fiction film about a gigantic bird of pterodactyl-like aspect that wreaks havoc on the country. Shemp studies the film as if it contains great secrets. "Ziz," he finally utters. "The *Ziz* opens his wings, and he's so big you can't even see the sun."

They resume watching. Back in her room, Debbie checks Ziz on the Internet. She gathers that it is a Jewish version of the Greek phoenix, except much larger. Rodan-sized. So Shemp is drawing connections between Jewish legends and the worthless movies Jacob watches? In which case the movies might not be so worthless? She joins them for the last film of the day: *The Beast from 20,000 Fathoms*, one of the better dinosaur films of the fifties. In one scene, the dinosaur crawls out of the sea and batters down a lighthouse.

"Leviathan." Shemp nods to himself, as if to confirm the correctness of his identification.

"What on earth do you mean?" Debbie asks.

"Leviathan, already. Sea dragon. Check your Bible, Leviathan's in there. Real bad *Tohu* stuff. Bet he eats people in the movie and mashes up cities and causes all kinds of chaos. Right, Jacob?"

"Yep!" Jacob grins. The dinosaur's lifting a policeman by the head off New York pavement has always been a favorite moment for him.

Wednesday is giant people day. They are just finishing *The Amazing Colossal Man* and moving on to *Attack of the 50-Foot Woman* when Debbie joins them. This one proves especially challenging to her. It is cheaply made, and it drags, even at the end, when the 50-Foot woman embarks on her rather sluggish rampage. Yet Shemp devotes to it the same level of scrutiny he has given to all of Jacob's movies.

"Jeez," he murmurs. "A *Nephilim* chick. Who would have thought it?"

"What does—"

Shemp cuts Debbie short. By now he knows the timbre of her queries. "Check your *Bereishit*. Chapter six. About the sons of God coming down to marry Earth chicks. The *Nephilim's* their kids, all right? Half giant, half—well, I guess there's no reason why some wouldn't be female." He snorts to end the discussion.

####

Nephilim.

Seated at her laptop that night, Debbie conjures a legion of online explanations. Some of the more staid commentaries assert that the "sons of God" were privileged males taking advantage of peasant girls. The more—how would Rabbi Hartman put it—*Twilight Zone*-ish interpretations tell of angels, called Watchers, drawn to Earth by the sheer allure of Earth women, enough so to abandon Heaven for the pleasures of having their way with these women. She tries to stop herself from imagining supra-worldly males, winged and smooth-muscled, forcing themselves onto female mortals. But the image burrows into her mind like a splinter. It pains her as she lies in bed, trying to sleep. How can there possibly exist a valid bridge connecting something as inept as *Attack of the 50-Foot Woman* to the sixth chapter of Genesis? Surely the Japanese who made *Rodan* were not of the Lost Tribes of Israel? Yet so many names in the credits on Jacob's DVD boxes have a Jewish ring to them. Sam Katzman, Lee Sholem, Sol Lesser, Albert Zugsmith, Samuel Arkoff—did some obscurely preserved gene in the collective memories of these Jewish progenitors of entertainments as pagan as they are puerile connect them to the eternal Hebrew myths that Shemp keeps citing?

Thursday is supposed to be a zombie day. But by the time Debbie arrives home, they have run out of classic zombie films and are about to move on to People and Animal Mixes. First up is *The Fly* from 1958. A scientist experiments with disintegrating matter in one booth and reintegrating it in another. Unfortunately, a fly gets into the first booth when the scientist tries to transport himself. It is a good film, in its way, one of the few Debbie has actually watched with Jacob. As usual, Shemp observes its unfolding with quiet attention. All goes well until the scene in which the scientist's wife pulls off the black hood covering the fly's head on the man's body. The wobbling appendages at the jaw, the twitching antennae, the shiny eye-bulbs multiplying the wife's face into a myriad of screams—

On a low groan, Shemp lifts himself off the floor and retreats to the back wall where he cringes, hands mashed child-like over his face.

"Better take this one off," Debbie whispers to Jacob. "Fast. What's next in your pile?"

"*Wasp Woman.*"

"Probably not. What else?" she asks.

"*The Wolf Man,*" Jacob responds.

"Not that one either. Why don't you jump to another category altogether?"

They move on to *The Exorcist*. Usually, Debbie would not have let such a film into the house. But she knows this one and somewhat admires it. It made a man in her old law firm become a practicing Catholic again. At least, according to him. Unless that was just another line. Another Trojan horse, to sneak him past her wall of defense. She had trusted the film more than the man. When she found the DVD in the clearance bin at Walmart, she chanced on bringing it home for Jacob.

"*Dybbuk* stuff," Shemp comments, more bravely now. He had returned to his place as soon as *The Fly* was off the screen. He seems his old self again.

"Tell me more," Debbie says, to keep him involved.

"You know. The spirit of some dead guy gets inside a chick. Her voice is his voice. Her head turns when he makes it turn. Do you know what I mean? Do you?" His eyes settle on her; his courage is back. In the room's dimming, near day's end, the violet in them now takes on the ice-blue transparency of pure sapphire.

"What got under your skin about *The Fly*?" Jacob intrudes upon the moment. For once Debbie welcomes the lack of social restraint he sometimes demonstrates, even with total strangers. "Ain't *The Exorcist* a whole lot scarier?"

"Tenth Generation stuff. Bad memories. Maybe I'll tell you. Sometime." And that is that.

That night, Debbie lies awake in bed, the words "Tenth Generation" nipping at her puzzled awareness. Something she had read online last night after the giant-people movies. Something about fallen angels imposing their carnal desires on animals as well as women. Monstrous beings now swarm the earth, along with the *Nephilim* giants—a plague of them, in the Tenth Generation, which directly precedes the punishment of the Flood. Hybrid mixes of the angelic and the bestial. *But not a fly. An angel wouldn't make love to a fly. Would he? Yet the abomination lies not in the creature spawned. The abomination lies in the mix. The unholy fusing.*

"Thou shalt not mate two kinds of animals," the book of Leviticus instructs. "Thou shalt not plant with two kinds of seed.

Thou shalt not mix threads of wool and linen."
Thou shalt not, thou shalt, thou shalt not, thou shalt.
Poor Shemp.
No.
Tall-as-a-basketball-player Shemp. Smooth-muscled Shemp. With his violet eyes changing to sapphire blue at sunset. Settling on her.
No, no, no.
Poor Orthodox-guy-from-Brooklyn Shemp. Who drops in occasionally at the Hartmans' Chabad. Without the Hartmans having any idea who he is.
He'd never said he was from Brooklyn anyway. Or had he?

####

Debbie awakes. Her usual morning despair has returned. *I put it on like a garment for the day,* she sometimes tells herself. The slightest confusion may set it off. And Shemp has confused her. Still, with no other choice, she leaves him with Jacob that Friday morning. As she drives to work, she determines to speak with the Hartmans about him tomorrow at Saturday services.

Work distracts her, though in no positive sense. The pall of last week's conflict still hangs over the school. Neither boy has returned. Derek Winslow is out of the hospital but recuperating at home. Josh Kim is still on suspension. The violence has deadened the atmosphere, drained it of its usual restlessness, the energy of insurrection that so often brews under the surface of even the most disciplined among the students. The halls possess a mausoleum quiet. Whenever Debbie passes the spot where the conflict occurred, her heart drums a recriminatory dirge; her mind clouds with guilt. *Maybe you couldn't have stopped Josh. You were too far away. But you could have shouted. You could have tried.*

Others do not know. They do not see past her somber mask, nor do they question it. Their faces remain marked by a certain somberness as well, albeit more resolute, more determined to make it through Friday to the weekend.

In this way, the day passes.

Driving home, Debbie debates whether to stop at the Kroger for more challah. She does not. She despairs of another aborted *Shabbat* evening. Another scene where Jacob provokes her anger, which in turn rends the already tenuous connection between them, sends both to bed suffering once more.

Outside the apartment door, she hears not the usual exchange of chuckles but squawks of frustration from Jacob. She enters to find him watching no movie but manipulating the controller to a new video game while Shemp stands, observing from behind. She picks up the game box and examines the front. *Raider of the Seven Earths*, reads the title across the top. The letters stand out in neon-white. An oily blackness drips down from them. At the center of the box, this viscous black surrounds the player avatar, who stands with feet apart, arms crossed masterfully, wand belted at his side. He has Jacob's thinness. His eyes possess the same shimmering black of Jacob's. His black hair is parted on the left, like Jacob's. The face is handsome, as is Jacob's, but less cherubic, more cartoonish. The player wears a sleeveless white undershirt, also like Jacob's. But here is a difference: whereas Jacob's arms are flaccid, the avatar's are muscled. He has on Jacob's favorite boxer shorts, black and printed with green faces of Yoda from *Star Wars*.

The video screen's landscape is a clearing of indeterminate location, cupped from behind by Sequoia-huge trees. Above this clearing, at the top of the screen, a dome of reddish-brown sky may be discerned. It is the color of rust, solid as iron, overbearing, seemingly impenetrable. The player-avatar that Jacob controls occupies the very center of the clearing. Unsheathed wand gripped in both hands, the player jerks forward towards the trees then freezes, to Jacob's barks of consternation; obviously, he is having some trouble manipulating its movement. Giants inch out at him from pockets hidden among the great trees. All are male, of varying shapes and heights. Some are naked, with groin areas obscured. Some wear loincloths, bristling with black fur, from which dangle half-chewed carcasses of animals. Brown hair coats massive, space-helmeted gorilla giants. None are of the human/animal mix that had so terrified Shemp on Thursday.

Luckily for Jacob, these giants move at him with lumbering slowness. With repeated pokes at his controller, he manages to advance on them as soon as they emerge. He confronts them with his wand of light, which has the lethal, sleek look so lacking in the flimsy plastic *Star Wars* sword that Debbie had bought for Jacob to keep in his room (he had thrown it away). Some circle away from the swings of his weapon. When he does succeed in slicing into a giant, it evaporates in gas-like streams of vapor that hiss like flattening tires.

Not so easily dispatched are the spheres that drop towards him from the top of the screen. These too he explodes with his wand. Pieces of them settle to the screen's bottom, where they congeal with other fallen shards into a pitch-like sediment that quivers in some vile manifestation of life. They distract him from dispatching the giants. And they multiply in number, all gaining speed as they plummet towards him.

What is this game? Has Shemp brought it?

"Jacob, please. I have to clean up, and Shemp has to leave. It's getting near dinner-time."

Her interruption breaks his focus. As he looks around at her, a sphere descends upon him. Like the others, it is creamy dark brown. It bristles with long hairs, uneven, unkempt, spread across a surface that glistens like a tumor, or at least how Debbie has imagined tumors. Jacob tries to toggle his player out of the way. Too late. With a comical whooshing sound, the player dwindles down to nothing.

"Look what ya made me do!" Jacob mutters to Debbie. Then to Shemp: "I told ya this game's too stinkin' hard!" Infuriated, he turns it off.

"It's an education game," Shemp counters. "You gotta learn how to get past the giants in this first screen. You know. Like *Math Wizard* was to you."

"I wasn't no good at that game either."

"You'll get better," Shemp answers. But his eyes stay on Debbie. "Hey, what time's candle lightin' for *Shabbat*, anyway?"

"We don't light candles."

"What do you mean, you don't light candles?"

"I don't have challah." It is all Debbie can think to say. Better a weak excuse than trying to go into more detail about last Friday night's debacle.

"Let me get you some of the good stuff! The real stuff, homemade!"

"I don't think Jacob will be comfortable...."

"I won't be gone but maybe five minutes. All right? Hey, if

you don't want us playing that game anymore, maybe Jacob and me can watch one of his movies tonight? You want me to stick around, don't you Jacob?"

"As long as we don't gotta play that giants game."

"No game already! How about watching *Star Wars* again? I can tell you where Yoda really comes from. Bet you didn't know he was Jewish, did you?"

"Okay!"

"That's all. I promise. All right?" Once more Shemp's eyes rest on Debbie. Only now their near-transparent violet-blue carries... what?

"All right." Her sun-deprived cheeks flush. Shemp does not see. Already he is heading for the door.

####

No comic books crowd the kitchen table. Shemp has deflected Jacob's lockstep routine from this habit as well, at least for tonight. The week's accumulation of bills and charity requests—triaged daily by Debbie for closer examination on Saturday evenings—has also been set aside. The table itself is simply adorned, yet it does not feel barren. The two unlit candles stand high in their holders. The Hartmans' *Kiddush* cup brims to overflowing with red wine. Shemp has covered the two loaves he has brought with a flower-embroidered cotton napkin Debbie dug out of a cabinet drawer. She forgot it last week. It had belonged to her mother.

Debbie has not seen the loaves. She hopes they will be sweet enough for Jacob to take at least a bite when the time comes. She stands in hushed expectancy beside Shemp at the table, Jacob sullen but quiet across from them.

"Is Yoda Jewish?" he blurts out of nowhere.

"We'll get to that. Right now, your sister has gotta do the lighting. Okay? And don't forget the blessing."

Debbie strikes a match. The blessing is uttered, the candles are lit.

"Wave your hands over 'em. Three times. Cover your eyes with your fingertips. Pray for something. Anything. Or just say thanks."

"For what?" Debbie asks.

"We're here, right? Got through another week, right?"

"I suppose so."

"Do I gotta do it, Shemp?"

"Not if you don't wanna, Jacob. Not if you ain't ready."

"I ain't never gonna be ready."

"Okay, lady of the house. Do your thing," Shemp instructs.

Three times Debbie circles her palms over the candles. It is so uncharacteristic a gesture, so out of line with all others she makes across a week. It seems artificial, like someone playing a charades version of religion. Then she covers her eyes: the darkness comes, the supplications roll out of her. Silent. But plentiful. *Send us peace. Heal Jacob. Send me peace. Give me rest. From Jacob. Help me to find a better job. Guide me to peace. Guide Jacob to a place in himself that is more than, well, more than what he is. You know what I mean, God. I hope you do. And thank you for sending us Shemp. Maybe.*

She lowers her hands. To her astonishment the room has changed. A vacuum has been created, one now filled by the silken glow of the two candles, the warm scent of tonight's meal, the lullaby of silence that puts the stresses of the week so gently to sleep. The timing is perfect. Somehow Shemp has engineered the moment of the Sabbath's arrival to coincide precisely with Friday afternoon's moment of departure. The kitchen holds no ordinary dimness but a magical one, as if the guardian forces of the day have been replaced by a night shift. The air carries strange energy, unique, benign. It is the exact moment of sunset. On Debbie's first real Sabbath. Thanks to Shemp.

"The sixth day." Debbie's voice quavers as she begins to read from the prayer book. "And the heavens and the earth were finished, and all their host. And on the seventh day God had finished His work which He had made, and He rested on the seventh day from all His work which He had made. Then God blessed the seventh day and hallowed it...."

Her voice cracks. She cannot continue; the moment overwhelms her. It is happening—finally, truly, happening. The brimming wine cup, the covered loaves, the two candles, their flames firm, unbending. And Shemp. Yes, Shemp. They are allies to her, companions and protectors, gathered about her in this precious hour that heralds the completion of Creating, the commencement of time as we know time. But pause first. Linger in this daylong oasis of time before time once more resumes its relentless march forward.

She grits her teeth, clamping down hard to stem the tide of emotion that swells in her. It has worked before. It works again now. She continues reading, her tone firmer, schoolmarmish, a voice she has used at work when reading a story to a group of restive sixth graders. She looks up. Jacob is staring at her, puzzled, as if her ears have just turned into flower pots. Shemp has positioned himself closer to her. When she glances at him, he simply nods at the wine cup. She reads the blessing for the wine; grudgingly, Jacob shares a tiny sip of it. After the ceremonial washing of hands, they proceed to the uncovering of Shemp's challah.

Never has Debbie beheld such bread. Each loaf is frost-white and round, like enlarged versions of the powdered donut nuggets she sometimes buys. Except the surface is not powdery but glistens, oily, wax-like. It does not look appetizing at all. She reads the blessing over it and breaks off pieces to share with Jacob and Shemp.

Jacob sniffs at his section. "Smells like Miss Nancy." Despite the smell, or perhaps for this very reason, he downs his bite without resistance.

Debbie smells her piece. It does carry a perfumed scent. Reluctantly, she presses a section past her lips—and is surprised by its airy texture, its pleasant taste. It is sweet, like honey. The crusted oily surface adds a burst of flavor as she chews.

"Where can I buy this?" she asks Shemp, as they sit down to eat.

"You can't."

"Where did you get it, then?"

"I made it myself. Special recipe."

"Do you have a nice kitchen where you live?" Debbie asks.

"Nice enough."

"Where *do* you live?"

"Oh, around."

"With friends?"

"I guess you could say that."

"All right." Debbie fights to overlook his secrecy. "Would you like some chicken?"

"Nah," Shemp says.

"Green beans?"

"Sorry. Stomach—"

"Problems. Yes. Okay. I know."

"The bread's enough for me. It goes down easy."

"Hey Shemp. Can you save me some? For tomorrow?" Jacob all but shouts, as much to be heard as for the bread. The ongoing back-and-forth between his new friend and his sister has left him feeling excluded.

"It ain't gonna be good tomorrow. Used to be it would last two days for *Shabbat*. But that was a long time ago. A real long time. There were secret recipes back then. Now I don't know."

Debbie and Jacob eat in silence. Shemp nibbles at the challah until it is finished.

####

Debbie and Shemp are alone together in the kitchen after dinner. Jacob is in the living room. He has started to watch *The Empire Strikes Back*, the second of the *Star Wars* movies, but has fallen asleep on the floor. He has seen it so many times that Debbie has memorized the pace of the film by the flow of its music cues. She begins to wash the dishes, but Shemp tells her to leave them until tomorrow night.

"C'mon, it's *Shabbat*. God didn't wash dishes on the seventh day, did He? Take your rest, already. You earned it."

"Okay." She sits across from him. Not next to him. His gaze burns into her. Does he do this on purpose? "Is Yoda really Jewish?" she asks, to deflect his stare.

"I don't know."

"Then why did you tell him?"

"It got him quiet, didn't it?"

"But it was a lie."

"Okay. So send me to that part of *Gehenna* where liars go."

"*Gehenna*. That was one of the words on the game box you brought. *Raider of the Seven Earths*. What was that all about, Shemp? It frustrated Jacob."

"Sorry about that. But he's gotta learn to get past that first screen. Or he won't be going anywhere."

"Where did you buy that game anyway? Surely stores don't carry something so... personalized."

"I made it. It's one of the things I do. I can custom-make

games like guys do with computers. I thought this one would help with, well, you know Jacob, he ain't too good at controlling himself sometimes," explains Shemp.

"Is there really such a thing as the Seven Earths?"

"Kind of."

"What do you mean, Shemp?"

"It's hard to explain. Unless you've seen it."

"You've seen the Seven Earths?"

"Well, I read a lot. Okay? I mean, you read your *Zohar*. It talks all about the critters scattered on those earths. You got giants, of course. You got two-headed guys, you got dwarves with holes where their noses ought to be. You got Cain's kids made out of smoke. Genies is the word, right? Some of these critters get squeezed down into Jacob's movies. From memories that go way back in people's heads. But not all of 'em are on the same level. When you get to *Gehenna* in the fourth Earth, it's got a whole bunch of levels. For people that are bad or maybe not quite so bad. The Seven Earths is like the screens in some of the games he plays. You move through one to get to the other. Sometimes you move back and forth. Sometimes you get stuck in one or thrown down lower. It depends."

"On what?" Debbie asks.

"On a lot of things. Hey, we don't need all those critters for the game anyway. Besides, I ain't gonna use all Seven Earths for the game. That's too much. Jacob doesn't need it. And you don't either."

What game? What do you mean? "You aren't going to make him play more games, are you?" she asks instead.

"Hey, I thought it would help him! I still think he might get something out of it. If it's okay with you, that is. Say, who's Miss Nancy?"

"A nurse at his doctor's office." She doesn't add how hard Jacob ogles her at every visit, how Miss Nancy somewhat good-naturedly takes his attention in stride.

"Well, he doesn't talk much about her."

"What does he talk about when I'm not here?"

"You, some."

"What does he say about me?"

"You don't wanna know."

"You're right. Please. What else does he talk about?"

Debbie continues.
"Going outside. Meeting people."
"Girls, you mean."
"Well, yeah."
"He doesn't know anything about girls."
"I know that."
"What else?"
"He complains about wanting to watch his kind of movies. With lots of weapons, lots of killing. Hey, look, if you were locked away inside that head, wouldn't you wanna break loose?"
"You seem to know a lot, Shemp."
"Sometimes maybe too much." His eyes fall from her. "Hey, I better get goin'. What time you want me here tomorrow? You're going to the Hartmans, aintcha?"
"I guess so."
"Rabbi's speaking about Noah. You don't wanna miss that, do ya?"
Shemp follows Debbie into the living room. Jacob is still asleep on the floor.
"Shouldn't we wake him up? Didn't you promise you'd watch that movie with him? He might be disappointed."
"Nah. Better just let him sleep. He gets tired real easy, you know. Sometimes sleep just sneaks up and clobbers him. Ain't nothing he can do about it. Let me put him in bed." With ease, Shemp lifts Jacob and carries him to his room.

####

Debbie is holding Jacob's *Sisters of Nightfall* comic book when Shemp returns. It was beside Jacob during dinner—on the chair next to him, below the table. She pushes the comic into Shemp's hands. "Put this on his night stand. He likes to keep it near him."
Shemp carries the magazine to his kitchen chair and sits down over it. He grins at the image of the two women on the cover. "Jeez, those two are everywhere, ain't they?" He flips through the pages. "You know, I might use some of this."
"I don't know what you're talking about!"
"For the game." Shemp frowns analytically through his

beard. "How come they make all those characters look so pretty and all? I mean, not just Lilith and Naamah, who they call the Sisters, even though they ain't. Not really. The guys too. Asmodeus and Gadreel. Heck, even Azazel! And he's the head bad guy!"

"They probably want to turn it into a television show. It's happened before."

Shemp goes back to perusing the story. At one point he laughs out loud. "How about that! Lilith and Naamah are do-gooders here! You heard of them, haven't you?"

"Well, yes. Lilith, at least. I've read a little."

"You know about the children that Adam had with Lilith when he ran off from Eve? One hundred thirty years of, pardon the word, nah, I better not say it. Bad bunch, their offspring. Real bad. They try to mess things up for humans every step of the way, right when Creation is brand new. So they get banished from Earth. But some find their way back. Nasty spirits, out-and-out demons. *Shedim* are goat ones, *Seirim* the ones like birds. There's lots more. And this comic wants to turn Mama Lilith into some kind of hero!"

"Well, it is a comic book. Listen, you better go ahead and put it where it belongs. If Jacob wakes up and doesn't find it there, it could throw him into one of his fits."

"He won't wake up anytime soon." Smiling, he rises from the kitchen table and takes *Sisters of Nightfall* to Jacob's bedroom. When he returns, he pauses to examine Jacob's latest puzzle in the living room. Jelly beans, this one is. Keeping her distance, Debbie joins him.

"How long did it take Jacob to put this together?" Shemp asks.

"Not much longer than you were gone for the challah."

"Jeez!"

"Jacob was born with savant syndrome," Debbie explains. "They have special gifts in some ways but no ability to function in others. Some can recite college football scores from games played on a certain date fifty years ago. Some can play an entire Beethoven piano concerto after only hearing it once."

"What's a Beethoven?"

"He wrote music. You don't know that?"

"We Orthodox guys are very sheltered."

"Which group are you?"

"Very traditional. Very, very traditional. People weren't even being called Jews yet. We weren't nothing. Call us the

Know-Nothings, okay?"

"I don't believe you." She sighs, more in gloom than confusion.

"I know that." He grins, an element of the imp in his expression. "Anyway, I hope you enjoyed your Sabbath, Missus *Shekhinah*."

Too tired to ask him to explain, she simply walks him to the door. Opening it, she turns to wish him good night. Her turning is met by his lips brushing her cheek. He has leaned close, down into her. She jerks back in surprise. Shemp steps away. His eyes disengage from her, hold to the floor, perhaps in apology. Then he speaks. "You shouldn't creep down that sadness road so often, like you do. It doesn't protect you, like you think it does."

How dare you! She wants to cry. *What makes you think—*
Instead she says nothing.

CHAPTER 4

The next morning Shemp arrives at his usual time, just when Debbie is set to leave for Shabbat services. He carries with him a box that is no game, he says, but a jigsaw puzzle for when Jacob awakens. The box has no illustration of what the finished puzzle should be. She gives Shemp instructions he already knows about Jacob's lunch, Jacob's pills. Her tone is formal, borderline off-putting.

"I'll be back before one o'clock," she announces. Avoiding eye contact, she leaves for the walk to her shopping center synagogue.

Her fingers probe her cheek, where Shemp kissed her. Despite the Atlanta heat, the spot feels cold, a patch of frigid skin the size of a quarter. It has not gone away. Nor has the hurt he put inside her last night. And not just with the kiss. Why had he made that comment about her traveling too often down the sadness road? What right did he have? More disturbingly, how could he have seen so deeply into that most private corner of her being—how at times her depression does protect her, how she would feel naked without it?

Perhaps Shemp's helping Jacob is just another Trojan horse, devised to sneak inside her. As other men have done. Last night's magical *Shabbat* evening may have been forged to get past her defenses. *Or maybe the problem is in me,* she thinks. At times despair does seem her chaperone, ready to chase off any male with thoughts of becoming her companion, much less her suitor.

Perhaps.

She will air her confusions to the Hartmans. Maybe they do know Shemp. Maybe one word from either of them about this Chabad guy with raw social skills will deflate her suspicions once and for all. Perhaps Shemp does bring good to Jacob. Yet his very presence makes her feel vulnerable. But to what? To having not just her physical self, but the very feminine core of her, probed every time his eyes linger on her?

With the High Holidays drifting into the past, attendance has dwindled. Two new female attendees occupy the middle. Seated side by side in front are the attractive, young Chabad woman and Rebecca Hartman. Today they are a study in even greater contrasts. The svelte young woman is dressed immaculately, in a narrow maroon skirt framed by a black sweater above and black stockings below. Her wig is blonde, this time. Its yellow tresses cascade down the back of the sweater, between her finely sculpted shoulder blades. Rebecca's shoulders are rounded slabs; her long-sleeved white blouse is more of a shirt that might belong to a man. A full black skirt balloons about her body. The plainness of her outfit acknowledges her bulk while denying her very self as a female presence. Her head covering is no gypsy-flavored scarf but a dark brown beret that puffs back floppily on a scalp that appears to have been shaved almost to crew cut length.

Fewer men occupy the other side as well, though with heart spiraling downwards, Debbie spots Saul among them.

The Torah portion does indeed recount Noah and the Flood. The tall, lanky Lubavitcher reads the Hebrew from the scroll. When it is done, the Torah is put away, and Rabbi Hartman takes the podium to speak. What will be his focus this week? Will he discuss the symbolism of the dove, the covenant of the rainbow?

He speaks of twilight. He mentions that in his years as an assimilated buckaroo galloping across the vast prairies of secularism, he had paused to refresh himself at the wells of Carlos Castaneda, an American anthropologist who became enamored with the shamanistic teachings of the Yaqui Indians. He speaks of the uniqueness of twilight in both Yaqui shamanism and Judaism. To Castaneda, it is the giving way of the *tonal*, which is the finite and material of day, to the *nagual*, which is the non-material, the infinite, of night. To observant Jews, it is the precise moment when the light of day recedes so that evening may advance.

Debbie sits forward.

"Nowhere is that moment more vital than in the instant of *Shabbat*'s arrival. And at no point in the history of Created Humankind was that moment more potent than on the evening of the Sixth Day, before the first *Shabbat*. It was the *nagual* to end all *naguals*. From which all subsequent *naguals* would unfold."

Last night... Shemp's perfect timing... the change in the very air when she brought her hands down from before her eyes....

"Many of you know *Ethics of the Fathers*. A section of the Talmud, it's often published on its own. And cherished for its gems of eternal wisdom. 'Do not judge others until you sit in their place; the more possessions, the more worry; hating others removes you from the world.' But it is also filled with mind-bending flights of fancy. 'Ten things were created on the eve of the first Sabbath,' we read. Right at twilight. Noah's rainbow, for example. Moses' staff, which becomes a serpent before Pharaoh. The physical shapes of the Hebrew letters themselves. The manna loaves that God sends from the sky to feed the Jewish people. Judaism teems with what's been called left-brained logic, to be sure. But our faith overflows with right-brained realities as well. The bizarre, the inexplicable—the Other Judaism—it too has been part of God's plan since the final day of Creation." He smiles, somewhat sheepishly, as if wondering if he has gone too far. "Does anyone have any questions?"

"Can you tell us more about manna?!" Debbie cries out fast, before Saul can hijack the discussion. Again she thinks of last night. Shemp's challah, what he called the real stuff.

"All right. Imagine the manna scene from the book of Exodus as if it were a movie. The people, all 600,000 of them, cry out for food. The Glory of God—the cloud, the pillar of fire—appears in a Hollywood sky to listen. The next morning they awaken to find the land around them blanketed with a substance they've never seen before. It's frost-white, feathery, baked sweet, with the taste of oil, of honey. It has a perfume scent to it. But it is not to be left overnight. Because it rots. Turns to worms."

Because tomorrow it ain't gonna be good no more—

"It stays with them for 40 years," Rabbi Hartman continues. "And maybe that's the true key to the manna. It gives daily focus to the people in their seemingly aimless wanderings. It is assurance of God's hand. Feeding them. Like a mother, a father. Only when they enter the Promised Land does the manna cease. They are on their own now. They will draw their own bread from the earth. I guess that's the lesson, isn't it? All of us wander through our own wilderness. Sometimes that wilderness seems impenetrable. Sometimes we need for God to send us something to guide us. Or someone." His last words, intended to show gratitude, trail off instead. His stare flits in seeming regret to the women's side of the room. To his wife Rebecca.

"Any more questions, Debbie?"

I need to ask you and Rebecca about this strange man that has entered our lives. I need to air all the mysteries he has brought past our door. The stretches of peace, the undercurrent of discord. Jacob's glee and frustration, my own self feeling simultaneously honored and stalked.

She doesn't ask.

####

To Debbie's relief, Saul leaves early. She lingers at the periphery of the small crowd, prodding herself to approach either Hartman, then backing off. How could she communicate with any degree of believability that she may have eaten actual manna last night? Perhaps Shemp had found an Italian bakery in Buckhead. Or a Greek one. Aren't Greek pastries extra sweet and soaked in oil? But would one be kosher?

"We missed seeing you this week." Rebecca has come up to her at the *Kiddush* table. Her round face is drawn, her cheeks pouched and reddened, her eyes made small by the smile she labors to hoist over the moat of some unstated defeat.

Debbie simply shrugs. Better that than to lie. Or to express the real reason clumsily.

Saul is waiting outside when she leaves.

"Come on. I'll give you a lift home. Or to whatever approximate location you want me to think is your home."

The first minutes in the car pass in silence. Finally, Saul speaks. "You must think I'm some kind of dirty old man. A masher on the make."

"I think no such thing."

Saul smiles, as once he might have at some fallacious testimony in court. "Listen. The old-man part fits, but that's about it. If you want to condemn a septuagenarian for admiring an attractive younger woman, then so be it. Guilty as charged."

Debbie crosses her arms and shrinks into the passenger seat.

"C'mon. Loosen up. You're turning into a regular Vashti, you know that?"

"Vashti?" The name rings a distant bell to Debbie.

"The queen in the Purim story. The one who won't show off her, what would one call it, her feminine attributes when her male chauvinistic pig of a husband the king orders her to parade in front of his cronies. Hey, there's nothing wrong with objecting to being treated like a sex object. But if it hardens, if it grows a shell around it...."

"I'm not that way."

"Sure you aren't." Saul is no longer smiling. "Anyway, you remember what Seth Hartman was saying about God sending us someone when we feel most lost? He was talking about me, among others. And himself. And Rebecca, for that matter. Most Chabad girls are married by the time they're twenty. Like that young Chabad couple you see every week. The tall guy and the glamour gal. Hillel and Adina."

"Those two married? They look like kids."

"They are kids. Go ahead, guess how many children they have."

"I don't know."

"Three of them. They've been with Grandmom and Grandpop up in Crown Heights for the past couple of weeks. And there'll be more. Most Chabad families shoot for a baseball team. *Be fruitful and multiply*, Torah tells us. The *mitzvah* comes in handy when you're trying to rebuild your people after losing six million to the Nazis."

"Is it allowed for Adina to look so, what was the word you used, glamorous? I mean, her hair and all?" Debbie shakes her head in disapproval.

"It's not her real hair. It's called a *sheitel*. It's not proper for a married Orthodox woman to show her hair in public."

"So she puts on something that's even more attractive?"

"I don't understand it either. Then again, I'm a growing boy. At least in my Judaism. But you'll notice that Rebecca veers in the opposite direction on the *sheitel* path. I don't know why. Maybe it's some Chabad form of sibling rivalry. Adina's Rebecca's sister, you know."

"No. I didn't know."

"Of course not. But back to Seth and Rebecca. I suspect that something not quite kosher is going on in their marriage. Hey, listen, it's not for me or anyone to pass judgment on a relationship's internal reality. But it's always been my impression that Rebecca has viewed her size as a wall between herself and any role she might ever play as a female in a man's life. Her family's efforts at matchmaking had ceased by the time their daughter reached 18. She married a career instead. When she finished her Chabad schooling, she began commuting from Crown Heights to Manhattan for a nursing assistant program. When her certificate opened the door to a job down here, her parents didn't object. She's still doing that now. Part-time. Even Hotlanta people get sick and need medical help, don't they? Somewhere during their separate wanderings in this Dixie Wasteland, Rebecca Moseson met Seth Hartman, and *bashert* bloomed. That's the Jewish word for destiny. What's pre-ordained. Soul-mate stuff. Except I don't think that shoe quite fits."

"They don't have any children?" Debbie asks.

"Not unless they've squirreled them away behind the Torah cabinet."

"How do you know all this about them?"

"Three years ago, I found my way to the Hartmans. Not too long before that, Seth found his way to Rebecca. Seth and I would sit and talk in that same room where services are held. At first I think Seth looked at me as something of a father figure. Until he learned what I really was—a fellow wise guy, out hunting for Something More. We eventually became antagonists, separated in age by two-score years and then some. Anyway, this smart-alecky little Jewish kid from the Atlanta suburbs had been floundering around in his own private wilderness when Rebecca came into his life. But I don't think we're talking happily-ever-after here. Something *is* off. Sure, she tolerates his secular baggage, like his Castaneda talk and such. But Rebecca was raised with different baggage. Lubavitch baggage. Also, there's the physical thing. He's this scrawny little weasel of a guy, and she's well, what she is. But I can't diss on them too much. The Hartmans became my manna during my wife's battle with brain cancer. Except it wasn't much of a battle. Not really."

"I'm sorry to hear that."

"Thank you. Listen, you can relax, counselor. It's not like I'm using Sophie's glioblastoma as a line to soften you up. You just tell me where you want to get out."

She directs him to the front of her apartment building. "There's someone I want you to meet," she tells him.

"A mother wearing a *babushka*? A father with a shotgun?"

"Please. I'd like your opinion. I need someone's opinion."

Shemp is gone. The apartment is silent. The TV is off, Jacob asleep in his room, sprawled atop the sheets in his undershirt and Yoda boxers. Debbie hastens to close the bedroom door. Not that Saul would have seen. He stands transfixed over Shemp's jigsaw puzzle, its pieces (only ten of them) still unassembled, on the living room card table.

"Where did you buy this?" he asks.

"I didn't. Shemp brought it this morning for my brother Jacob."

"Who is Shemp?"

"I don't really know. He appeared out of nowhere, one Sabbath morning, a week ago. He dresses like Orthodox Chabad. He says that the Hartmans sent him, but they say they didn't. I was hoping that you might have seen him. Anyway, Shemp has been taking care of Jacob while I'm at work."

"How much does he charge?"

"Nothing."

"Does Jacob like him?"

"Dotes on him. I've never seen Jacob so happy as when Shemp's around. Something in him just opens up. And it's all the more unusual because Jacob was born with a mental handicap. Savant syndrome. Have you heard of it?"

"They used to call them idiot savants," Saul responds.

"He takes medication to control some of—" reminded of Jacob's regimen, she hurries to the kitchen. The pills are gone. In their place lies a note, scrawled hurriedly: *He took all the pills like he was supposed to. You were late. After one o'clock, like what you said. I waited. Had to go. By that time Jacob was asleep. Sorry.*

Back in the living room, Saul is examining the puzzle box. "There's no picture on the box cover, no company name either. No label, no scan code. Maybe he bought it online?"

"I don't think so."

"Why?"

"He doesn't seem the computer type," Debbie says.

"What do you know about him? Where does he live?"

"He hasn't said. I've asked him, but he sidesteps."

"What does he look like?"

"He's very tall. He dresses in a black robe and always wears a *yarmulke*."

"Does he have a beard?"

"Yes. But full. Mountain-mannish."

"What do you mean?"

"It isn't groomed like Rabbi Hartman's or Hillel's. Instead it rather tumbles over his cheeks and lips. It sounds wild, but it adds to the friendly impression he gives off. Sometimes."

"Sometimes. I see. Has he made a play for you?"

None of your business, she thinks to say. "Not really," she answers instead.

"No such thing as not really. Anything else about him?"

"Well, he got Jacob to join us last night for a Sabbath meal. And he knows Torah."

"He knows about Kabbalah too. The Tree of Life. That's what these pieces are. They're all here, all ten of the Kabbalistic emanations, from *Keter* on top, down through *Chesed* and *Gevurah*, all the way down to *Malchut* at the bottom. Look at the puzzle board, where the pieces go. It looks like a tree, doesn't it? The ten spheres are meant to fit into empty circles embedded in the trunk and branches. Just ten! It should have been easy to put together. Unless Jacob's savant syndrome stopped him."

"He's put together puzzles with 500 pieces," Debbie explains. "A thousand. He does it in a matter of minutes."

"Maybe it's the Hebrew words underneath that confuse him." Saul picks one up. He flicks his hand hard, as if it has stung him. The piece crumbles to particles that spread upon the air.

"Did it hurt you?"

Saul doesn't answer. All insouciance has vanished from his manner.

"Maybe it was old material," Debbie volunteers, in an effort to settle him. "Kind of like fabric that sits too long on a shelf. Maybe that's why it fell apart. Maybe it gave you a splinter."

"I don't know if I'd let this guy back into your home, Debbie."

"Why not?"

"Let me speak to Seth about him first."

"No. I'll do it. Please. Let me do it. You haven't seen everything."

Saul nods, then sighs, then shakes his head. "What the heck have you gotten yourself into, kid?"

CHAPTER 5

Sunday morning. Shemp appears earlier than his usual time.

"We want the day to ourselves," Debbie tells him.

"Hey, listen, I'm sorry about leaving early yesterday."

"It's not that."

"I know." He bends closer, down over Debbie. His eyes are a transparent blue in the hallway's morning dimness. They do not bore into her as they did before. If anything they have softened. "You want me here tomorrow?"

Debbie freezes.

"You don't want me to come around at all anymore. Right?"

"Thank you for all you've done."

"You don't gotta thank me. See you around, okay?"

See me around where? At the synagogue? The bread aisle at Kroger? Lurking outside my place of work? Tomorrow she will take the day off. She will make phone calls to adult daycare agencies until she lines up someone to be with Jacob during the day. As she is thinking, Shemp retreats. The door closes behind him.

Instantly, DVD cases clatter past her. *Trader Horn, Tarzan's Greatest Adventure.* Today was to have been for jungle films. Now it is tantrum day. She has not seen Jacob throw a fit like this one for years. He whines and groans and sniffles, orbiting the room in his boxer shorts.

"Jacob! Let's go out. I'll take you to breakfast. We can stop at Walmart. For movies."

The offer makes him pause. He stares at her, his widened eyes seeing not his sister but the potential of the day. "Help me get dressed," he tells her, and fetches from his bedroom the black *Star Wars* T-shirt and blue jeans that are his uniform for such rare excursions.

"You need to shower first."

"I already did."

Don't lie, Jacob. You know you didn't. "You need to take your medications before we go," she answers instead.

She drives him to a pancake house. Their waitress is a young woman of color. She is tall and slim, her skin a vibrant ebony sheen. Her hair is cropped short, all curls that frame her rounded cheekbones and long eyelashes in a way that accents her attractiveness, her vitality of youth. The exaggerated rims of her glasses and erect, attentive posture lend her an academic aura. She is perhaps in college. Debbie places their order. Jacob cannot cease scanning her sleek figure, its firmness heightened by the snug fit of her green uniform. Before she leaves their booth, he launches into interview mode. He wants to know her name (Fana); what that name means (brightness); why she speaks with an accent (she is from Ethiopia); where that country is (Africa); if she likes living in America (very much); where she may have traveled this summer (Lookout Mountain). Physically, Jacob manifests no visible indications of his savant syndrome. His dark features radiate a perpetual sweetness of inquiry, cherubic in their boyish innocence. Only when he begins to speak do others detect that something is not quite right with this eager fellow. The questions pour, one upon the next, with a relentless yet guileless persistence, as if he were a boy of twelve, not a man in his thirties.

At first Fana grins, inwardly congratulating herself, as others have, by braving the arena of Jacob's handicap. Then Jacob accelerates his queries. He wishes to know if she has a boyfriend (yes); how old is this boyfriend. (24); is he African (no); what is he (American). What time does she leave work to go see this boyfriend? Where do they go, what do they do? At this point, a warning alarm goes off in Fana. She retreats to official waitress manner. Then she leaves them, Jacob trailing her with his gaze.

When they have finished, an older waitress, this one Caucasian, brings them their check. The woman squints suspicion above her sagging cheeks. Then, seeing something off in Jacob, she smiles, her disfavor softened, and goes away.

Debbie wants to get Jacob home. But she has promised him movies, and if she does not follow through, she will never hear the end of it. She drives them to Walmart, all the while pondering Jacob's ogling of that young waitress—of the beast, so long caged in Jacob, set to pounce and have its way, even if it does not know what that way is. He has never known a woman. Not in the biblical sense. Debbie is the only female who has touched him. She and an occasional nurse like Miss Nancy. Something is about to run loose, her inner voice cautions, as they park. She has no wish to believe herself. But she cannot quiet that self either.

Inside Walmart, Jacob spurts out of sight. Debbie finds him all the way in back. Has Mrs. Benederet trained him to find his way? With much intensity he is poring over the new releases in the DVD section. Debbie beckons him to the clearance bin. "Choose any two that you want," she tells him. He is not interested.

"Let's go home, then," Debbie says.

Jacob hangs behind Debbie at the entrance. Does he not want to leave? The automatic doors part; Jacob shoots through. Alarms go off, whooping sounds that cause two security personnel to descend on Jacob. He crumples, arms clasped tight about his middle. A low whine erupts out of him, culminating in a wail of absolute bafflement. Hands are upon him. Debbie tries to stop them. One security guard stops Debbie. The other pulls Jacob's hands away. A DVD pops out of his jeans, where he has tucked it.

"Okay, sport, come this way," the second security guard demands.

Jacob does not obey. He cannot obey. He falls to the floor, clutching his chest.

"Call an ambulance!" Debbie screeches. "He needs medical assistance! If anything happens to him because of what you've done, I'll hang lawsuits on every single one of you!"

The hyperbole gives them pause. One squats by Jacob and endeavors to utter calming phrases. The other picks up the DVD case and hurries to a back room behind customer service. Debbie glimpses the title: *Noonday Holocaust*. Blood-red flames dominate the cover.

She rides with Jacob in the ambulance. The attendants have taken Jacob's pulse and blood pressure. His heartbeat is unstable. This much they have determined. They have tried to question him about what he is feeling, what bothers him. He responds with back-and-forth gyrations of his head.

"He has a handicap," Debbie explains.

He is admitted immediately to the emergency room. Debbie identifies herself as his sister and answers all medical questions: what happened, his medications, this heart problem, the savant syndrome. She is allowed to accompany him as he is wheeled into an area for his vital signs to be taken. A heart-regulating medication and a mild tranquilizer are administered to him intravenously. Debbie watches him drowse off to sleep. Then she is told to return to the waiting room. To wait.

She chooses a plastic chair, away from others. She perches on its edge—spine straight, hands clasped in her lap. The whole of her turns rigid. Otherwise, she would scream. Everyone in the waiting room would know her desperation, how foolish she feels, how alone. No. Not alone. Confused. She wants Shemp gone. She wants him there, to settle Jacob. Without Shemp, Jacob will throw more tantrums, which will lead to his death. With Debbie herself as his assassin. While Shemp waits in shadows. Shemp. Her deliverer. Her assassin.

####

They keep Jacob overnight. When Debbie is allowed in to see him, he is propped on pillows, arms flung out, an IV needle in the right one. He looks cross, disgruntled, a king in exile from his domain. The beeping and blinking of monitoring lights provide bleak distraction to the reality at hand. Jacob's alertness has returned. His scowl holds to her for scarcely a moment before turning away. His resentment approaches hatred, that of an animal that has tasted freedom then been recaptured.

They are sent home with instructions to resume his medication and to follow up with his physician as soon as possible. They drive in silence, separated by the ocean of discord now between them. It is too early, this Monday morning, for the school to be open. Debbie leaves a message explaining that there was an emergency in her family; she will not be coming in. The school knows something of the "Jacob situation," as the assistant principal once called it. Debbie will not lose her job due to absenteeism. Not yet.

She helps Jacob off with his clothes. He reeks of hospital ointments and perspiration. Again she avoids suggesting that he take a shower. She suggests nothing. He climbs into bed in the same Yoda boxer shorts of yesterday morning. His expression has hardened in icy coldness towards his sister, his caretaker, his prison warden. She tries to hand him his *Donald Ducks*, his *Uncle Scrooges*, his *Chip and Dales*, comics she has bought for him. He does not take them. She worries that, without Shemp, she has lost control of him. *He will run out the door while I am sleeping,* she fears. *He will pay me back for chasing off Shemp by returning to Walmart to shoplift again. He will corner the Ethiopian waitress down a side street while she is walking home and ask her how to have his way with her.*

Yawning, she leaves him. She is too exhausted to screen more catastrophes on the wall of her imaginings. One can at best doze while sitting all night in a hospital chair. She barely peels off her blouse and slacks before collapsing into bed. Her mind drifts into quiet. No sooner has sleep claimed her than she is jerked awake by repeated honking brays. Above her, the upstairs neighbor's footsteps accelerate. Back and forth. Louder and harder. Building up to come back down. Administer the final blow. Break the last straw.

Debbie drags herself out of bed and pulls on a bathrobe. Jacob's croaks wedge themselves into every corner of the headache that accompanies her abrupt awakening. The pounding in her skull gives way to raps on the door. She does not even prepare a smile for the neighbor. After all, one is under no obligation to smile for one's executioner.

It is Shemp.

"Gimme a minute." On his weird gliding walk, he rushes into Jacob's bedroom. Instantly, the croaks cease. Shemp comes out. "You want me to stay?" His gaze finds the exposed flesh below her throat. Debbie tightens her bathrobe across it. And nods.

She leaves a follow-up message at work saying that she will be able to come in after all.

####

All is silence beyond the apartment door. Home from Monday work early, Debbie dreads knowing why. *They've run off*, she thinks. *They've left me to stew in my own errors.*

The living room is empty. So is Jacob's bedroom. She finds them, seated across from each other, at the kitchen table. One of Jacob's *Donald Duck* comic books lies between them. The cover shows Donald risen off the ground, his orange-webbed feet elevated on exclamation-marked puffs of rage. His fists are clenched, his duck bill quacking in anger over some antic his three giggling nephews have performed. Jacob appears to be staring at the cover.

Yet his eyes are closed. Shemp focuses on the air between them, as if he sees something above the comic book.

Jacob's eyes blink open.

"You learn fast," Shemp tells him. "You got the makin's of a natural."

"A natural what?" Debbie smiles her interruption.

Shemp stands. His height, abruptly sprung on her, sends a shock through her. She expects his gaze to invade her. Instead, he walks ahead of her to the apartment door.

"What just happened?" she asks, with Jacob out of earshot.

"*Gerushin*," he says. "That's what you saw."

"Is that Hebrew?"

"Yeah."

"What does it mean?"

"Tough to explain. Why don't you ask your boy rabbi?"

"Do you mean Seth?"

"Why not?" Shemp leaves. His responses have carried no barbed insinuation, no hint of lewd suggestion. Perhaps he has simply sought to exit on words whose innocuous nature will not bar him from returning.

Why not indeed. Because Rabbi Seth would come here. He would want to meet Shemp. Speak with him, size him up. Odds are he will sense something wrong, some kink in Shemp's presence. He will urge Debbie to banish this man from their apartment. In which case Jacob will go ballistic once more. There will be more screeching, more trips to the emergency room, more irregular heartbeats to stabilize. More discord, more guilt. More counting the days, in her moments of greatest weariness, to her brother's demise. Or her own.

Jacob, now at the kitchen sink, is washing down his pills.

"Shemp forgot to give those to you?"

"Nah. He doesn't want 'em to get in the way."

"What does that mean?"

"He wants me to learn."

"To take your pills on your own?"

"That's part of it." He sits back down at the kitchen table. His focus locks on *Donald Duck*. He seems to be sucking in the comic book's cover with the power of his stare.

"Why are you doing that, Jacob?"

"I told you already. Shemp wants me to learn."

"Learn what?!"

"*Gerushin*, already! How to tune out the static."

"What does that mean?"

"It's tough to explain." He smiles at Debbie. She recoils. Has he also absorbed Shemp's smile, one of seeing Debbie, not as his sister, but as a woman? No. It can't be. It is something more. Some quality she has never read before in Jacob's innocent savant face: alertness, clarity.

Gerushin, tuning out static, tough to explain—

Jacob's words run rings around her, poke at her, like a child matador tormenting a bull with plastic swords. She has to talk to someone about what's happening. But who?

It comes to her while she showers. Contact Saul. Not by phone. The Hartmans may not be willing to give out that information anyway. No. Ask for his email. And that is exactly what Rebecca Hartman gives Debbie when she telephones the *shul*. Saul Fishman's email.

####

yesodguy@hotmail.com.

Surely it has some meaning that she would prefer not to know. *So I will not email him after all.* She strains to hold to her decision. Until past dinner, she holds out. But the urge nips at her awareness. It bores holes through her concentration. She cannot read. She tries to blame the distraction on the riotous clamor of Jacob's Abbott and Costello discs, which he plays one after another. But it is not that. She helps Jacob change for bed. She makes sure that he washes his face and brushes his teeth properly. Then she sits, fully dressed, on her own bed. Laptop propped on her thighs, she stares at the keys as if they were enemies. *Yesodguy.* Surely an email to Saul will erect a bridge for him to cross. Or for her to cross—to a foreign land, no doubt hostile, glutted with hidden dangers. A land where creatures of the male id roam in search of female fodder. Propelled by a sigh, she goes ahead and types.

Do you know the word Gerushin?

His reply appears quickly: *How nice to hear from you! And with so warm and cordial a greeting!*

Please. She does not apologize for her abruptness. She is surprised that he is at his computer, as if he had been lurking in the cyber brush for her to appear.

It's Hebrew for divorce. Why? Are you separated? Do you need a lawyer?

Is that the only meaning?

His response takes longer. *Why do you want to know? Is this another curveball from that fellow who babysits your Jacob? Where has that guy dragged your head now?* Sparks of jealousy fly off his text. He won't even type Shemp's name. *You didn't get rid of him after all?*

I tried, she types, then erases the line. *Not yet,* she writes instead.

Gerushin is a type of Jewish meditation. You choose a verse from Torah, an insight from Talmud. Or an image. A Jewish letter, let's say. You visualize it. You hold it in your mind's eye for as long as you can. If it is a word, it helps to repeat it over and over. Like a mantra. Do you know that term?

I've heard of it.

It separates people from distractions. The sixteenth-century mystics of Safed used to meditate, Gerushin-style. They'd wander away from the city and lose themselves in nature. Luria, Cordovero, Caro, Vital—our boy Seth has spoken of them. You remember, don't you?

But why a Walt Disney comic book? Donald Duck isn't a verse in Torah. A Donald Duck illustration can't be Gerushin.

Maybe it is. To Jacob. We all have our sacred texts, don't we?

I suppose so, she replies.

What else did your guy explain?

Nothing. He told me to speak to Rabbi Seth.

And did you?

No.

Why not?

I don't know. Her finger punches the send button. Immediately she regrets it.

So you emailed me instead?

Yes.

Do you want company?

Her fingers curl back from the keys. Then she types. *I am not as easy as you think. Do you really think you can smooth-talk your way past my door? Well, you won't.* She smiles defiance at the computer screen. *I only wanted information. Just information. Why can it not simply be that I, as a human, have asked you, another human, for feedback on a word? Why does everything have to be the man looking for an opening into the woman? No. I don't want company. Not yours. Not any man's. Not—*

She highlights the entire text and deletes it.

####

Tuesday afternoon. The walk from the air-conditioned car to the door of her apartment building brings sweat to the white blouse she has worn to work. Reaching behind, she peels the fabric away from her spine then adjusts the waist of her skirt. It is black and over the knees. *My concession to Orthodox modesty*, she teases herself. Its tubular fit hindered her patrolling of the youngsters during their recess break. The building is not air-conditioned. Outside has been cooler than inside in this latest of Atlanta early fall heat waves.

She finds Shemp and Jacob sitting across from each other on the living room floor. The legs of each are crossed. Jacob's hands relax on his thighs. Between them lies a white card with what appears to be, from a distance, a tiny black spot at the center. Stepping closer, she recognizes the shape. A curl, plump and pointed, on top; a thinner spur sprouts comma-like from the bottom.

One of the Hebrew letters?

Eyes shut, Jacob's head inclines towards the card. Shemp monitors the air between them; he seems to be timing Jacob. When Jacob's eyes blink open, Debbie crosses her arms and stares her unstated query at Shemp.

"It's a *Yod*," he tells her.

"I know that. It's the first letter in one name for God. We studied it in Hebrew school."

"God doesn't need a name. You can forget all that 'I Am What I Am' stuff. He had to say something to Moses, didn't He?"

"That's what Popeye says anyway!" Jacob injects himself into the conversation. "'I yam what I yam and that's all what I yam.' The Fleischer Studio made 109 Popeye cartoons for movie theaters. One hundred five are in black and white, four are in color. I've seen all of the color ones. Except *Poor Cinderella*. Popeye

Meets Sinbad the Sailor, I've seen 13 times. *Popeye Meets Ali Baba and the Forty Thieves,* I've seen 13 times too. *Aladdin and His Wonderful Lamp—*"

A rap on the door halts the digression.

Debbie opens the door to Saul Fishman. He waits, white beard combed, vest loose, shirt half-unbuttoned, hands jammed in the largest pockets of his multi-pouched khaki shorts. "I have come to meet Mr. Shemp. Is this a bad time?"

"It's okay," Shemp calls from the floor. "We're about done here anyway. You wanna join us, Mr. Saul?"

"How did you know my name?"

"Devorah must of said it."

"You mean Debbie?"

"Well, she ain't Devorah yet. But she's gonna be."

Saul seats himself, cross-legged, to Shemp's right. "Engraving, you're teaching him?"

"I don't know that word."

"It's visualizing. It's almost like what you did with him yesterday."

"Yesterday was *Gerushin.*"

"With a comic book?"

"For him. For Jacob. Yeah."

"Today is *Yod.*"

"Yeah." Shemp is saying as little as possible.

"The father of all letters," Saul continues. "The one from which all other letters are formed."

"Who taught you that?"

"I read. And I go to a Jewish meditation group."

"That's the word. Meditation. Thanks."

"That's all I can stand, I can't stand no more!" Jacob is scowling now. He resents the imbalance Saul's intrusion has created.

"*Yod.* It's the tenth letter. Its numerical equivalent is ten," Saul explains.

"Lots of tens," Shemp comments.

"Ten Commandments. Ten plagues. Ten things made on the first day of Creation. Ten generations from Adam to Noah. Ten men for an Orthodox minyan, Ten *Sephirot.*"

"You sure read a lot."

"*Yod* is the smallest letter. It's humble. Little more than a dot. But it's the spark, the beginning point of God in all things."

"You sure know a lot." Shemp's disinterested gaze drifts to where Debbie is standing. "You wanna join us?"

She sits across from Saul. She has trouble folding her legs under herself. Finally, she tucks them backward and leans on one hand. Her skirt rides up over her knees. She tries to tug it down but cannot. Her blouse is unbuttoned, though not down to the bosom. Never down to the bosom. *Today's heat*, she would explain. *With the children outside, I had simply forgotten.*

All four now face the *Yod* card. Debbie holds her eyes to it. It is a raft to which she clings in the sea of male undercurrents swirling around her.

"*Yod*," Saul resumes. "It's the seminal drop. The concentrated power of God. The primal vibration." No one is listening to Saul. Not even Saul himself. His attention trails Shemp's to the exposed portions of Debbie's body.

"Seminal. Like semen!" Jacob laughs his raucous bray.

CHAPTER 6

"You wanna join us?"

It is Wednesday afternoon. Home from work, Debbie finds Shemp and Jacob again on the living room floor, across from each other. She is wearing slacks this day. It would be easier for her to sit without having to worry. She stands over them. Jacob ignores her. His eyes are closed, his face inclined towards a new card on the floor between himself and Shemp. The new card is another Hebrew letter. It has two parallel vertical pillars with a horizontal line as a kind of flat roof. At the top, this line nears but does not touch the vertical pillar on the left. It is the *Heh*. The second letter in the ineffable name of God.

"Do you wanna join us or not?" Shemp again asks.

She lowers herself into their cross-legged posture. She does not need to be told to stare at the *Heh*. Her eyes remain open.

"You gotta stop thinking," Shemp advises her.

It is not an unwelcome suggestion. "How do I do that?"

"Close your eyes. Let all the sparkles settle. When they do, put the *Heh* up there where the sparkles were. Got it?"

"I'll try."

"What's in your head?" Shemp asks after a few minutes.

"The *Heh*." It is a lie. Images from the day fill the curtain of her eyelids. The smiley face on Derek Winslow's eye patch, the cinnamon Danish she wishes she had bought at Kroger, the sunset hue of Shemp's eyes—

"Okay. You see the *Heh*. What does it look like?"

Debbie's eyes flutter open. She shakes her head in defeat.

"What about you, Jacob? What do you see?"

"I see the *Heh*."

"What does it look like?"

"A jar."

"What do you mean?"

"That gap at the top is where things get poured in. I mean the side of the top. Where it's open."

"What things get poured in?"

"I don't know."

"What about the bottom? Won't all those things just pour right on out?" Shemp asks.

"I guess so," Jacob answers.

"So where do all those things go?"

"Onto people."

"What do people do with them?"

"Use 'em."

"Is it good stuff or bad stuff?"

"Good stuff. Because it comes from the top. And it comes from a Hebrew letter."

"So all the Hebrew letters are good?"

"I guess so."

"What do you think, Miss Debbie?"

"I don't know." She flattens her voice to come across as uninvolved. She does not like that he called her Miss Debbie. It makes her sound like the host of a children's TV program.

"You gotta stop thinking so much. Your brother, he doesn't need help with that. His savant thing is his help. He jumps on the letters and rides them, like he does with his movies and games. He's barely here when he's into those things. Sometimes he isn't even here at all."

"I know that. I try to control it."

"That isn't the way, telling him to stifle himself. You don't stop it. You guide it."

"That's not what his psychiatrists have said."

"I yam what I yam!" Jacob barks.

A flustered Debbie escapes to the kitchen. Never has she felt intellectually subordinate to Jacob. In other ways, yes. When their father was showering attention onto Jacob. Or at all those appointments with Jacob's physicians and Jacob's mental health specialists and Jacob's test givers. But today is different. If that floor was a classroom, Jacob would make an A. And Debbie Forman would fail.

She thinks to contact Saul that night but does not. Nor can she sleep. More pictures rampage through her head. *Heh's* jumping over a fence. Count them like sheep. Humor does not make her drowsy. It never does. Popeye and Bluto in the ball of smoke and fists that is one of their cartoon fights. Only it is Saul and Shemp. She cuts off the image before Saul loses. The opening at the top of the *Heh*. A receptacle. For what pours inside it. The thought surprises her with sudden desire. Rising from her bed, she drinks a full glass of water to wash it back down. She wishes she had bought that cinnamon Danish.

####

Thursday. *Vav* day. The third letter of God's name.

"A skinny man wearing a lop-sided cap." This answer Debbie contrives, when Shemp asks what she thinks it looks like. Her focus is no stronger than yesterday. It is weaker, in fact. Her frustration erupts in continual squirms. Her legs shift in constant motion on the floor.

"You're blocking it," Shemp tells her. "Like you block everything."

The comment is meant as no criticism. It comes across as matter-of-fact, a statement of reality, almost scientific, as if Shemp were explaining the suspension of salt in a glass of water. Still, it wounds her.

A fishing hook is what Jacob sees.

"What do you mean?"

"It reaches down under the *Heh* and pulls up what's dropped there."

"Then what?"

"I dunno, Shemp."

"That's okay. You're kind of right. You just keep your eyes closed. Hold the *Vav* up there for as long as you can. If you have room for Tuesday's *Yod* and yesterday's *Heh*, hold them too. Can you do that?"

Jacob smiles. Jacob nods. Jacob sees.

####

Friday afternoon. Shemp and Jacob sit in their usual positions on the floor. Four cards lie between them. *Yod-Heh-Vav-Heh*. God's Name, at least one of them. From somewhere in the Torah. The *Tetragrammaton*, it is called, though Debbie cannot remember why. It's Greek, she recalls. And has something to do with the four letters. No one is ever supposed to utter God's Name. Out of respect. Or fear. Or something more.

She does not join them.

Am I not the woman? She has prepared this response for Shemp in case he presses her. *Does it not fall upon me to ready the house for Shabbat? FALL UPON ME? Isn't that the right term for what I do while you men sit?* She is not asked. Nor would such a response express her total feeling. She sees herself as no feminist. It is no less a human construct, so therefore imperfect, than any other of mankind's isms. Humankind's, make that. At the same time, she will never bow to the chauvinist whims of any man.

A regular Vashti.

Isn't that what Shemp had called her? Or had it been Saul? They continue their meditation. Debbie cleans what does and does not need to be cleaned. She makes great show of her efforts in the clattering of dishes, the swishing of cloths across kitchen surfaces. Snatches of conversation come out to her at one point. Actually, only Shemp's murmuring. Something about the *Yod* and the first *Heh* being the man part of God, pouring into the lower letters, the woman part. Of God.

She pounds a half-thawed pack of chicken legs against the kitchen counter. She has no wish to hear more. Yet she does. She cocks an ear towards the living room. Shemp is saying something about the seed being planted into the final *Heh*, which is Earth. He gives Jacob a Hebrew word. *Yichud.* Which means Uniting.

"Why is the *Yod* the man part?" Shemp asks in a teaching voice.

"Because it's pointed?" Jacob's answer is a question.

"Why is the *Heh's* gap at the top, Jacob? Why not the middle, where a real woman has—"

I do not want this in my home.

She marches through the living room to the closet where the vacuum cleaner is stored. She plugs it in and turns it on. The two men are not disturbed. The direct sunlight of late afternoon sets the two seated male forms to shimmering amidst all the dust particles. She tries to blink away the glare. She vacuums close to them, around them. The sound does not stop them. She shuts off the vacuum and returns it to the closet. Through the overbearing slivers of sunlight, she squints at them once more. *Ask Shemp to go now for his special challah. Yes. That will stop them.* She steps forward. For the briefest of moments she makes out what appears to be the likeness of the four letters of the *Tetragrammaton* swirling in the air, like blown leaves, between Jacob and Shemp. Jacob's eyes are still closed. His whole body strains to keep this image afloat. Shemp is smiling in approval. Then the image is gone.

It was the sunlight, she tries telling herself. The direct rays fracturing the wholeness of the moment into an illusion. Of something that could not have been there.

####

Shemp returns with his manna-resembling challah. And a rose. It is a deep and vibrant red, with small thorns running down the stem. He holds it at the place where the green sepals support the petals, separating them from the thorns below.

Do I thank him? Curtsy like a prom date? She rushes to find some holder. Having no vase for flowers, she places a tall glass between the two unlit *Shabbat* candles now rising at the center of the kitchen table. Shemp positions the rose in the glass.

"It doesn't need water." His words stop Debbie from going to the sink.

For the second week in a row, the Sabbath is welcomed without resistance from Jacob. Shemp insists that Debbie read aloud the prayers in Hebrew.

"It's for you to do, Missus *Shekhinah.*" Debbie does not protest his labeling of her. She understands that welcoming God to the home on Sabbath Eve falls to her by virtue of gender. She does not understand why he has again used "missus" to denote her marital status. Shemp's eyes stay on her as she reads. They are vermilion now, a shade of amber that borders on rust. The glow in them pulses then fades, the power of Shemp counterbalanced by some sorrow she now senses he hides. Desire followed by the restraining of desire. Then desire again.

After the meal, Debbie clears the plates. Shemp and Jacob stay seated; she does not mind. *Not all is roses for Missus Shekhinah*, she thinks, as she washes the dishes. She wonders if Shemp is still staring at her. She tries to imagine the flow of her shape when seen from behind. The window before her captures Shemp and Jacob's reflection, silhouetted in the night-darkened pane; the rose floats, at eye level, between them. As the letters of God's name had swirled between them in the living room this very afternoon. Only now there is no sunlight to blame.

"More *Gerushin* practice?" She tries to sound casual as she returns to the table. There is no more denying that she has witnessed the levitation of the rose. Or its having been visualized into concreteness in midair. It could have been either. She can only hope for an explanation that will allow her to sleep.

"Kind of."

"I didn't know...." Debbie trails off.

"Sure you didn't. How could you? The way you are, the way he is."

Shemp's remark is no insult. It is delivered matter-of-factly, a statement of truth regarding fundamental differences between herself and her brother. Again her dunce cap blooms. Then she remembers. Is there not a term for the power that Jacob is demonstrating? Telekinesis or some such? Had not one in the parade of neurocognitive specialists to whom her father had taken Jacob explained that savant syndrome manifests itself in untold forms, many of which have not even been touched by research?

"I'm sure there's a rational explanation for it."

"You wanna try?"

"All right, Shemp. Tell me what to do."

"Just stare at the rose."

Debbie does so.

"Tell me. What do you see?"

"I see a rose. It's red. It's framed by two candles."

"Is that all?"

I see only confusion. Why have you brought it for me? Is it a sign that you wish to embark on a romance? Or is it more practice for Jacob's Gerushin or whatever it is you are teaching him?

She says nothing.

"Help her out, Jacob. What do you see?"

"I see a key."

"What do you mean?"

"To what's up there." He points at the ceiling. Debbie knows that he does not mean their upstairs neighbor.

"Very good." Shemp's tone has turned tutelary. "What do you mean, what's up there?"

"I dunno. I just know what you tell me to know."

"What did we say this afternoon?"

"Everything down here is a key to what's up there. Where God lives."

"Do you believe that yet?"

"I dunno. You told me."

"Come on, Jacob. Try. What do you really see?"

"I see the 13 whatchamacallit's."

"Petals."

"Yeah. Petals. Eight of 'em. They're the beautiful part. Then you have the five green-pointed parts that wrap around the bottom of the petals and support them. Protect them, too. From all the thorns underneath. Which are bad."

"Why?"

"Because they're always trying to stop the petals from opening. They just want to tear them apart. Like sometimes she—"

"That's not true!" Debbie interrupts.

"Is that true, Jacob? Your sister's upset."

"I dunno. She gets me things. Sometimes."

"Come on, Jacob. What about you? Are you such a sweet piece of candy?"

"I dunno what you mean, Shemp."

"How about you, Missus *Shekhinah*? Do you know what I mean?"

"You want me to see the petals, not the thorns."

"Kind of. But not really."

"You want me to look more at the good in life?"

Jacob bellows a yawn. It is time for the evening to be finished.

"Let him have his power." Shemp murmurs, when he and Debbie stand together at the door. Never has he tried to counsel her. Never has he sounded gentler. He hovers over her, his face bent close, the vermilion eyes parting her. Opening her. She closes her eyes and braces for him to try to kiss her. She does not know if she will turn away. He does not try. When she opens her eyes, he is gone. She carries into her bedroom the feeling born in her when they were standing at the door. Her steeling herself to repulse his advances, her desperate longing for his touch—

She turns on her laptop.

"Rose in Judaism," she types into the search engine. The first hit is a line from Song of Solomon: "As a rose among thorns, so is my beloved amongst the daughters."

By this I am not the thorn. I am the rose. Do you hear that, Jacob? I am the rose. And maybe the beloved. Maybe the beloved, do you hear me?! She wants to scream these words in Jacob's face. But

what about "amongst the daughters"? Does Shemp have one-night stands? *With me his special intended?* A school-girl jealousy fills her. It is a sweet feeling. Not negative at all.
Let him have his power.
The words loop in her mind and ease her into sleep.

####

Saturday morning. Shemp has brought another puzzle box. He empties the pieces onto the living room table. Debbie recognizes the circular pieces as resembling those of the puzzle Jacob failed to assemble earlier in the week. Again, as with the Tree of Life puzzle, there are only ten of them. Except this time the Hebrew words are transliterated. She studies the box cover, which this time holds an illustration. Instead of fitting onto tree branches, the pieces are meant to be put into the shape of a man. *Chesed* under the right palm, *Gevurah* under the left. *Tiferet* over the chest. *Yesod* at the genitals.

Yesodguy indeed.

So that's what Saul was up to, Debbie fumes. Anger flushes her cheeks.

"Listen, it isn't really a naked man. It just shows how what's in God fits into what's in a person," Shemp explains.

"Does Jacob have to play it today? On *Shabbat*? Isn't this a day of rest?"

"Yes. You're right. I should have known. Me, of all people."

"I got cartoons!" Jacob has joined them now. He stands bleary-eyed but excited in his undershirt and boxer shorts. "We can watch 'em all day! I don't wanna do a puzzle today anyway. Not a hard puzzle like that one! And the one from before!"

"Which means you ain't ready for it."

"Hey, I can put together any puzzle! Except that kind of puzzle! It's a trick, Shemp, and you know it! Why do you wanna trick me?"

"You're tricking yourself, kid. You want me to go?"

"No! I want us to watch cartoons!"

"Okay, okay." Shemp turns to Debbie. "You go on ahead to *shul*. I'll tell Jacob to get dressed. You got his pills laid out?"

"Not yet, Shemp. Can you help him?"

"Jacob can handle it. It's about time, right? He's gotta learn. About getting dressed too."

Jacob is in the kitchen as she leaves. A pill box pops open. Several bounce across the floor. Shemp, at the kitchen archway, does not help pick them up.

Debbie's thoughts veer between questioning Shemp's help and condemning Saul's trickery as she walks. *At least Shemp doesn't try to insinuate his male presence into me with not so subtle allusions to his virility through an email screen name.* Should she avoid him today? No. Confront him. Ask him point blank to explain that screen name. See which way he squirms.

After services she lights out after Saul.

"Hello. Mr. Yesodguy." Her voice trembles, her resentment patent.

"Aha. So somebody told you about *Yesod*? Our boy Shemp, I suppose?"

"I saw a picture."

"A picture's worth a thousand words." He gropes to extend his retort but does not. "Look at me, Debbie. You see a guy at the end of his hippy rope. His guy rope too, for that matter. You try turning 70 sometime. You won't like it. Time's a bitch, honey. It always takes but never gives."

"Can you drive me home?" she asks, letting the 'honey' remark pass.

In his car, her hostility thaws. Silence seems pointless. "He brought another one of his puzzles this morning. It had those same ten spheres."

"The *Sephirot*. Did Jacob figure it out this time?"

"He didn't even try."

"Something's going on. Something really... queer, if I may float the word in both its classic and more contemporaneous sense. Are you sure it's okay to leave those two alone?"

"I just don't think there's a problem. Not in that way. Shemp really wants Jacob to figure out the puzzle. I can tell you that much." She doesn't bring up about the levitations of Donald Duck, the letters of God's Name, last night's rose. One perplexity at a time is more than enough.

"Tell me, was the face of a woman in the lowest sphere?"

"Yes. I saw the drawing on the puzzle box."

"Which Shemp didn't show to Jacob. Otherwise, Jacob wouldn't be able to figure it out on his own. Right?"

"Right. That's all, then?"

"Debbie, I don't have to say that things are hardly that simple. Not to you, of all people. Your boy Shemp was using an image of A*dam Kadmon*. It's another way of visualizing the spheres. Not as a tree, but as a man. The First Man. God's blueprint for Creation, with the *Sephirot* positioned strategically throughout. From the top, the *Ein Sof*—the Hidden Essence of God's Presence—filters down through the other eight *Sephirot* emanations to... well, to the *Shekhinah*. Who dwells in the *Malchut* sphere. The lowest *Sephirah*. The one where we mortals live. Or try to live."

"Please, Saul. You're losing me." She holds back from questioning what Shemp has called her. Missus *Shekhinah*. It should be enough that the woman leads the welcoming of the *Shekhinah* to the home on Friday night. It should be simple, not a tangle of interpretations within interpretations spinning off more interpretations.

"Hey, I'm losing myself too, for that matter. The *Shekhinah* is the feminine aspect of God. She's down here with us in *Malchut*. Exiled with us by her own choice. In *Malchut*. Which is the tenth *Sephirah*. Our very own *Sephirah*—this blind, long-suffering wasteland world. And the *Shekhinah* is not happy at all about where she is or what she sees while she's sharing our exile here, in *Malchut*, on Earth. But there's nothing she can do about it. Except follow us. And hope we don't get hurt too badly. Because the *Shekhinah*'s that aspect of God that always loves us. No matter what. She's like a mother who can't give up on her kid, no matter how many times he drops out of school or gets thrown in jail. All she can do is hope that someday we'll get it all straightened out."

"By *Tikkun Olam*."

"Why not? That's as useful a condensation of the Ultimate Complexity as any."

"Why do we welcome her on Friday night, then?"

"Oh, if you tie in another several hundred legends, rabbinic and Kabbalistic or otherwise, you get to Friday night. When the *Shekhinah* returns from exile to God's bedroom, as it were. And they get to, well, how did Shakespeare put it?"

"Don't be vulgar, Saul. Why not just say unite? Find unity."

"I yield the floor to the counselor from Buckhead." Saul has pulled up in front of Debbie's apartment building. "Listen, do you want me to come in?"

"I can take care of myself, Saul. Thank you, anyway."

"I'll let you off right here, then." His tone is restrained now, dutiful to the point of subservience. It is enough to make her miss the wise guy. Almost.

CHAPTER 7

Her afternoon nap lasts for several hours. Her few surfacings to wakefulness are underscored by the reassuring cacophony of cartoon humor played, for her sake, at a respectfully low volume. Occasionally she tunes in to their murmurings. Jacob, telling Shemp about the waitress from Ethiopia, that *Noonday Holocaust* movie he tried to steal. Shemp, asking Jacob for more details about the characters in the *Sisters of Nightfall* comic book, especially the one called Azazel.

Fall has deepened; the days have grown shorter. Debbie's bedroom, with its solitary, east-facing window, has already been claimed by evening dimness. The *nagual*, as Rabbi Seth would put it.

The television is off, the living room empty, when she comes out. Shemp's new video game box is nowhere in sight. No covert intention unfolds here, only quiet. Jacob is asleep in his bedroom. Shemp is leafing through *Sisters of Nightfall* at the kitchen table.

"He loves this stuff."

"I know." Silence rises between them. An Orthodox warning flashes through her mind: an unmarried man and woman, not to be alone together. "I'll get the *Havdalah* candle. It's in the other room." She starts out.

"There's another way to finish *Shabbat*. Luria used to do it. Out in a field. Under the stars."

"I'll go wake Jacob."

Shemp leads them away from the erupting Saturday evening Buckhead traffic. He walks them into a pocket of older Atlanta homes, mercifully sequestered from the grinding roars of Peachtree Street. Debbie has never been in this area before, nor to the small park beyond these residences. Here Shemp stops. An unpaved walking path loops a pond on which ducks and geese float and fly and skim the water. The three of them settle on the grass. Tall pines and low bushes rim the pond, enveloping it in shades of green so special to the Atlanta that she has loved. They enclose it in an even greater peace than the pond already possesses. The twilight is giving way to night. No one else is there. For several minutes no one speaks. Free of the lights of Buckhead, the sky pales to streaks of orange and blue that soon fade as well.

"Are you two ready for a game? Lie back on the grass. Put your hands behind your heads. Watch the sky. Point to three stars as soon as you see them. But you can't point before. First one wins. If you point too soon, you lose. Got it?"

Shemp is reclining between them. For once he addresses Debbie without locking his gaze on her. "That's how they used to do it in the villages," he explains softly. "You wait until you spot three stars in the sky. Three means *Shabbat* is over. The week begins. All your headaches come pouring back in."

Debbie smiles. Shemp does not see. She observes him in profile, his eyes a pure liquid violet now, filled with what she can only deem a mystery of sadness. A longing, akin to regret. It seems a stricken melancholy, much like that which accompanies guilt. For what? *What tortures you so, Shemp?* She wants to ask but remains quiet. She has no wish to shatter this charmed twilight. *If charmed it is,* she warns herself. *It's the oldest trap in the world, is it not? A woman braving the dark chamber of a man's torment to heal him?*

Yet who fashions the trap, the man or the woman?

Her attention returns to the night sky. The three stars are there. Already, Jacob points to them. She is glad to let him win. This time.

####

Monday morning. A steady rain cools Atlanta. It also creates a power outage at Debbie's school during lunch time. Parents are called, children sent home. Those whose families could not be contacted remain behind in the care of the teachers, who will be paid for the day. But not the assistants. Which is just fine with Debbie. For the first time in as long as she can remember, she awoke in a happy mood. Thanks to Shemp, there have been interludes when she has opened to the positives of this world. Two Sabbath evenings of peace in a row. Saturday's sunset, at the pond.

Where might she take Shemp and Jacob today? She considers options as she drives home. None come to mind. None really matter. *The world is your supply,* she has read. The bracing thrill of the unexpected. It is life, this thrill, this opening to life's bounty. It is a garden which flourishes when watered by the unplanned. She parks close to the door of their apartment building. On Monday spaces are more plentiful, with so many tenants at work. As soon as she cuts off the engine, the rain picks up. At first, she sits to wait it out. Then she ventures into it, glad to feel the natural soaking through her clothes, embracing her skin.

Music blares out to her from beyond the door. Some ancient rock and roll song, one of Jacob's 45 rpm records, scratchy with jumps where Jacob has let the needle fall too clumsily onto the grooves. "Dr. Feelgood", this one is called. "Now you talk about women... I love 'em all... so good, so good..." It ends. There is a click and a whir, the slap of another record dropping from a stack on the spindle of Jacob's old player. "Louie Louie", is this one. *It hides dirty lyrics,* she has read. But most of the song is unintelligible to Debbie. Had there been any off-color lines, Jacob's savant syndrome would have detected them like a mine sweeper. She has no idea why Jacob dug out this device and these records. Perhaps it is another face of the unexpected? Hoping to surprise them with her early return, she puts on a smile, unlocks the door, and slips inside.

They stand side by side, backs to her, swaying to the coarse and thrusting glides of the song. Shemp has taken off his black robe. His white shirttails flop loosely against the seat of his pants. Jacob wears no shirt at all.

"Stop this right now! You have no right—"

And they do stop. Taken by surprise, they whirl to face her. Shemp's shirt is unbuttoned. His exposed chest, his uncovered throat, even his face and hands—they possess a scarlet iridescence. His translucent body seems more a shell encasing crimson fire that flickers and licks across his surface as flames do.

I'm seeing through him. Debbie sinks to her knees. She does not look up but only hears the scrape of the needle jerked from the record, the shuffle of garments being put back on. Shemp pauses over her on his way to the door. She risks staring up at him. His form is once more concealed within the folds of his black robe. His face and hands now possess human flesh tones. His eyes linger upon her, longer than ever before, the rose-pink of them unearthly, feral, in a way that stirs in her an animal longing so strong, so beyond any logic of control, that she can only avert her own glance to temper it. His black robe blurs as he leaves her. The door quietly closes.

And she is alone. With Jacob. He is sliding his 45 rpm records back into the sleeves. He takes them into his room, the closet where he keeps them. She waits for him to put away the record changer as well. He will not speak to her until he has finished setting this particular compartment of his life back in order. It is one of the laws of his condition. Everything must be in its place.

Rising from the living room floor, she stands in his doorway. Jacob is lying on his side, back to her, on his bed.

"What is he?" she asks.

"Shemp?"

"Who else?"

"He's an angel. You didn't know that?" He speaks to the wall, not to her face.

"What makes you so sure? Maybe he's something else."

"He ain't no demon."

"I didn't mean that. I meant maybe he's a man with some peculiar condition."

"Like me?"

"That's not what I meant either."

"It is too."

Debbie makes no reply. To do so would drag her into one of their arguments, never more pointless or ill-timed.

"Shemp's an angel," Jacob repeats.

"What's he doing here, then? Why were you two dancing that way?"

"It's more *Gerushin* stuff. How to work up some joy first."

"I don't understand."

"I know ya don't understand. Ya never understand. Not the important stuff."

"What do you mean, the important stuff?"

"I dunno. If you dunno, I dunno."

"Why is he here?!"

Jacob pulls himself around on the bed. Sitting up, he stares straight at her.

"Because you ain't."

Debbie backs off. She stands frozen in the living room. *Where to now?* Choosing her bedroom, she shuts the door behind her. On the edge of her bed she sits, bolt straight, knees tight, hands clasped in her lap—her favored posture, one that allows her time to regrow a shell around herself. It has worked in the past. It does not work now. This time the world has tricked her too well. It is an old lesson of hers, never well learned. *Open yourself to the world and it will shut you down fast. With a kick to the gut. A blade to the heart.* It has killed her many times over in her lifetime. Not physically but emotionally. Spiritually, if that is the word.

This time is different. It is not like the bait-and-switch of a man who feigns to court and respect her then puts his hands on her when she least expects it. Not like the phony smile and false praise of a father who wants only that she stay with his son when he, the father, needs or wants to be someplace else. This trick paralyzes her. It makes her feel stupid. And helpless. *And to think, I was beginning to love him.*

####

Hours pass. She remains seated on the edge of her bed, the rain her only companion. She welcomes the sound of the drizzle. It is white noise that obscures the spiritual cacophony of the world outside her bedroom, a malevolent cartoon universe full of translucent phantoms with rose-pink eyes and crimson skin. With the door shut, she feels safer, though *safe* is not the word. *Sealed off for now* would be better. From the dinnertime sounds of Jacob foraging through the kitchen for something to eat. From the deformed realities that prance like goblins in their living room.

So Shemp's an angel, eh? Then where are his wings? What's he doing here anyway? Don't be so gullible, Debbie. Had not some behavioral therapist in Jacob's past cautioned that savants are capable of extreme interpretations of reality? Perhaps this Shemp interfaces perfectly with Jacob's illusions? No doubt he bears some syndrome of his own. That must be it. They met at some specialist's office. In the waiting area. While Debbie was in with the latest professional to hear his or her summary of the session with Jacob.

She turns on her laptop. After it loads, she types "angels" into her search engine. Many thousands of hits come up. "Appearance of angels," she types instead. Among the relatively fewer hits that register, "meanings of angel colors" is among them. She scrolls through various explanations of angel colors. It amazes her that anyone has actually put so much thought into such a topic, much less to quantify it. The yellow of goodly radiance, the blue of holiness on high, the green of miraculous healing. How do these people know? Do they meditate on rainbows and make up what they want? And white. Of course, white. Pure as the clouds below

Heaven. Or as the white people who have cornered the market on such fabrications. Where are black angels? Do the blue *devas* of India count?

One website reproduces not only the colors but their shades. The compiler makes claim to having researched a variety of sources within the "admittedly disparate" field of angelology but asserts that much of what is presented elsewhere is at most a compendium, a putative consensus, of what has been written about archangels, throne angels, ruling angels, messenger angels, destructive angels, and the whole host of types within the "constellation" of angels with which legend, mythology, and "pure religion itself" have provided humankind. She scans on, down the colors, not the explanations beside them. And there it is. The exact shade of red that had been spreading up Shemp's chest to his throat and face. This explanation, Debbie reads. It uses two of the same words that had come into her mind upon beholding him. Crimson. Iridescent. *The color of shame. Most often associated with the fallen angels of Genesis.*

Not too far down is the color that had flooded his eyes. Rose pink. *The color of sexual desire.*

In an angel?

She shuts down her laptop. The sudden cessation of its artificial light allows complete darkness to fill her bedroom. Darkness, and something more. Somehow, the entire reality of the space around her has changed. Some menacing foreign energy has entered. Or is that just her imagination? Which she must learn to trust more. Isn't that what Shemp has been telling her? Jacob as well?

Ya never understand.

She snorts a quiet laugh to dismiss the rebuke. It does not help. Nor does it change the blackness of mood now filling her bedroom. It is alive, this blackness. It has taken over this room, this space, no longer safe. *Unless I am making this whole thing up.* She stands to stretch the hurt from her muscles. What would she normally be doing at this hour? It is past dinner-time. She has no hunger anyway. *Why not change into your bedclothes? Yes. That is what you would be doing. Normally.* She opens the bureau drawer that holds her nightclothes and reaches in. Her fingers brush not cotton, not flannel, but something rounded, hairy, hard. She jerks her hand away. Some creature has taken refuge in her night clothing. Some spider perhaps? No. Too large. Perhaps some small mammal that, seeking shelter, wormed its way inside and curled up to sleep? Not likely. It did not move when she touched it. Maybe Jacob is playing a trick. Except Jacob does not play tricks.

She takes hold of the flashlight atop the bureau. She shines the light into the drawer. It is filled with objects the size of coconuts, mud-brown and sphere-shaped, bristling with hairs. An odor rises from them, the fetidness of things dead. Yet life stirs in them. It is no manifestation of life she has known, much less quantified. And quantify she must. It is her life's protecting impulse. She must understand these presences, impose logic on them. They are not *Sephirot*. This much she knows. Otherwise, she cannot begin to make sense of them.

Instinctively, she tries to pull away. She cannot. Why? Another tug fails. She looks down at herself. A tendril extends, from one of these objects, into her middle. She feels no pain. She had not been stung or bitten. Still, the tendril joins her to this sphere. It is the newest sphere. Perhaps. For it is on top of many others, the one nearest the front. It is a dark liquid brown that borders on blackness. Yet it is shiny with the richness of light. Its surface possesses an excrescent viscosity that puts her in mind of online images she had found when researching her mother's tumor. Yet it does live. It thrives. *On me. It knows me. Though it has no eyes, it sees into me.* It is like an umbilical cord. Except umbilical cords do not have dark hairy coatings. And it pulses. She feels it probing inside her chest, beneath her heart, that very spot where her isolation gnaws, where the denials of her mind have established their last rule in her body, the exiled throne of her urge to constrain, contain, control.

The sphere-like object feeds on that denial. It sucks at her, and as it does so, a single eye opens on its surface. She has no desire to meet its stare. It causes feelings of guilt to rise in her. Why? *I have done nothing. Nothing.* The more she protests, the more vitality the sphere gains. More complete shapes begin to take form around the eye. Human shapes. Two of them. One tall and muscular, one short and slight. With that one eye. It is the eye of Derek Winslow. Standing beside Josh Kim. Both glare up at her from within that foul sphere. Both shout contempt in a silence so loud that she clamps both hands over her ears. Still she hears them. She squeezes her eyes shut. Still she sees them. And a word from Rabbi Seth's lectures comes to her mind.

Kelipah.

She longs to slam the drawer shut. But she cannot renounce it, cannot sever her connection to it. To do so would be the same as to deny a baby milk from its mother's breast. A baby the mother hates. Even as she hates herself for having conceived it.

At this admittance, it lets go. It has fed enough. It leaves her spent, exhausted; despite her drowsiness, she manages to shove the drawer shut. Then she retreats to her bed, collapses upon it, and sleeps.

####

Daylight fills her bedroom. She has no wish to awaken. To do so is to face yesterday. And last night. But there is work. And there is Jacob.

Of course Shemp's an angel. You didn't know that?

She climbs from her bed. She is surprised to find herself fully clothed. For the first time in years, she has not brushed her teeth before sleep. Her mouth breathes the same foulness she smelled from those awful things in her dresser. *Those Kelipot spheres.* Were they still there? As long as she doesn't open that drawer, she won't have to know. She looks down at herself. The hair-coated tendril no longer probes inside her. Perhaps never had. She is not prone to dreams, much less ones that leave the detritus of illusion in their wake. As long as she stays away from that drawer….

But she must get ready for work. She can't lose her job. *So go ahead. Brush your teeth. Cleanse your mouth of that taste. Take a shower, put on fresh clothes. If Jacob isn't hogging the bathroom, that is. Go ahead,* she rails at herself. *Throw the door open.* Which means letting in the outside world. Jacob and Shemp's outside world. With its Seven Earths and sex-charged jigsaw puzzles and exercises in *Gerushin* and telekinetically elevated roses. But that is only in her apartment. *Most of the world isn't what Seth calls right-brained,* she reminds herself. The morning sunlight pouring in through the window, car engines coughing to life as people drive off to work, even the blue fluorescence of the numbers on her digital alarm clock—

Reluctantly, she turns the doorknob and steps through.

The heat strikes her first. It is strong enough to push her back a step. Thin veils of smoke obscure a form that extends pillar-like from her living room floor to its ceiling. *My apartment is on fire,* she briefly thinks. Yet the smoke is more like dry steam. It does not burn her eyes. She blinks anyway. Her focus gathers; she sees. Shemp's form rises at the center of her living room. His head all but grazes the ceiling. He is naked. Yet it is not the normal nakedness of human males. There is nothing human about it. Three pairs of scarlet wings adorn him. The first spreads wide, in majesty, from his shoulders. The second folds to cover his loins. The third pair opens at each thigh. The whole of him is of that same crimson iridescence she found in her online research. Yet no words would capture the texture of him. It is not so much indescribable as undefinable. One might describe a being whose surface is of flames that flow upon him like cords of water. One may state that he is not made of flesh. But to define such a being? One who burns yet does not burn? Who glows from within like water reddened by some subterranean sun? Who is utterly foreign to any human or animal, alive or imagined, that has ever been seen, much less known of?

His face is human. But it is a face alive with sparks. Crimson to be sure, of a cosmic radiance that awes her, as might an intimate view of a giant planet. His beard is gone. His cheeks are smooth, as is the whole of him. He might have been a statue. Except that he moves. Not much, only a faint rotation towards her, a downward incline of his head to allow his eyes to hold her. They are not the rose pink of sexual desire. But crimson as the rest of him. *The color of shame,* she has read. Only by these baleful eyes does she find any hope of safety in his presence. She recognizes the sad longing in them, the blend of desire and regret that now constitutes the least of his mysteries.

"Are you a demon?" Her question is bold, one that has to be asked. Yet there would be no stopping him if he wished to tear her apart. Burn her alive. Take up residence within her and make her head swivel. Or whatever it is that demons do.

"He ain't no demon. I already told ya." Jacob stands in his bedroom doorway. He too stares up at Shemp, but not with his sister's level of awe. Has he seen Shemp this way before?

"I will tell you what I am. Then you will know my story." No longer is his inflection colored by B-movie Brooklynese.

"May I use the telephone, Shemp?"

"Shemhazai is my true name. Of course you may use the telephone. You may do anything that you wish. You may ask me to leave. Is that your wish?"

Debbie edges her way across the living room. In the kitchen, she lifts the phone's receiver and dials work. This time she calls in sick and means it.

CHAPTER 8

He speaks in a voice surprisingly soft, one whose smallness belies his size. His tone is crystal-lucid, melodious, as befits a being once numbered among the ranks of the Seraphim, the highest of angels that hover above God's throne, to sing praises to the Lord.

He tells first of how two of these exalted Seraphim, he and the one known as Azazel, became leaders of the 200 angels that descended to Earth in the epoch of humankind's dawning. The Watchers, these angels were called. *Irinim.* Those Ever Wakeful, Beings Who Never Sleep. At their request, God allowed them to walk the earth—to observe God's final creation, to report the actions of newly forged mortals to the Heavenly Court. Yet God doubted the Watchers' strength to withstand the pull of the evil inclinations built into the fabric of this new earth. It was God's challenge to humans. Learn to control your darker impulses. Resist the challenges that will constantly assail you. But for angels to do so? Watchers in human form, with human shells?

God warned them. Still they descended. The Watchers found instant distraction in mortal women. The enticements of their most casual postures, the inviting sway of their hips, the moods that etched their faces in different shades of allure—everything about the Daughters of Men chanted siren calls to angel eyes that had been shielded from such sights by the walls of Heaven. The first sweet tug of lust emptied the Watchers' resolve; how they desired these Daughters of Men, in whose forms the Watchers' angelic seed might be planted, their earthly hungers satisfied!

In coming to Earth, the Watchers had assumed the forms of men whose size and power should have drawn the objects of their desire to them. Yet the human exteriors by which the Watchers enabled themselves to become visible in the lower realms were not sufficient to win over these females of the new earth. The women of these First Generations were raw, simple creatures, lovely yet primitive, far removed from any understanding of the trove of eternals brought down from the Heavens by the Watchers. They knew not what to make of these strange males entering their villages. New to their natural wiles, they were scarcely aware of their power over mortal males no more evolved than they were.

It was enough for them to be taken by whatever man would have them, to be sheltered in that man's dwelling, to be safe by the fire that warmed her, beside the male who fed her, wrung children from her. And if a man passed her by, then so be it.

So it was that the Watchers began to woo humankind with higher teachings.

Those led by Shemhazai shared with the Daughters of Men the Heaven-sequestered secrets of primal allurement. See how these dye-brightened garments draw men's gazes. See how the painting of bold colors beneath your eyes and upon your lips slow the males who once passed you. See how they pause as if hypnotized by the glitter of precious jewels that adorn the smooth flesh of your throat. And if your adornments do not slow them, then the roots and powders you add to their food or drink most certainly will.

Azazel's generalship schooled mortals in more literal war. Males were taught the secrets of metal forging, the fashioning of ever more efficient forms of weaponry. So war came to be. War spread, and with it the hunger for killing. While their men were slaughtering each other, the women invited the Watchers' heavenly seed into their earthly wombs. Soon were born giants that roamed the land. *Nephilim*, these were called. Offspring that spliced the purity of the upper realms with the taint of the lower realms. In this profane mix, the downward slide to the purge of the Flood found true momentum. Through ten generations, from Adam to Noah, humankind piled vileness upon vileness, abomination upon abomination.

In the time of this Tenth Generation, corruption reigned with a level of savagery unknown on this earth. Lust satisfied was not lust banished; glutted with the flesh of mortal women, both the Watchers and their *Nephilim* offspring forced their passions upon the beasts of the field. The earth swarmed now with all manner of beings. The 200 Watchers and the *Nephilim* giants, the men with their instruments of violence, the women with the enhancements of their flesh—these were joined by the monstrous hybrids born of matings with beasts by the half-human children of the angelic. The mingling of spirit and flesh was further corrupted; the land teemed now, as well, with creatures in whose genes the divine, the mortal, and the bestial combined.

"Like that man with the fly's head that frightened you in Jacob's movie," Debbie interrupts.

"Wasp women and alligator people and werewolves too," Jacob kicks in.

"The creatures in your movies are at best pale approximations of the mongrel horrors that roamed the earth in the time of the Tenth Generation. They were terrifying even to the Watchers. And to me. Only Azazel took delight in them. The more extreme their deformities, the more pleased he was."

The appetites of this profane menagerie were not limited to the carnal, Shemhazai continues, resuming his story. The denizens of the Tenth Generation lusted for meat as well. Daily, the *Nephilim* devoured camels and horses, cattle and oxen, by the dozens. When they had supped full of beasts, they turned on humans. They became cannibals. Carcasses of man and beast alike lay discarded, unburied. The whole earth reeked of decay. To satisfy their thirsts, the *Nephilim* washed down what they had eaten with the blood that pooled across the land. In this blood, an ever more inventive humanity found further uses for the powers of divination with which the Watchers had gifted them. They summoned, from the blood, the spirits of slaughtered *Nephilim* to fight beside them in their endless civil wars. These remain among the host of demons that lurk among mortals to this day.

God was grieved to His heart by the actions of this Tenth Generation. God knew pain; God knew regret. Other worlds He had created and destroyed before forming this one: worlds rendered imperfect by an excess of severity, a dearth of mercy. So God determined that this world would not be destroyed. It would be purified. The very land itself pleaded for cleansing. And God heard. The Flood began. The waters rained from above and burst upwards from the sea bed below. Humans and wildlife, the *Nephilim* and their hybrid offspring—most perished. Immune from the ravages of the Flood, the immortal Watchers were chained away in exile, Shemhazai and Azazel as well.

Suspended upside-down from the Sky as his punishment, Shemhazai was cursed to witness below him the devastation wrought in this Tenth Generation as well as in future times. His own legion of offspring had died: some in the *Nephilim* wars, others in the Flood. Daily he suffered for his actions. He found no peace. He longed to find a way to repent.

Azazel knew no such regret. Chained in his cavern beneath the earth, he continues to this day to contrive snares of destruction that he shares with all who make pilgrimage to him. He pleasures himself with female demons that survived the Flood and visit him in his abyss. But as long as he is chained, the world need not fear him.

Shemhazai's thoughts also turned to his want for a female—one female this was, the solitary one among thousands upon whom he had not pressed his desires, for she would not receive them. Istahar, she was called. A mortal virgin now risen among the stars.

But of Istahar Shemhazai would not speak, beyond murmuring her name in brief longing, in briefer regret. And there ended his story.

####

The three of them remained at the kitchen table. Shemhazai has resumed his human form, complete with Orthodox black garb and mountain-man beard.

"Why are you here?" Debbie asks. His story has not been enough.

Jacob rushes to answer. "He's gotta finish his, what do ya call it, Shemp? Your mission?"

Shemhazai nods.

"See? I ain't so dumb after all." Jacob shoots a glare at Debbie. On one of his bellowed yawns, he retires in triumph to his bedroom.

"What mission?"

"All right. My mission. Every angel is sent to Earth with one mission only. Consider the three angels that visited Abraham at his tent. One tells Abraham and Sarah that Isaac will be born to them in their old age. Another saves Lot when Sodom and Gomorrah are destroyed. The third enforces the destruction. Their missions done, all three return to Heaven."

"So, what is your mission?!" She cannot screen the impatience from her voice.

"Jacob needs to find a woman. Before he dies, he needs that woman."

"All right! That's enough!" She stands, shoulders stiffened, her signal that he has overstepped his bounds. She walks him to the door but stays behind him so that his eyes won't roam her. Fallen angel indeed. An extremely talented illusionist, is more like it. One capable of changing size and shape and color with a skill that would put the Houdinis and Copperfields and Blackstones of this world to shame.

At the door, he turns to face her. She is close enough to feel the heat of him. Still his eyes burn into her. The rose pink has returned to them. The color of desire.

"Do you want me to come tomorrow?"

"I don't care."

"For Jacob, I mean."

"Of course that's what you mean."

"Angels don't lie. Though the information they give may be incomplete."

"That's not very reassuring."

"Nothing is reassuring," Shemhazai says.

"Not even God?" Debbie counters.

"God wants to help humans. But they must help themselves first."

"I've heard that before."

"But you don't believe it?"

"I no longer know what to believe."

"That doesn't have to be a bad thing either."

"Shemp, please."

"Do you want me here tomorrow or not?"

"I'd better not miss more work."

"Is that your only reason?"

"Why not? Is Jacob really going to die?"

"Don't all humans die?"

"But you have to find a woman for him first. Isn't that right?"

"He must find his own woman. To rescue. Then to...."

"Rescue, is it now?! I don't care what you call it! He doesn't need a woman! He needs discipline! Not like spankings or time-outs. Like self-control. And that's impossible with his condition. I know. I've lived with him for years. And you've only been around him for what, a couple of weeks? Unless you were spying on us from a cloud? Or wherever it was that God dangled you from the sky?"

"You don't know what you're talking about." Shemhazai smiles through his beard. For yet another moment, his rose pink eyes hold to her. Then he is gone.

####

Dinnertime. Darkness. Debbie hears the flat-footed swish of Jacob beyond her bedroom door.

Has he told you where to find a woman, Jacob? How about the bars in Buckhead? You two would make a real pair on a Saturday night. If Buckhead fails, surely there are houses of prostitution in Atlanta. But I won't find them for you. Let that be Mr. Shemhazai's job. If he can sprout wings, he can find whore houses.

The living room is empty. So is the kitchen. The door to Jacob's bedroom is open, his bed unoccupied, a different issue of *Sisters of Nightfall* open on its rumpled sheets. She breaks their most sacred unspoken rule by entering Jacob's bedroom without his permission. The issue of *Sisters of Nightfall* is indeed not the one she knows about. Is it yet another secret gift from Mrs. Benederet? She picks it up. On this one's cover, the Sister of flaming red hair is shown from the back. She kneels astride a supine male figure while the blonde Sister looks on, smiling eagerly, awaiting her turn. The recumbent figure lies with three pairs of wings spread out from him. It may be a Seraph. But it is not Shemhazai. His body is massive, muscular, the burnished amber of molten iron. Ram horns curve alongside broad cheeks. Yellow goat eyes with horizontal black slits stare up as if dominating the Sister atop him. His grin is at once feral and evolved, animal-like but of high intelligence. Circling the scene are vignettes, like numbers on a clock, miniature depictions of winged demons using a daunting array of weapons to bring death to everyday twenty-first century mortals. Blood pours in crimson streaks from knifed torsos. It gushes in bright red jets from sword-severed limbs. Decapitations abound. Heads are blown apart, eyes gouged to pools of jelly. Fists split cheeks open; bullets penetrate faces; arrows penetrate chests, all accompanied by more blood spewing in arcs that might be termed graceful. Along the bottom, in letters dripping red, are these words: "IS THIS THE END?"

"Please don't touch that."

Jacob's voice. It comes from deep in his walk-in clothes closet, across the room from his bed. Debbie puts down the comic and goes to him. As she approaches, she is met by the same stench that assailed her from her own dresser drawer last night. One hand clamped over her nose and lips, she steps over the lip of the closet. Jacob is seated, facing her, in the darkened far end. Cross-legged, round-shouldered, he hunches over something cradled in his lap. Head down, he studies it so intently that he takes no further note of his sister's presence. She slips forward in order to see more clearly. Black, oily spheres fill the closet shelves behind him. Dozens of them. She coughs out a gasp. It draws Jacob's attention up to her. Whatever he has been holding falls from his hands. It rolls near Debbie but halts at her feet. Imprinted on its surface is an image of Jacob himself, lying on his bed, an unclothed female kneeling over him. It is not a Night Sister but a tall, slender young woman with ebony skin and large-framed glasses. The Ethiopian waitress from the pancake house? Fana, her name was. Brightness, it means. Not bright here but discomfited, submissive. The coitus is imprecisely imagined, as by one with no experience of it. A hair-coated tendril joins this dark, slimy sphere to Jacob's chest, just below his heart.

"Get outta here," he orders Debbie, without conviction. When she does not leave, he retreats to his new, head-of-the-class tone of voice. "I bet ya don't even know what these is called."

"I do know. You don't have to tell me. *Kelipot* is the word." She does not say how Rabbi Seth explained *Kelipot* in one of his sermons. She makes no mention of what she has seen, attached to herself, in her own bedroom.

"The bad in us makes 'em. Shemp says so. That's what they feed on. The bad in us."

"All right then. How do we get rid of these husk-like excretions from discarded worlds, this parasitic waste matter from every human breach of good?"

"I dunno what you're talkin' about."

"I didn't think you would." The acid comment escapes before she can censor it. Instantly she feels a pull, a probing in her chest. Below her heart. Another *Kelipah*. *How easily we form them,* she thinks.

"I ain't so dumb." Jacob's response is sullen, defeated.

"The *Kelipot* empower the Other Side. The Dark Side, if you prefer your happy talk from *Star Wars*."

"Okay. All right. You win." Jacob yawns. His chin drops. An exhausted sigh escapes him.

Debbie retreats to her room. It is her turn to know triumph. So why doesn't she feel any better? To the contrary. The tugging in her chest has strengthened. She feels it feeding on the one-sided duel for intellectual superiority that she has just won. But lost. *My resentment was perfectly justifiable,* she would counter, in way of defense. *It wasn't my fault. Do you hear?* She will shout this latest *Kelipah* out of existence. She opens the dresser drawer which last night had been packed with them. This newest one rests atop the other ones, all rotten yet vibrant, all black yet bright, all hard as keratin yet viscous as slime. And no more likely to honor her justifications than a barrel of leeches.

####

Debbie sleeps until morning. It has been a sleep of dimly shifting shadows, one that gives no respite from the exhaustion to which she awakens.

Beyond her bedroom door, she hears Jacob in the living room. She knows it is Jacob from the clatter of *Sephirot* puzzle parts, his abbreviated bark of frustration as he flings pieces to the floor. With no words of greeting, she enters his space. Jacob has left the puzzle table and sits cross-legged on the floor, before the TV, his youthful cherub face aged, haggard, drained by gloom and defeat. Again he is attempting to get past the first screen of the *Raider of the Seven Earths* game. As usual, this screen is filled with giants. They lumber out at him from among the trees. For every one of them that he manages to destroy with his wand of light, several more smash his character, which kazoos down to a blob before reshaping. The *Kelipot* continue to rain down around him from the game's rust-iron sky. Each time one hits the base of the landscape, it resurrects as a small winged demon that attacks Jacob's player character with the fierceness of a hornet. Jacob now tries pursuing a small blue sack that bobs throughout the landscape screen, impervious to the deluge of antagonists around it. Debbie has not noticed it before.

"What's that bag?" she asks in an attempt to reclaim a modicum of connection between them.

"What do you care?"

"I'm just asking, all right?"

"It's an Escape Tool. All right? I get to use it four times. But I gotta capture it first. For the game Shemp is gonna send me into."

"Never."

"He knew you were gonna say that. So I'll go by myself."

"No you won't."

Jacob glares at her over his shoulder. In this instant of distraction, another giant smashes Jacob's player down to a blob. "Now look what you made me do."

"I don't care. It's enough with these games. I won't let—"

Before she finishes, Jacob turns off the TV. Rising, he stalks round-shouldered back to his bedroom. His door slams shut.

Shemhazai arrives. Despite his presence, Debbie calls in sick to work. Again. She wonders if they will fire her. In truth, she does not care.

####

Shemhazai and Debbie sit across from each other at the kitchen table. Usually, Jacob comes out to greet his pal. This morning, he clings to the silence of his bedroom.

"Did you give this to him?" She holds before Shemhazai the *Sisters of Nightfall* comic book she found last night in Jacob's room. Again, she is trying to play the cross-examiner. Shemhazai's glee as he peruses the image on the cover renders her tone of accusation clownish.

"Do you really think that my powers are so compromised as to create so paltry an illustration of Azazel? Goat horns indeed! Why not give him claws and a trident! This isn't a tenth of Azazel's appearance, not a hundredth. If you saw the real Azazel... would you like me to include him in the game?"

"No more games, please!" They sit in silence. Debbie knows that Jacob will play regardless of her protests. "All right. What about this new game, then? Where will you be taking him? A video arcade somewhere?"

"Down into *Malchut*."

"*Malchut*? That only exists in Kabbalists' imaginations."

"It's in the old game. Let me show you." He motions for Debbie to follow him into the living room. He turns the television back on. *Raider of the Seven Earths* swirls into view, its oily spheres forever dropping, its giants roaming back and forth like fish in a bowl. "This is part of *Malchut*. The lowest part of the lowest sphere. It is only the threshold landscape. Jacob will have to figure out how to get past it. He's not been very successful from outside of it. So he'll go in."

"You're taking him into the television?"

Shemhazai nods.

"You'll be hypnotizing him, then?"

"In a way. In a way, not."

"And why are you doing this?"

"I have told you."

So that he can get—

The words do not escape her lips. Nor can she think of a comfortable way to repeat Shemhazai's words of yesterday. *He needs a woman, Debbie. Before he dies.*

Jacob has appeared now. He stares from his bedroom doorway at the image on the TV.

"Are you afraid of dying?" Shemhazai directs his question to Jacob.

"I gotta complete my mission first." Jacob mumbles. His flat tone indicates that he is feeding back something he has been taught by rote.

"And what is your mission?"

"I gotta find that woman. I gotta rescue her. From the bad guys."

"If she lets herself be rescued. Isn't that right, Jacob? Her degree of openness depends on what is inside her. And the power of the negative forces surrounding her. And your actions. Most important of all, your actions. Don't forget her other name, Jacob. I have taught you."

"*Shekhinah*," he recites. "She-What-Wanders-In-Exile. Down there."

"Among the forces of the *Chitzonim*. The inhabitants of the Other Side."

"The Dark Side! Like in *Star Wars!*"

"This is insane," Debbie interjects.

"Do you want to go?" Again, Shemhazai addresses Jacob.

Jacob nods with an eagerness his sister is meant to see, as she is meant to note the defiant glide of his eyes to her. *I'll pay you back good,* his glare warns her. *If you block me again.*

"Is it safe?" she asks.

"Either he comes back or he doesn't."

"In that case, he's not going."

"Come back into the kitchen, Debbie. Let's talk some more."

When they are settled, Shemhazai continues, low-voiced, so that Jacob will not hear: "Have it your way, then. Go ahead and let him suffer behind the bars of his, how did you call it, savant syndrome until his heart finally gives out. Go ahead, Debbie. Pile on the grief. See how much his heart can take."

"What about my heart? Don't you think I have one?"

"Of course you do. But it's buried under all those, what is the word with which your mystics have labeled the negative emanations that human failings bring into being?"

"*Kelipot.*"

"Yes. Husks, it means. Shells. Why not?"

You tell me why not. She doesn't make this answer. She makes no answer.

"You see how weak he looks. How depleted. You have to let him play. And you have to go with him."

"Don't be ludicrous."

"I don't know that word."

"It doesn't matter. I didn't mean it anyway."

"You'll go with him, then."

"As his chaperone, I suppose? But I guess you don't know that word either."

"You have another choice," Shemhazai answers, ignoring her thrust.

"And what is that, may I ask?"

"You could watch more boys crash on the rocks. Watch them lose control and kick other boys' eyes out. Or stand by and watch while your brother crashes on his own rocks. It's the same thing, isn't it? The impulse to witness a train wreck and secretly enjoy it; to witness a catastrophe for the novelty of it. Or for no reason at all. All you humans have it. But some control it better than others. Do you know what I mean?"

"Well, I never—" in a great show of offense, Debbie crosses her arms and marches to her bedroom. Behind her, Shemhazai smiles victory.

####

Debbie and Jacob sit side by side before the television screen. Shemhazai stands behind them. He has instructed Jacob to wear what he wishes. Jacob has chosen his usual white tank shirt and Yoda-checked boxer shorts. At Shemhazai's suggestion, Debbie has put on a high-buttoned white blouse and loose black skirt. *You'll be less conspicuous that way,* he has told her, though to whom or in what way he has given no hint.

"Do your *Gerushin*," he tells Jacob. "Use anything."

Jacob closes his eyes. In moments, the image of an enraged Donald Duck imprints itself upon the air.

"Do not return from where you are going," Shemhazai murmurs, his voice mellow yet firm, the commanding drone of a hypnotist. "Not unless you win. Now you do *Gerushin*, Debbie."

"I can't."

"You have to. Or Jacob will be there by himself."

"May I use Donald Duck?"

"No. That is Jacob's. Think of a distant memory. Or a word. You're a woman of words, aren't you?"

She tries. Shemhazai waits. Jacob's eyelids flutter.

"I simply can't." Her own eyes blink open. She shakes her head.

"All right then. We will use a different way. Close your eyes. Just close them."

She does so. It is less strenuous now that he has released her from the burdens of meditation. *How long must I stay like this?* The question is scarcely formed before heat envelops her. It is neither a fiery heat that burns nor a suffocating heat that makes her long for cool air. It is more the reassuring warmth of her oven pre-heated to bake some treat. She does not ask if she can open her eyes. She simply does so. Shemhazai has settled behind them. He has revealed himself once more in his six-winged Seraph form. Sparks flash from his reddened surface. His beardless cheeks are smooth. Arms reach out from under his middle set of wings.

One encircles Jacob. The other snakes around Debbie's waist. She stares at him in surprise. The color in Shemhazai's own eyes alternates from the rose pink of desire to the crimson of shame. But this time his gaze makes no retreat. It does not melt the wall of her defenses but renders it transparent. Freely, Shemhazai now roams inside her mind. Debbie does not resist. To the unmoored craft of her will, he becomes pilot.

His hand pulls her body closer to him. Still she does not resist. She cannot. *Why has he not taken advantage of me earlier?* She does not know. She cannot think. She only knows that she is being lifted, Jacob as well. Shemhazai bears both of them towards the TV screen. *It's only a game,* she tries assuring herself, as they enter this lowest sphere of the Kabbalistic Tree. Down they go, down, down, into Shemhazai's *Malchut*. They sink along a tunnel vortex that spirals towards a living blackness. His hand continues rising on her waist. She cannot protest.

The vortex blackens.

Part II

CHAPTER 9

Ogville: The Landscape of the Amorites

*The Weapon is his companion,
Who eats uncooked meat,
Who knows no submission,
Who has no house in his lifetime,
Who does not bury his dead companion*

—ancient Sumerian hymn mocking the Amorites

Jacob didn't have to be told that Shemhazai was no longer with them. He and his sister were alone, and together, though unified by no single track of thought, no shared sympathy. The clearing to which Shemhazai released them was the same, yet not the same, as the one that gave Jacob such fits in the video game. Those trees that had towered even in their smallness now loomed with genuinely imposing height. No giants shambled from them. No *Kelipot* rained from the sky. The small blue sack—their Escape Tool, Jacob had called it—alone carried over as a moving form in this landscape. It hovered, just out of Jacob's reach. How to grab it? What was to stop him? The emptiness gave Jacob hope. Maybe actually going into this first landscape would make it easier for him to get past it?

The dome overhead had the same rust-colored iron sheen of what was in the video game. Here, it spread with the massive totality of an earth sky. Its brightness glared onto this landscape. Yet Jacob felt no heat. Would his senses be dead inside the game? Yes, he could see, but would he be able to smell those stinking *Kelipot* if he stumbled onto a patch of them, like in his closet? Or taste food if he got hungry and something was given to him? Or touch the woman he was supposed to rescue, even if he didn't know how or where to touch?

And was there hearing? All had been still. So still. Then great pounding that shook the ground gave evidence of some gargantuan presence approaching through the green monoliths. Jacob imagined a Tyrannosaurus Rex crashing past broken trees and bounding into the clearing. Then what? *I have no weapon*, he realized. He reached high for the Escape sack just over his head.

He tried to jump for it, but his grasp did not even graze its base. Could any of its four protections, whatever they were, really stop a dinosaur anyway? What else could he do?

He wasn't about to ask his sister for advice. His stupid, scared-of-everything sister, who cowered behind him. Debbie laid down no rule, made no threat of what would happen if he didn't listen. Here he was the one in charge instead of the other way around. If she barked at him to run, he could bark right back. *Run to where? You turn tail.* He liked that expression. Turn tail. Even if he had no idea where he had learned it. Or how it might save them from whatever thundered at them from among those high trees. So they froze in place. Both of them. And waited.

There emerged a giant—not vast-sized, as in legends, but at perhaps 12 feet in height, certainly of greater-than-human stature. He wore a dark brown loincloth whose bristling fur reminded Jacob of Alley Oop in the caveman comic strip whose reprints Debbie once ordered for Jacob, allowing him to read "healthy" funnies, as she called them. His strapping chest widened to shoulders with muscles that rippled down his arms, a stream of bulges that denied even a pinch of loose skin. Could he possibly be friendly? Jacob couldn't tell. A mop of hair obscured his facial features. His thighs and calves were thick as the club that he clutched in his meat-slab hand. His other hand dragged a large bag. Something alive inside caused it to bubble with spasmodic pokes.

Whatever task he was about to perform prevented him from noticing these two newcomers.

Setting down his club and bag, he stomped back into the woods. Moments later he returned with a pair of stone pillars, each as long as Jacob, one under each arm. These he jammed, ends up, waist-high, into the ground. Disappearing once more, he brought out a third pillar, this one flat, which he laid across the two already standing. Rolling over a boulder, he sat on it and opened the sack.

An axe came out first. It was short, with a handle not much longer than a butcher knife, and a squared blade that took unhealthy gleam from the glare that coated the clearing from above. A large silver goblet came out next. The giant set it to his right on the horizontal slab. He looked to have fashioned a table for a meal, an inference sealed in fact when the giant drew forth a zeppelin-shaped roll, large enough to hold a slab of meat well over two feet in length. He laid it flat upon his stone tabletop. From deep within the bag, the giant now drew out two sticks topped with diagonal splits. These too he pushed into the ground until they stood erect. Straightening, he flexed his great hand. On a truculent snort, he plunged the hand far into the sack. The fabric churned with panicked lurches, accompanied now by mewls of protest. The squealing accelerated as the animal was lifted out. Except it was no animal. Its lower torso had the slick gray gleam of a worm writhing to escape the punishment of a hook. Human arms ended in talons. Nubs of wings marked the shoulder blades. Tiny horns bloomed atop slanted eyes and a round bald head that might have belonged to an Asian child.

    The giant gripped this creature by its neck. From the sack he took a metal rod whose point he jammed through the worm end and pushed until the point protruded from the mouth. Ignoring the creature's bleated howls, he set the rod in the diagonal notches of the upright sticks, forming a spit, beneath which he bent to ignite a fire in the bed of grass and twigs below. Before the flames could jump too high, the giant took the goblet and axe and stood by the creature's head. He placed the goblet under the throat; with one deft swipe of the axe's blade, he sliced off the head of this creature whose abruptly terminated shriek found added length in Debbie's groan.

    The giant spotted them. He waited until the blood from the headless creature filled the goblet. After setting the goblet down on his stone table, he lumbered towards them. Hands on hips, he stood over them. His face was clear now. Its skin was a rich beige, as if a mix of all races. The teeth were broad white blocks, like bloated piano keys. The mop of hair shared the same bristled look of his loincloth. His cheeks, beardless and wide, punctuated the coarse breadth of his whole head. It made Jacob think of pictures he had seen of anvils.

    His eyes narrowed in a barbarian squint, a scowl both hostile and questioning.

    "Who sent ya hyar?!" He spoke with a twang, like that of male characters in hick TV comedies Jacob watched. Except the giant's voice thundered, strengthened yet limited by its primitive edge, sheathed in a provincial suspicion which the slightest wrong move might fast unleash.

Jacob stepped back. He wished he had a weapon, but what good would it do? He backed into Debbie, still frozen behind him. Stymied, his knees sank.

The giant grinned. "Looks like I don't gotta lunch on roast demon after all. Something better done come along. Ain't nothin' as tender as pale-skinned little human boy meat. With a real live earth gal to pass around like after-dinner smokes." He eyed them once more. "How'd you say ya got hyar?"

"Shemp brung us."

"Shemhazai," Debbie corrected.

"You shet up!" The giant hammered Debbie with his squint. But he had blinked at the name she had given, as if a bug had flown into his eye. "You know Shemhazai, son?"

"He's my friend," Jacob answered.

The giant rubbed his chin in thought. "Whose side are you on anyway? Did old Shemhazai send you hyar to get even with Azazel or to buddy up with him?"

"He sent me here to find a woman."

"Which woman?"

"I don't know yet."

"You mean he just wants you to get some gal candy? That don't surprise me. Old Shemhazai had more earth gals in his day than all of them Fallen Ones put together. Except maybe Azazel." His gaze slid over to Debbie. "Say, you one of his trophies?"

"How dare you." They locked stares.

"Oh, a sensitive one she is. This your wife?"

"She's my sister."

"Ha! I heard that story before. Old King Og used to tell it around the campfire while he was roastin' his demons. About Abraham the Jew tellin' old Pharoah that Sarah was his sister. When she was his wife all along. Story goes how the Big Boss sealed up all them Egyptians' oh-ree-fices 'til things got straightened out. Say, you Jews?"

"Yes we are," Debbie answered.

"Well then. Maybe you gonna be on our side after all. Maybe Shemhazai wants you to help us conjure up the Big Weapon. For when we get attacked."

"By whom?" Debbie asked.

"When's more the question. Say, Little Brother. Did Shemhazai ever learn you about makin' predictions? Readin' the future and all that?"

"He's what's called a savant," Debbie told him.

"Didn't I tell you to shet up?" The giant paused in thought. "What's a sah-vunt anyway?"

"Sometimes he sees everything. Before anybody else can see." Debbie said nothing about the idiot side. They were buying time here. As long as this giant didn't know....

"Well, it just so happens we're lookin' for a seer. Job's vacant. Had to fire the current one. The one before her was a gal too. Pretty good one. But she got eaten up."

"What happened?" Jacob asked.

"Big mistake. Or small one. I dunno. Well, I do know. One of us *Nephilim* got a little too drunk and a bit too hungry. It happens around hyar in Ogville."

"You're a real live *Nephilim*?" Jacob asked.

"Amorite's more like it. Live's for sure. Real I don't know. There's too much mixed blood in us. Shemhazai ought to of told you about that. About how the Flood took out most of the giants. Except for Og. Story goes how he held on to Noah's ark for dear life while that thing floated along, with mountain tops ticklin' his butt. Except life ain't the right word. When you got angel blood in you, you live longer. Anyway, when Og climbed off the ark, he was plenty gal-hungry. Waited for the world to repopulate then picked up right where he'd left off, nailin' earth gals. He made his way up hyar to Amorite Land. Made himself king. Back then, the Amorites were pretty much easygoin' folks. Which made their gals easy pickins'. All Og had ta do was show folks he was a giant and tell 'em, 'I'm your new boss.' They went right along. That was three, maybe four thousand years ago. So what you got now is three, maybe four thousand years of mixin'—human and angel, and human and human, and human and animal, and *Nephilim* and animal, and everything in between. Which is pretty much what you see walkin' around Ogville. Hey, it ain't but a stone's throw away, Ogville. You come on with me. Spend the night. We treat you like a king. And no one ain't gonna touch your... sister." The giant snorted a laugh. "Besides, we got all the gals you want. You see one you like, she's all yours."

"I'm supposed to rescue her first."

"All women gotta be rescued. Why do you think we men's got what they don't got? We put it to 'em, they get rescued. It's either that or kill 'em and eat 'em. What else is women good for? Except makin' more human babies for us to hunt down when they grown. That's why we let humans and animals mix in with us. What else you supposed to do around here? Wait for some baby demon to come wanderin' over here when them *Chitzonim* Up-and-Ups ain't lookin'?"

"What in the world are you talking about?!" Debbie blurted. She braced for a blow from this giant. Instead, he mashed his butcher-block hands against his knees and doubled over in laughter.

"You worried what I'm talkin' about? And you don't even know where you are? Why don't you go ahead then, Miss Brown Eyes? Go on out in them woods. See how long you last. Well? Go on, do it!"

Debbie tightened her arms across her chest and turned away.

"You come on with me then, Little Brother. Say, you hungry? Roast demon ain't that bad. Wonder how this one got over here anyway. A Chink one at that. Don't see many of them. Musta wandered off from *Chitzonim*ville. Or maybe Azazel's crowd just didn't want it hangin' around there. All juiced up on prejudice, that bunch. Not that we ain't. Wish we could kill off all them *Chitzonim* before they do it to us. But it don't look like it'll be that way. Less'n maybe you can help, Little Brother. Less'n' maybe you the one we been waitin' for."

"I only want—"

"A gal needin' rescue? I got one picked out already! You follow me. I'll take care of you. She will too. You just leave that sourpuss sister of yours behind. I don't like her. I'd cook her up and eat her, but she's too scrawny." The giant spit on the ground. "Anyways, let's you and me go over here and eat. No use wastin' good demon meat. Say, you ever drink blood? Nothin' like it. Especially when it's hot."

####

> *"...if the eye had the power to see them, no creature could endure the demons... they are more numerous than we are and they surround us like the ridge around a field...*
>
> *Every one among us has a thousand on his left hand and ten thousand on his right hand."*
>
> —Talmud, Trachtate Berachot, 6a

Little Og, the giant called himself. He talked freely as—Jacob by his side, Debbie behind them—he led them towards the town of Ogville. He had taken the name of Og from his great-great-great-great-great-great-great grandfather King Og. Whom he hated, but feared, even though King Og had been dead for over two thousand years.

"Old Moses himself was the one killed King Og. His Jew-people was headed right for the Promised Land, but bad old Og wouldn't let 'em pass through Amorite territory. Instead he brought out his army. Moses came face to face with Og. Well, not face to face because humans can't really do that with a giant. So, Moses smacks his magic rod down on Og's ankle. And down Og topples. But Og was a *Nephilim*. And you don't just kill a *Nephilim*. They come back as demons. Well, Moses may have sent Og to Demon Hoo-Hah Land a long time ago. But for all I know, he's still hangin' around, watchin' and waitin, makin' sure we pen up as many demons as we can collect. Heck, he could be floatin' around us right now. And I don't want him thinkin' I mean him no disrespect. So, I took his name. Just like my daddy. And granddaddy. And great-great-great—"

"Wow!" Jacob interrupted. "You really collect demons?"

"Have to. It's part of the system. Gotta build up our demon army for when the Big War happens between us and them Up-and-Ups over there in *Chitzonim*ville. They're tryin' to kill off as many of us as they can. So, we kill off as many of them as we can. We kill one of them, they become one of ours. They kill one of us, it becomes one of them. That's the game. But they been killin' off a lot more of us than we done of them. Which means we gotta start killin' off some of our own to spring demons, which ain't near as strong as theirs. Them Up-and-Ups over there, they got more muscle, damn 'em. They ain't just fallen angels either. They got some of the worst bad apples you can name."

"Like who?"

"Like Lilith. Sometimes that high-nosed demon gal comes scroungin' over here to see what children got abandoned outside so she can take 'em back and cut the demons out of 'em. Or maybe she's reconnoiterin' to see what kind of Noonday Critter we got corralled to carry the Big Weapon we done built to wipe her kind out. Except we ain't got no Critter, and we ain't got no Weapon. Not yet." Pausing, Little Og eyed Jacob. "Say, you know anything about buildin' weapons?"

"Can't say as I do, can't say as I don't." It was a line from one of Jacob's movies.

"You sure about predictin' the future? Ya didn't gimme a yes or no. Thanks to her."

"Well, they call me a savant, and that's kinda what that means."

So Shemhazai's game had inserted Jacob and Debbie into the midst of what had been a long-standing war between these Amorites and the residents of this place called *Chitzonim*ville. From which the demon child that Little Og had devoured (Jacob had said he wasn't hungry) had either strayed. Or been banished.

"Them no-good Up-and-Ups," Little Og continued. "They think they so high class. Just because they ain't mixed like we are. Ain't no giants over there. No *Nephilim*, no mixed bloods. No humans either. They's only on our side."

"Wow! Humans fighting side by side with giants! Wow!"

"No, Little Brother. 'Our side' don't mean they's with us. They just one of the types that fill Ogville. You gonna see all kinds. You gonna see folks that's half-human and half-angel, half-human and half-demon, half-human and half-animal. You'll see. You ain't nervous, are ya?"

"No way!"

"Your mean, scrawny sister can tag along too if she wants. Unless'n' she wants to stay out here and get taken by a *Chitzonim* raid. They'd have fun with Miss Scrawny. They'd have their way with her, then kill her and leave her out for the crows to eat. Bet she'd cough up a tasty little demon too. But if she stays with us, worse could happen is we use her for breedin'. We gotta keep humans around. Sometimes we hunt 'em for fun. Sometimes we train 'em to wait on us. The womenfolk, we especially need 'em to keep up the population. The cute ones, well, everybody needs a plaything once in a while. Anything wrong with that?" His cold gaze slanted to Debbie. "But you don't worry. We ain't gonna do that to your sister, if you don't want it to happen. Say, what's your name anyway?"

"Jacob."

"Like your great-great-great-great-great-great-great Jew grandfather. I know about that one. Original mixer, our kind of guy. He mixed speckled sheep with striped ones to trick his cheatin' uncle. Had lots of women, too. Four wives, 12 kids. You sure that ain't what you want? Lots of women?"

"Just one."

"Oh yeah. I forget. Well, if you don't like the one I picked out, we got gals by the bunches, and they all in need of rescue." Little Og grinned ridicule at Debbie. "Guess you ain't been rescued, have you?"

Debbie kept silent.

"Say!" Little Og called to her, in the spirit of one throwing darts. "You ever tell the future by pokin' through animal guts?"

"I should say not."

"What about you, Brother Jacob?"

Jacob shrugged. In truth he did not know how to answer.

"Well, like I said, we got what you might call a vacancy here in Ogville. Shame what happened to our good seer gettin' eaten up and all. Big mistake. This *Nephilim* feller gets drunk one night and goes after her. She shouldna' been out that late anyway. He looks at her, and he don't see no oracle. All he sees is gal-treat and hamburger. Gal-treat first, then hamburger. Everybody hears the screamin'. Nobody cares. Lots of screamin' in Ogville. Hey, at least we got a demon out of it. Not much of one, but we got one. Then we went lookin' for a replacement and come up with, well, you'll meet her. Miss Sybil, we called her. She kept blabberin' around town about 'seein' what kinda Noonday Critter was gonna carry that weapon was gonna slaughter us all. Last time, it was somethin' about a huge snake. Before that, it was a dragon. And all the time, she's jumpin' around like some kid makin' up tall tales that she wants grown folks to believe. Anyways, these tales, they just don't make sense. Then she clams up. Hasn't said a word since we fired her. We was all set to roast up Miss Sybil and eat her. Then you come along. And I'm thinkin', why not match up Brother Jacob with Miss Sybil? She's got plenty where it counts. And what with what we was plannin' to do to her, ya might call her your rescue bun."

"Would you please stop talking that way?!" Debbie cried from behind them.

"Awww, Miss Nasty is all upset. Say Jacob, you wouldn't mind if we played with her a little bit? Wouldn't kill her. Just play with her?"

"Well...."

"Okay. Forget it. Come on. Let's get goin. Time's a wastin'."

And the landscape changed.

####

"Behold! Og's bed was an iron bed... nine cubits was its length and four cubits its width [13.5 feet by 6 feet according to the standard cubit of a man]."

—*Deuteronomy 3, 11*

Now they were climbing a steep mountainside. At its peak, a stone wall of daunting height amplified the foreboding nature of whatever lay within. Jacob stayed next to Little Og. Debbie labored to keep pace behind them. Jacob sent few thoughts and even less concern her way. He knew that Little Og tied her stomach into knots. He knew that she hated Little Og, who spoke to her in ways Jacob never would have dared. It was sweet revenge to Jacob. He had worn the yoke of her rule for so long. Now it was his turn.

The fetid stink of unburied corpses bore into their nostrils as they neared the entrance to Ogville. The mountainside was littered with the remains of giants and humans and animals, some devoured to the bone, others chewed on then discarded, others still whole and evidently hunted for sport then left to rot. Jacob raised questioning eyes to Little Og. He was, at best, half as tall as his companion, who did not acknowledge Jacob's stare. *This is how things are here,* the giant's aloof manner suggested. *Take it or leave it.*

Heavy bars, narrowly spaced, formed the front gate. Beyond these bars, a slumbering giant stirred in the dim entranceway. Uncurling from his bench, he shambled up to the gate. One eye, centered on his forehead, peered through.

"Jeez," Jacob murmured. "A real live Cyclops."

"That's what you call him?"

"That's what movies call him." Jacob knew none of the Greek myths, though Debbie had tried to read them to him. It had been one of her favorite books, the Bulfinch. Jacob had made it a point not to listen.

"Okay, Mr. Dumbbell Cyclops. Open up. These two is safe."

With a grunt of assent, the giant rotated a turnstile. The gate creaked, squealed, lifted. The doorkeeper's bulging eye roamed Debbie up and down as she passed him.

"Not this one, you! Now get that gate down before somethin' slips in ain't supposed to be here!" The gate groaned closed behind them.

The tunnel-like vestibule opened to a central courtyard. The structures surrounding this area were of varying heights. Some were as tall as the guard wall itself; all were of similar gray stone, some lopsided, some straight, a jumble of mismatched structures punctuated by narrow passageways that snaked off into Ogville's unseen pockets.

The city center swarmed with the mixed multitude Little Og had described. Giants were everywhere. Most of the males were of Little Og's height, though some loomed higher. Most carried axes and spears. A few held bows. The giant females were all long-haired, raven-tressed. Some were tall and spare of build, like Debbie herself. Smaller humans scurried past, hunched as if to avoid being spotted. All manner of animals—sheep and cattle, free-roaming dogs and a tight-knit brace of ducks—moved along in much the same fashion. The human females skittered, diminutive and defenseless, a wily grace Debbie was in the process of envying when the twang of a bow brought one down with a screech. The giant predator grabbed her hair and dragged her through a dolmen-shaped portal.

The abrupt attack initiated a chain reaction among the passersby. Violence infected the air. The atmosphere turned predatory, the city square a seething cauldron of hunter after hunted. Size and speed were the sole determining factors of who survived. Larger giants savaged smaller ones with axes similar to Little Og's. Two suddenly broke into a trot, ran down a smaller human, and clubbed the man to death. Arrows flew into fleeing humans and the more ponderous animals. Several women were thrown to the ground, then beaten and ravished as they screamed. Fleeter females joined faster animals in bolting for the safety of Ogville's maze-like side paths.

"C'mon." Little Og paid the carnage no mind as they crossed the courtyard. He stopped at a door on which hung a sign: *Oracle Wanted.* Little Og unlocked the door; Jacob, then Debbie, followed him inside. A narrow cave, shaped as a long arch, ended at an elevated throne atop a squat pyramid. Rough-hewn steps ran up the front of the pyramid to the throne itself.

"Go ahead," Little Og told Jacob. "Scramble up it."

Jacob did so. Seating himself, he laid his arms across the stone arms of the throne. Its size swallowed him. Still, a king-like sentiment seized him. To be so exalted, to be staring down, not up, at his big-mouth, know-it-all sister—

"That's for you, Little Brother. All you gotta do is say the word."

"But—"

"The gal thing? We got that covered. Climb on down now. I got another surprise for you."

Behind the pedestal area, a second door opened to an actual room. Debbie slipped in after them. Little Og didn't stop her. She wished that he had. Then she would not have witnessed the room's only two presences: a bed, and the naked woman standing beside it.

The bed was huge, a good 14 feet in length, half that across. An oblong slab of stone, it rested on two squared boulders at its head and base. It had no sheets, no pillows.

"King Og didn't like pillows," Little Og said, anticipating Jacob's question.

"You mean this bed belonged to King Og himself?"

"Yep. It'll belong to you now. Sybil, too."

The naked woman was as tall as Little Og, though as lithe-figured as the giant was muscular. Her skin possessed a black sheen so bright that Jacob blinked.

"Fana?" Jacob's savant side retrieved a name that Debbie had put out of her mind. The waitress at the pancake house—Fana, whose name indeed meant brightness. Her hair was all short curls, like Fana's. Yet the face itself was not the same. A high nose, solemn slit of lips, and long chin fronted the angular thinness of her head. Unlike that waitress, she had sad eyes that stayed on Jacob, begging him, perhaps, for rescue.

"She ain't gonna answer. She don't talk at all anymore. Best that way," Little Og added, with a mocking glare at Debbie. "Anyway, it ain't Fana. It's Sybil. Don't know where she got that name. All I know is, she was the oracle that got picked to replace the one that got eaten. And she wasn't no good. Were ya, Sybil? Scared the speech outta ya, didn't it? Or are you just plain dumb? All we really need to know is what them Up-and-Ups in *Chitzonim*ville got up their sleeve. And how we're gonna beat 'em. Ain't that right, Sybil? Well? Ain't that right?"

The girl fixed her baleful stare on Jacob. He stepped back, only to be stopped by Little Og's hand against his spine.

"She's all yours," Little Og insisted. "And you don't worry about her bein' so tall. When she's lyin' down, that ain't gonna make no difference. Say, this ain't your first time, is it?"

Jacob made no response.

"Well, well. I shoulda known. Miss Sybil can help you along that way too. Ain't that right, Miss Gal Treat? You take Little Brother here under your wing. Teach him all he needs to know. Things gonna be fine. Tomorrow, when you come outside, Little Brother, we gonna have a parade. Whole city of Ogville gonna line up and cheer. Then you gonna come back in and ascend your throne. You gonna be above everybody. I mean everybody. Ain't no big sister gonna tell you what to do no more. Sound okay to you?"

"I—"

"Jacob, get out of here! Right now!"

Little Og whirled on Debbie. "Now you listen," he warned. "You wanna stay in one piece, you shut up and get out. I'm gonna close that door on Jacob and Sybil. You gonna sit and wait. Below that throne. Below it, not on it. You hear? Then I'm gonna go out and lock the cave door from the outside. Ain't nobody gonna bother you. Unless'n' I say so. You comin'?"

Debbie stood her ground.

"Have it your way. All I gotta do is say three words to that crowd out there, and your meat's gonna be wishin' it was that roast demon I just ate. You wanna know what them three words are?"

Debbie nodded slowly.

"She's... all... yours. Now, you comin' or not?"

####

Debbie sat alone on the pyramid's lowest step. The throne that would be Jacob's loomed above her, severe in its dominance, as if Jacob had already thundered down judgment on who she was, what she had been to him. She tried to gather her thoughts to defend herself; to assess what was occurring here, as if by tallying the facts she could explain more favorably her role in Shemhazai's game.

Like it or not, she and her brother were now participants in this war between the realms of Ogville and *Chitzonim*ville. The dwellers of Ogville must be primitives by comparison to their adversaries. Their weapons were of the Iron Age, their garments (when they wore them) downright prehistoric. They feared some Doomsday Weapon that the Up-and-Ups, as Little Og called them, would send against Ogville. It would be borne by some creature whose identity was just as vital to discern as the nature of the weapon itself. Maybe if they could destroy the bearer, the weapon would fail. Maybe. They longed for the services of a seer sufficiently gifted to provide them with oracular visions from which solutions might be drawn in advance of the attack.

Ain't no mixed-bloods over there, Little Og had said. The realm of the Up-and-Ups contained no motley stew of *Nephilim* giants, Amorite humans, or whatever else populated Ogville. He had spoken not with grudging admiration but scarcely concealed dread of the purity of the *Chitzonim*, their advanced status. Were Lilith and Azazel figures in the game for later? It would surprise her if they weren't. Would Lilith be as sensual, Azazel as carnal, as the illustrations in Jacob's *Sisters of Nightfall* comic book had portrayed them to be? Perhaps Shemhazai had drawn inspiration for some of the beings in his game from Jacob's own world. For some reason, this thought reassured her. After all, the giantess now with Jacob bore more than a passing resemblance to the Ethiopian waitress at the pancake house. Sybil, the name of a Greek prophetess, had somehow leaked into Shemhazai's game. But others had no patent link to Jacob's reality. Like Little Og himself, with his Alley Oop build and hillbilly twang. And the bald-headed demon-child misfit with slanted eyes and a worm's torso.

Both Rabbi Seth and Shemhazai had cited references in Genesis to fallen angels mating with women of Earth. Giving birth to *Nephilim*. Half-human, half-angel. "Men of renown," the Bible called them. Renowned at what? Rape and murder? Bestiality and cannibalism? Were these Ogvilleians not fashioned to resemble the dwellers of the Bible's Tenth Generation?

One dweller of Ogville—an ebony-skinned giantess whose naked allure was matched by her apparent need of rescue—lay alone with Jacob now. What would be the outcome? How could Jacob resist the caresses of this willing female? Would years of being looked down upon, marginalized, lead Jacob to accept more readily the mantle of seer that Little Og dangled before him? What would happen to Debbie then? Would it break the rules of Shemhazai's game were she to be destroyed? Would Jacob's ascendance trigger the mechanism by which her actual Atlanta self could be raped, even murdered? Inside a game, no less?

Maybe it was for the best. Never had she felt more superfluous: alone, in a foreign place that harbored equal contempt for what she thought and how she looked. Perhaps this was an adjunct function of the game. To force her to stare the truth in the face. And what was that truth? *That you do not matter. That your every effort to build a wall of protection around yourself was in reality a wall between you and human contact. That you were never Jacob's caregiver but always his jailer.*

She thought back to the moment before Little Og had emerged into the clearing, how part of her had hoped that the presence crushing its way through the forest was some meat-eating predator that would sweep her off the ground, violate her not sexually but by dismembering her, devouring her, thereby silencing the voices that had warred in her during her time on Earth. Solitary, unwanted, in this alien cave's dankness, she wished for the pain of living to end. But what if the pain did not end? What if the entity that was Debbie Forman continued on in whatever demon the Amorites collected out of her dead self? Would Jacob protect her, even at that point? Probably not. Not if his tentatively uttered "well...," when Little Og asked if he and his fellow giants could "play" with her a little, was any indication.

Please. It has to end quickly. That is all I want. The plea droned in her head. No. Not in her head. The droning came from outside of her, a faint yet definite buzzing. Above her, that blue Escape Tool sack from the game's initial video screen flitted past like a giant housefly. She thought to try to catch it. But why? Wasn't that Jacob's business? She raised both hands towards her ears. She would clamp out its sound so that she could concentrate on her fate.

Then it vanished through the door to King Og's bedroom, and the buzzing ceased.

####

"If one wishes to influence anything in the physical universe (space), he must make use of the physical shape of the letters."
—Sefer Yetzirah (The Book of Creation), Aryeh Kaplan trans.

Jacob came storming out of the back room. Clutched high in one hand was that blue sack. At last he had captured it! No pride of completion lit his eyes. They quavered with confusion as he rushed past Debbie. She caught up with him at the cave's door. Before Jacob could bang on it for Little Og to let them out, his stinking sister started in with her stinking questions.

"What happened?"
"Nothin'."
"You mean you didn't—"
"She ain't the one."
"But she looked so sad. Surely she wanted you to...rescue her."
"Yeah. She looked sad. But the other one looked sadder."
"There were two women in there?"
"Yeah. Kinda."
"I only saw one."
"That was at first. Okay? The other one came later."
"Not through that door. I would have seen. Was there another door?"
"Nah."
"Then how—"

Jacob banged on the door. He didn't want to put his confusion into words: him, back in that room, next to Sybil the Fana Giantess on that huge stone bed; him on his back, Sybil curled towards him on her side, legs hiked up so she wouldn't seem longer than he was; him trying to talk, to ask where she was from, what language she spoke, whether she had a boyfriend or not; her not saying a word but just staring at him with those big eyes, then running one hand up and down his chest, all with his shirt still on.

He had closed his eyes. And his savant side had fed him the image of a figure. One that was tall, but not giant tall. The waist tucked in at the center while widening at the small bosom, the narrow hips. And Jacob had known it was a female. He had known, too, the depth of her sadness. He saw nothing of her face but the eyes. They had held to him, pulling him to her, away from Sybil. They had drawn him with that power of gloom which opens under you and drops you all the way down to where the falling never stops. Both arms had poured out at him. Not like she was inviting him. More like she was pleading. But for what?

His eyes had opened. And she was gone. Back to where? Disappointment had filled him. He had turned away from Sybil the Fana Giantess. In that instant, the blue Escape Tool from Shemp's first landscape had appeared, hovering just above him, well within his grasp. Had he finally done something right in Shemhazai's game? With ease he had reached up and taken hold of the sack. It had tingled, soft in his palm, there yet not there, when he had squeezed it. Then he had felt Sybil the Fana Giantess's hand on his shoulder. And he had known to get out of that bedroom. Fast.

"Jacob—"

His sister's failed whimper of authority caused Jacob to glance behind him. Beyond Debbie he saw Sybil the Fana Giantess. She was following them. At a distance, but following. Hesitating, like a stray dog that wants a home.

The cave door scraped open. Outside was still awash in Ogville's pulverized glare, light mashed down by the iron dome of sky. Little Og was waiting. All of Ogville was waiting in a semicircle behind Little Og. Male giants had bulled their way to the front of the crowd. All were holding bows and spears and small axes.

Jacob's fingers tightened around his Escape Tool. He stepped into the glare; Little Og studied him, but only for a second. The giant knew right away what Jacob's decision was: not to become Ogville's seer. Little Og made a slight nod. But not to Jacob. The Ogvilleians raised their spears, cocked their throwing axes, threaded their bows. Jacob was quicker. His nimble fingers untied the bag. A letter flew out. *Yod*: the first letter in God's name.

Jacob flew too. So did Debbie and Sybil the Fana Giantess. The landscape changed.

CHAPTER 10

"Chitzonim... the external ones... the most exterior forces, the 'waste' of holiness that constitutes evil."
—Mystical Concepts in Chassidism,
Jacob Immanuel Schochet

They found themselves at the center of a street lined with stores as clearly ordered as Ogville's were cluttered by chaos. None of the stores were more than two stories high; all had the well-groomed look of high-end businesses whose affluence was restrictive, intended to keep out all who did not belong.

They were three now. Sybil the Fana Giantess still followed them, still at a stray-dog distance. Jacob was glad she had not been harmed when Ogville tried to unleash its violence upon them.

Beyond the stores to their left, an immense sea stretched without limit to the horizon. Colorless yet opaque, it reminded Jacob, in his shame, of body secretions; Debbie thought of Rabbi Seth's descriptions of *Tohu*, the indefinable chaotic substance from which the order of Creation had been shaped. This sea had no waves at all—a disconcerting calm neither Jacob in his savantness nor Debbie, behind her fortress wall of logic, could begin to explain. The sky above them was the same iron-like dome of Ogville, casting light both glaring and stifled on this landscape.

The sidewalks were crowded with couples, all dressed in varying shades of yellow that lent their collective movement a rhythm at once lock-stepped and casual. At first, none took notice of these three interlopers. Most seemed young, in full flush of vitality and physical appeal. The males were of a uniformly dark handsomeness against which their bright garments stood out in greater boldness. Their slacks were well pressed and of a sheen that radiated expense to the point of indulgence. All wore short-sleeved shirts on whose fabric the yellow pulsed.

Yellow also dominated the garments of the females, though with greater variation. They were not naked, as had been some of the women in Ogville, yet the manner of their adornment signaled a carefully engineered sensual allure even more potent than had they been unclothed. Some wore translucent blouses above skirts that flounced against their thighs. Others favored dresses whose tightness delineated every detail of their figures. Still others had draped themselves in evening gowns from whose strapless tops their flesh bloomed, fresh as newly opened flowers. Yet there was no innocence about them. Their beauty seemed calibrated to draw the attention of male eyes. They certainly drew Jacob's, whose scrutiny wandered from their sculpted bodies to rouged lips and painted eyes, hair curled to ringlets or shimmering down their backs, the sparkle matched by the necklaces that adorned their throats, the diamond rings amassed on their fingers, the gold bracelets emblazoning their wrists, the gleaming pendants that dangled from their delicately shaped ears.

A collective pause halted the strollers. At first, they seemed taken aback by the sudden appearance of these uninvited presences at the center of a street on which no cars or buses or any vehicle traveled. Then, as one, they began to close in. In that instant there came from behind Jacob and Debbie a rush of scuffling, a screech of alarm. Four males had thrust Sybil the Fana Giantess to the pavement. Two grasped her arms, two more her legs; despite her size, she was carried, squirming but helpless, into one of the stores.

"Hey!" Jacob cried.

His voice catalyzed the males into motion. Their scowls turned hostile as their circle tightened around Jacob and Debbie. Jacob held up his bag to fend them off. He didn't want to use up another of the Four Escapes; still, the males hesitated, leery of some alien power the bag might hold. Before Jacob was forced to summon a letter, there sped from one store a figure whose menace of authority quelled the advance of the mob. He placed himself before these Yellow Shirts, Jacob and Debbie behind him. He stood taller than everyone. Though not of the raw bulk of the Ogvilleians, he radiated an aura of otherworldliness greater than that of those giants. He too wore a T-shirt, not yellow but of a black that crawled up his shirt, like liquid flames.

The crowd settled; this figure turned to face Jacob and Debbie. He did not ask who they were or where they had come from. He simply studied them; then with a curt nod, he motioned them to precede him into his store. As the Yellow Shirts dispersed, Jacob could not resist eyeing one of the done-up young women. In the moment of her turning, he glimpsed behind her fair female face a hideous swarm of goat-like features, malevolent of expression, with curling horns and tufted beard and silken brown hair coating the cheeks. Swallowing, Jacob hurried inside.

####

"And the name of the third is Gadreel; this is the one that showed all the deadly blows to the sons of men... the shield and the breastplate, and the sword for slaughter...."
—I Enoch 69, 3

GADREEL'S WEAPONS EMPORIUM, read the sign above the door. Once inside, Jacob studied the figure who had followed them into the store. The Gadreel of his *Sisters of Nightfall* comic book looked so different. That one had a movie-star-handsome face and flame-blue eyes.

"Are you really Gadreel?" he went ahead and asked.

This Gadreel assented with an impatient nod. His was the raw height of a tight end in football, more rangy than bulky, with biceps of such muscularity as to bulge out from his black T-shirt. His head was so narrowly shaped as to mimic a chisel. Blonde hair hung in waxen strings around paper-white cheeks. His beard, equally blonde, was tailored to a refined point. Reddened eyes fixed on Jacob with a bloodshot intensity that held intelligence.

Jacob didn't understand the word "emporium". It didn't matter. He had entered what was, for him, a paradise better than anything at Walmart. The store divided into two spacious rooms. Each side displayed, table after table, an array of treats for which his imagination had long hungered. The Yesterday Room, so labeled to the left, exhibited ancient weapons both exotic and formidable. Hatchets and clubs filled the Stone Age table. The Bronze Age table had wonderful copper daggers and bronze-headed spears. *For Distance,* read the plaque to describe the grouping of blowguns, crossbows, bows and arrows, and slings. *Asia* presented dragon stars, combat spikes, nunchucks. *Stabbing and Chopping* included knives for hunting and throwing, machetes, stilettos. The *Swords* table offered polished sabers meant to be wielded by gladiators, would-be Conans, and Civil War officers. *Clubbing* showed blackjacks, maces, and tomahawks.

The right side of the store was the Today Room. Derringers, pistols, and other handguns filled one table. Next to it lay rifles, muskets, and shotguns. Assault rifles had their own display. One table held a mortar, another a grenade launcher encircled by artfully placed grenades. A handheld rocket launcher intrigued Jacob, as did the *Explosives Collection*, the *Hybrid Insect Weapons* (especially the chemical-bearing scorpions on wheels), and the *Electrified Shock Probes.*

Branching off from the front of the Today Room was a short corridor labeled the *Future Alcove*. Mounted high on the wall at its end was a single item illumined from beneath by a pair of spotlights. Jacob approached this item in awe. *Plasma Wand,* read the label. Then in subscript: *Shaped charge explodes within victim. Sends killing in all directions. Defies all matter, solid or liquid or gas. Available in black or gold sheath.*

"How much is that one?" he asked Gadreel. His voice quivered in longing. The notion of money in Shemhazai's game had not occurred to him.

"Not for sale. Not to you. Not without a permit."

"Where can I get a permit?"

"You have to see Azazel. He's in charge of everything around here. Everything."

"Where is he?"

"You can't see Azazel. Not without a pass."

"Where can I get a pass?"

"Lilith might give you one. Then again, she might not. She and Azazel didn't exactly part on what you would call friendly terms."

"You mean *the* Lilith?" So Shemp had put one of the *Sisters of Nightfall* in here too?

Gadreel crossed his big arms and nodded.

"Where is she?"

"Down the street. But you can't go there."

"Why?!" Jacob asked, his frustration seeping through.

"You wouldn't make it very far. Not even five feet with your stupid wife trailing you."

"She ain't my wife! Tell him you're not my wife!"

"I'm not his wife. And I'm not stupid," Debbie retorted.

"You'll find out what stupid really means if you get too near that door," Gadreel warned. Outside, on the sidewalk, a crowd of male Yellow Shirts had gathered. All were eyeing Debbie.

Gadreel turned his attention back to Jacob. "What's that bag in your hands?" he asked.

"You can't have it."

"Didn't ask if I could have it. Asked what was in it."

Jacob opened the bag, just long enough to show Gadreel the three remaining letters before closing it.

"Well, well. Azazel might be interested in what you have there. Catch him in the right mood, and he just might be feeling generous enough to arrange a swap."

"The bag for that wand?"

"Maybe."

"Is the Plasma Wand good for protection?"

"The best."

"Better than these letters?"

"Only one way to find out. And once you use up those three, you have nothing. The Plasma Wand never runs out of juice."

"Where's Azazel?" Jacob asked.

"Can't tell you. You have to have a pass."

"And where—"

"I already told you! Down the street. Lil's Orphanage."

"How do I get there?"

"You can't. Not by yourself."

"Can you come with me?"

"What about her?"

"I'll be fine," Debbie countered.

"Sure you will. As long as you stay away from that door. Which'll be tough for you. Women's curiosity pretty much did in your world. Eve and her apple, Pandora and her box. You know."

"No. I don't know."

"A feisty one, eh?" Gadreel grinned. "Come on, young man. Let's take a stroll. We'll leave baby sister here to her own devices."

They left before Debbie could correct him.

####

"Ten things were created on Sabbath eve, at twilight.... some say also destructive spirits."

—*Perkei Avot Chapter Five, Section Nine*

> *The Kabbalah teaches that Adam had a first wife, Lilith, who was rooted in Din (severity).*
>
> *She soon passed away as the young, fresh world was not ready for harshness....*
>
> —Likkutei Torah Bere'shit, Rabbi Schneur Zalman of Liadi

LIL'S ORPHANAGE, the sign read, above a door of polished iron.

"It keeps them from escaping," Gadreel explained, before Jacob could ask. "That's what iron does. In case one gets loose before Lilith has broken it."

"Keeps who from escaping?" There wasn't anything in his *Sisters of Nightfall* comic about Lilith running a prison or an orphanage. And he didn't want to find out about "broken".

"You'll see. Now you go on inside."

"You ain't comin'?"

"Go in!" Gadreel barked. Then more calmly: "No males around here speak to Lilith. She does her job, we do ours. We pretty much stay out of her way. Now do you want your permit or not?"

Jacob entered a large space bereft of furnishings or decoration. A plaintive screech drew his attention across the room to where a female figure kneeled, her back to him, struggling as if to hold something down. Was this Lilith? One thing was the same—the scarlet hair trailing down her back, its tips red-orange like the afterglow of a spent match. But if this was Lilith, she sure wasn't dressed like in the comic book. For one thing, she wasn't naked under her hair. Just the opposite. A loose-fitting garment of mud brown draped below where her feet would have been. Twin bumps raised the garment at the level of her shoulder blades. It spilled onto the floor around her, obscuring her shape from the neck down.

"Close that door tight!" The command was a growl. Jacob did as he was told. "You may come closer," Lilith instructed, her back still turned.

Jacob did so.

Lilith was indeed fighting to subdue a small creature she had pinned to the floor. Its ebony sheen matched that of the black giantess that had been abducted from the street. Its slender shape and buds of breasts might also have been those of Sybil the Fana Giantess. Except Sybil had been maybe 12 feet tall, this being scarcely 18 inches long where it lay. Its face lacked any sign of human features. The head was a ragged black-ink smear interrupted by white slashes where a face should have been.

"Is that from inside Sybil?"

The white slash of mouth widened as if to affirm. Again it screeched, a wounded bleat of protest over its apparent excision from Sybil's body. Lilith cut off the shriek. The talon-like points of her right hand curled around its throat but did not penetrate. Deeper they pushed, all but entering, until the creature gave up and fell still. It had not died. At least life, if life this was, had not passed from it. Leaning forward, Lilith murmured something to the creature, at whose nod of acquiescence Lilith lifted herself off and turned to face Jacob.

Jacob gasped in desire. Maybe this wasn't the Lilith of his comic book. But in some ways she was better. Because she was alive. Every breath pushed Lilith's chest high against the brown garment. He ached to behold her nakedness, as he had longed to see so many human females undressed. Yet it was her face, at once more and less than human, that drew him most. The red hair pulsed, as flaming embers might, around alabaster cheeks. Her beak-like nose curved downwards, towards lips both sullen and succulent. Her eyes were black-irised ovals of amber; they held to him, unblinking, like the stare, unsparing and exact, of an owl set on its prey.

"Why are you here?" Lilith asked.

"I need a permit. To buy a weapon. Gadreel said so."

"Gadreel." Lilith snorted. "That vulgarian."

Jacob had no idea what this word meant. He repeated his question more carefully: "Is that... creature from inside Sybil, the giant girl that followed us here?"

"Sybil? That is what this interloper from the land of the Amorites was called? Yes, then."

"Is everyone over there evil?"

"All are evil. Everywhere. Or perhaps it would be better to say that all have a demon inside them. Some are more strongly caged than others. But all can be... pried loose, shall we say." On that, Lilith gathered the Sybil thing in her arms and glided to a side door, also of polished iron. It opened to a room whose cacophony of demented cackles and bruised wails and wrathful howls blended, the dissonance that of a monkey house. Lilith released the creature into the room. Stepping away from the door, she motioned for Jacob to look in and see.

Dozens of monsters swarmed the air. Pointed ears and ram's horns, bald heads of obscene smoothness, goat heads on squat human forms, human heads on elongated owl forms, bellies distended over cock shanks, bodies coated in coarse hair or feathers—it was a true menagerie of the awful, the abominated conjoinings of their shapes their sole denominator. One possessed the horn-nubbed head and worm-like torso of the creature that Little Og had roasted. Another had the fully articulated curved ram horns, goat snout, and chocolate-brown goatee of the face he had glimpsed behind the human-seeming female outside Gadreel's weapons store. Some were transparent, with insubstantial bodies and unfinished faces aflame with sparks of fire. Except for these inchoate wraiths, most leaned towards what might be called human or what might be deemed bestial in the obscene melding of their features.

All had wings and flew. And all were demons. Jacob did not have to be told that. Baby ones, perhaps. But demons. And more horrible than any he had seen in any of his movies or games or comic books. *This is the real side of that make-believe,* he was thinking, when one flew at him. Instinctively he raised the Escape Tools bag without opening it. The creature bolted off. The whole room erupted in panic. The demons flew in every direction, their panicked howls so loud that Jacob's eardrums quivered.

"Take that out of here! They don't like it, and I don't either!"

No sooner had Jacob cleared the entrance than Lilith slammed the door shut behind them. Quiet returned. At first she glared at him, as if he should have known better. Then her glare somewhat softened.

"What did you think of them?" she asked.

"I'm glad you keep 'em locked up."

"And why is that?"

"They're, I dunno. Kinda disgusting. For an orphanage."

"Some of them are mine, you know."

"I didn't know."

"Of course you didn't. How could you?" Her face sagged in some private sorrow. Jacob wondered if she could be the one in need of rescue. He hoped not.

"I'm sorry I got you mad. About your children and all."

"They're not all mine!" Lilith snapped. "Only the unfinished ones."

"I don't know what you mean."

"Come sit with me. Let me see you." She glided ahead of him, to the center of the room. They settled, facing each other.

"How old are you?" Lilith asked.

"Thirty-seven."

"The age of a man. Yet you are not a man. You too are unfinished. Like my orphans."

"I'm sorry." It was all he could think to say.

"It's not your fault. It is the fault of, how is it said in your world, the One Above. For not finishing you. As my true children were not finished in the twilight of Creation's final day. The One Above had no time to complete them before the Day of Rest brought down the curtain on the act of Creation. And my husband said nothing. My pathetic worm of a first husband."

Jacob struggled to remember the story. There was Adam, and there was Eve, and later there were Cain and Abel. But no Lilith. And there were trees and plants and animals.

"Who was your husband?" he asked, hoping she wouldn't say something weird like a Venus fly trap or a dinosaur. Or something else that existed when only one man was around.

"Adam. Of course. I was his first wife. But most humans don't know that. Unless they read the renegade texts of your earth's blind religions. To Muslims, I am the mother of Jinn. The Jewish and Christian witch-hunters of history make it much simpler. To them, I am the mother of the first demons. Those you saw of fire and air. They long for completion. But they cannot have completion. Still, they will fly in the army of demons. When the Final Day comes."

"What day?"

"The day of our triumph."

"Over who?" *Humans,* he expected Lilith to answer. So many comics and movies and video games were full of stories about, what was that word, Armageddon. Which meant the final battle of good and evil. When all half-bad and quarter-bad and mostly bad people get swept off the earth after everything almost gets destroyed. Or something like that.

"The other camp. The Amorite descendants of the *Nephilim*. That entire vulgar brood."

"But they have demons too!"

"Not our kind of demons. That is our purpose. To build an army of our kind of demons. As many as possible. To run our kind of world."

"You don't send 'em up to our world?"

"That too." Lilith shrugged with impatience, as if this last thing wasn't worth mentioning.

He was about to say he was sorry again when Lilith rose from the floor. She stood close over him, staring down, the most inexplicable heat pouring from her.

"What is your name?" she asked.

Jacob told her.

"Jacob. Listen, Jacob. I flee Adam in that Sabbath twilight. I take my unfinished children with me. My Jinn. My demons, if you will. And why do I leave? Because I am told to lie under Adam. Under that weakling, that fool, when he should have lain beneath me. My act is not pleasing to the One Above. He sends his angels to find me. But Azazel finds me first." Lilith's cheeks paled. "Azazel. My second husband. Who forced me to his way. Who brought more demons out of me. Before the emissaries of the One Above discovered where I had hidden. They changed me, Jacob. They prevented more children from issuing from my loins."

Loins. It was a word Jacob didn't know. But he could guess. "How?" he asked.

"Tell me, young Jacob. Do you find me attractive?"

Jacob nodded.

"Would you consider to be my third husband?"

Again, Jacob nodded. This time he figured he had better do so.

"You want your weapon badly, I see." Lilith smiled bitterly. "Let me show you, then. Behold, Lilith's beauty." Her taloned fingers clutched the base of her garment and pulled it over her head. She stood before him, slowly pivoting so that Jacob might see the whole of her. The shoulders were strong, the whiteness of her face and throat enhanced within the nest of her red hair, the bosom as high as he had imagined. But the waist tapered to no legs. Instead a pillar of flame extended to the floor without touching it. She continued to rotate so that he might see her back. There hung a pair of charred wings, withered and black and useless.

"Now get out of here." She tried to speak with harshness. Instead her voice heaved sadly. "Jacob," she called after him. "Jacob, if you ever need...."

He did as he was told.

####

"And there was one male who came into the world from the spirit of Cain's side, and they called him Tubal-Cain. And a female came forth with him, and... her name was Naamah.... This Tubal-Cain brought weapons of killing into the world. This Naamah became aroused and adhered to her evil side. To this day she exists... she comes forth and makes sport with the sons of man... she takes their desire, and from it she conceives and brings forth other kinds of spirits into the world. And those children whom she bears from the sons of man come to the women, and they conceive from them and bear more spirits. And all of them go to Lilith the Ancient, and she rears them...."

—*Zohar iii: 76b, from Gates to the Old City, Raphael Patai*

A smaller group of Black-Shirted males had replaced the Yellow Shirts on the sidewalk outside Gadreel's Weapons Emporium. Through the front window they ogled Debbie without cease, tacit in their desire to storm her, vocal in their lures.

"Come with me," invited one called Genun. "Let me show you my store of musical instruments. You may admire them while my fingers pluck sweet melodies from your flesh."

"My store holds lustrous pets," tried a Kasadya. "You may stroke them as I stroke you."

"I promise you the secrets of the stars," smiled one Kokabiel. "I will whisper them in your soft ear while we lie together beneath them."

"The phases of the moon I will unlock for you as our bodies lock under its glow," enticed a Sariel.

"I will teach you sun signs while its rays warm your nakedness," promised a Shamsiel.

"There's no sun here! No stars, no moon either!" Her sharp retort was meant to push them off. But these Black Shirts only laughed over having been exposed. Then their grins dropped. Their hungers turned murderous. With a shudder, Debbie retreated farther into Gadreel's store. At the very back she came to another room beyond whose door she heard a familiar sound.

The tap-tap-tap of fingers against a computer keyboard? She knew to knock first.

"Yeah?" A male voice. Thick and low and somewhat dumb. But also not angry over having had his work rhythm interrupted.

She opened the door to a room whose walls put forth stifling heat. The male at his computer desk wore no shirt. His goal could not have been to show off his body, for it was no body to show off. It was rotund, burly, past plump, with beefy shoulders covered in hairs curling high as the back of his bull neck. Seeing that his visitor was a female, he grabbed a sky-blue T-shirt off the floor and tugged it down over himself.

"Come on in," he told her.

Debbie hesitated at the doorway. Standing, he straightened, as if inviting her to evaluate him. He was dark-skinned, swarthy and stocky, his arms flabby bulges under the T-shirt's short sleeves. Black hair flopped about his sweat-grimed cheeks. His eyes were sunken purple hollows, like the ringed sockets of a raccoon.

"Name's Tubal-Cain."

"I know that name."

"Everyone knows it. Everyone who's read those Bible legends, that is. I don't come off too good, do I?"

"I don't know about that." But she did know. Rabbi Seth had spoken of the descendants of Cain, how Tubal-Cain had been civilization's first blacksmith, from whose hands humankind's first weapons had been forged under the supervision of Gadreel, the command of Azazel. When he made no answer, she let her eyes roam the room's interior. An iron chunk with winged points occupied a squat pedestal against one wall. Scars coated its faded silver.

"My first anvil," Tubal-Cain explained, with some pride.

Above it hung a large photograph. It looked to be of a family—a single father, perhaps, flanked by smaller figures, presumably his children. Yet this grown-up male wore the hunted, fear-laced grimace of a fugitive. A red scar marked his forehead. Those flanking him were not children but a variety of misshapen beings. Debbie had imagined several of them from Shemhazai's depictions of the Seven Earths. A two-headed being exchanged glares of discord with itself. A noseless dwarf peered out blank-featured, its pancake-flat face void of memory. A sad-eyed presence had fangs down to its hairy chest. Interspersed were the by-now familiar if not downright ubiquitous humanoids, their reptilian or mammalian or avian features melded with human forms in all manner of combinations.

"First-generation Cainites," said Tubal-Cain. "And the old man's Cain himself. My, let's see, great-great-great-great-grandfather, if I'm countin' right. Actually, the old man part's half-wrong. He was part man, part demon."

"I thought Adam and Eve were Cain's parents."

"The Adam part's right. His real mother's right down the street."

"She must be pretty old."

"Lilith ain't old. First-rank bitch demons like that one don't get old."

Debbie ignored Tubal-Cain's profanity. Something inarticulate in this homely figure made him less threatening to her.

"So you're Lilith's descendant? Which means you have within you elements of that other part too?"

"Everybody's got a demon in him. Or her. Everybody."

"Is Cain here too?"

"Nope. Got murdered. Had enough human in him to leak blood. His grandson shot him full of arrows. Hope he suffered."

"Why, Tubal-Cain?"

"I hated him. Nasty old man. Jealous about everything. What was his, was his. What was yours, well, that was his too." He blinked hard to dismiss the thought. Sitting once more at his computer, he stared at its screen in frustration.

Debbie stepped closer.

With a defeated slap at the keyboard, he switched his computer off.

"Here I am, supposed to be designing the Doomsday Weapon to kill off all those Amorites. And all I'm killing is time." Leaning back, he eyed her with sudden suspicion. "What are you doing here anyway? You some kind of spy?"

"Gadreel told me to stay away from the Black-Shirted males gathered in front. At least those Yellow-Shirted ones aren't around anymore," she added.

"Of course they aren't. They make themselves scarce when the Black Shirts come around."

"The Black Shirts outrank them?"

"Listen, we're not running an army around here. At least, not like what you think an army is. Black Shirts are top rung. Those Yellow Shirts are on the lowest rung. Like pawns in a chess game. Except the Yellow Shirts are demons."

"But they looked like humans. Some were even, well, attractive."

"All of them are. Now that they're grown. All the newborns get sent to Lilith. She raises them. Trains them. When they're old enough, she lets them out to roam our little village. They take human shape for two reasons. First is practice. For the Big War. Second, it's better for when they fornicate. They don't have to see each other like they really are."

"Demons... fornicate?" Such a word.

"They make more demons that way. Besides, it's fun for them. Ain't it fun for you?"

"Tell me more about the Black Shirts," she asked, attempting to shift the subject.

"Highest rung. Kokabiel, Shamsiel, Sariel, Genun, Kasadya—all fallen angels. You know that story? About the Watchers and the earth gals?"

"I do."

"Only Lilith and Azazel are higher. And those two, well, let's just say they don't get along."

"What happened?"

"They had marital problems, you could say. So they split. No, that ain't right. Azazel ran off."

"You mean they were married?"

"Well, you sure could say they were spendin' lotsa time together. And they were havin' fun at it too. It was right after Lilith ran off from Adam. And right before Azazel teamed up with Shemhazai to lead the 200 Watchers down to your world. Lil was quite a dish in those days. And she let him do it whenever he said the word. Demons were springin' outta those two like they were bunnies. But then You-Know-Who"—Tubal-Cain jutted a chubby finger skywards—"put a stop to it. Things were getting out of hand. Too many of our kind, not enough of His kind. So He killed off as many of Lilith's little demon kiddies as He could locate. Hundreds of 'em, popped or punctured or squashed. And He fixed Lil so she couldn't have any more demon babies with Azazel or anyone."

"How?"

"Never you mind. Anyway, that didn't make Azazel any too happy. He's not exactly the type to sit home by the fireside, if you know what I mean. So he started doing a bit of his own midnight creeping. Except it wasn't just at midnight. He found other ovens to bake up baby demons. Human gals. Oh, did he find them. Him and Shemhazai and the 200 Watchers, they were cutting a good-time path through your world right up to that damn Flood. But before that, oh boy. All them dumb-brained Daughters of Men— it was like shooting fish in a barrel. Pchoo, pchoo!" Tubal-Cain shaped his hand into a mock-gun and aimed it at Debbie.

"Why is your shirt blue?" She managed to choke the question out of herself.

"I'm middle rung. Over the Yellow Shirts and under the Black Shirts. Part human stuff mixed in with the higher-up stuff. Or lower stuff. Me and my sister both. Say, you wanna meet Naamah? Might do you some good. If ever I saw an outfit that stiff-arms a guy, it's that white blouse and black skirt you're wearing. Can't see nothing of the real you. Leastways, nothing to make anyone want to for-ni-cate with you. You could learn a lot from sis. Lots of *Chitzonim* come banging on her door. Except they don't have to bang too hard. Naamah's a friendly kind of gal. And fertile as, well, a regular little bunny." He slapped his computer back on. "Listen, you don't even have to leave here to visit. Step closer. Look over my shoulder."

Tubal-Cain clicked several buttons on his keyboard. There appeared on his computer screen the exterior of a different store. *NAAMAH'S COSMETICS BOUTIQUE,* read its sign. The computer's camera eye tracked fast through the entrance. Inside it rotated, right then left, passing through garments of flaming pinks and iridescent purples and blazing whites; of the liquid blue of sapphires; of the ruby reds of royalty. The colors were as bright as the weapons in Gadreel's store were dour. *Yet here are weapons for females,* Debbie thought. Thong panties, wireless bras, satin slips and silk kimonos, glittering sequins, powders and lipsticks, eye shadow and nail polish and perfumes... all possessed a spirit, festive and liberated, that Debbie had always renounced.

The camera eye came to a stop behind a female stretching to straighten a stack of lingerie on a high shelf. Her summer dress, the same sky-blue of Tubal-Cain's T-shirt, hugged her every contour. Yellow hair, bright as sunflowers, tumbled down her back. The act of extending herself sculpted a shapely tautness into her calves. It indented her waist and lent a graceful arch to her spine. From the strapless peak of her low-cut garment bloomed creamy shoulders, a smooth white neck. The twist of Naamah's reach lent her form the sinuous flow of a Greek statue.

"You want to say hello to my sister? You can speak right into the computer."

"No. No. I have nothing to say to someone like that."

"Oh, you don't. Well, tell me. What makes you so special?"

"Well, I never," Debbie responded, backing away.

"Of course. You never." With a dismissive laugh, Tubal-Cain resettled his watery stare onto his computer screen.

Debbie slammed the door as she left. She wanted him to take note of her exit, but all she heard was more keyboard clicking. And to think, she had liked him at first. Something in his pudgy, little-boy self had led her to want to trust him. Sighing, she went back up front. The Black-Shirted fallen angels still crowded the sidewalk. She took an all-but-involuntary step towards them. Collectively they arched, like predators set to pounce.

Go ahead, a now-familiar voice within her urged. *Give yourself to them. Let them have their way with you, as long as it is quick. Let them ravage you, demolish the part of you that thinks, so that you may find release from—*

The words swirled in her mind like gossamer threads. The winds of Tubal-Cain's final question blew them away:

What makes you so special?

Nothing.

CHAPTER 11

"Blood is symbolic of Gevurah (judgment). Since judgment is the root from which all the demonic forces draw their energy, we honor the blood by covering it. Now that Gevurah has been honored properly, it will not 'look elsewhere' for its honor."
—Rabbi Menachem Recanati, Kabbalistic commentary on the Torah (13th century)

"... the one who loves violence, His soul hates"
—Psalm 11:5

Outside Lilith's door, Jacob tried to decide which way to head. Should he go back inside to Lilith? That sadness under her severe surface—maybe he could use one of the letters to help her. But what if she was bad and got hold of the sack of Escape Tools? Hadn't Shemp said something about how anyone, good or bad, could use the letters of God's name for any purpose if they knew how?

Now you go. And if you ever need....

What? Lilith hadn't said. And there was so much he hadn't asked. Like about that permit to see Azazel. Most importantly, about that permit. Maybe the savant side of his head had warned him not to ask. Not after the way she had spoken of Azazel, all those words coming out with a slight tremble in her fierce voice. Maybe he shouldn't go see Azazel after all. But how else could he get the Plasma Wand, which he wanted more than anything else in the world?

Where was Gadreel anyway? Was Jacob supposed to walk back alone to the weapons store? He looked both ways. Nobody was on the street. No Black Shirts, no Yellow Shirts. Nobody. He started up the sidewalk. As if triggered by his moving, a wave of Yellow Shirts streamed around the corner of a side street and headed in his direction. He shrank back against Lilith's door. It didn't matter. With nothing to hide behind, he was easy to spot. And he wasn't that fast a runner. He wasn't fast at all.

They passed right by him and stopped, one block down, in front of some other store. No. Not a store. A movie theater. He knew because of the movie-sounding name spelled out on the marquee part jutting over the crowd. The name jumped his blood in eagerness. *Shriek of the Haruspex.* He didn't know that last word. But some real good movies Mrs. Benederet had snuck in for him had titles with unusual words. Like *Suspiria* and *Ringu*.

The Yellow Shirts all rushed inside. The sidewalk emptied. Except for Black-Shirted Gadreel. "Get a move on!" he shouted to Jacob from down the block. "Show's about to begin!"

Inside, excited Yellow Shirts circulated through the lobby. Some eyed Jacob, but when they saw Gadreel, they kept their distance.

"Let's go find seats." Gadreel aimed Jacob into the auditorium. "Where do you like to sit?"

"All the way down front." In truth Jacob had never thought about it. He had only been to the movies four times in his life. Three times were from when he was six and seven and nine. *Snow White* and *Peter Pan* and *Pinocchio*. His father had thought that being around people at a movie would do Jacob some good. He was wrong. The fourth time was *Star Wars.*

The same gabbling and cackling that had filled the demon room at Lilith's Orphanage dominated the auditorium. Except here were no groans or howls. Only the raucous clatter of anticipation. The noise flattened to silence as Gadreel led Jacob down to the front row. They settled in middle seats, the screen looming above them. The theater darkened. A deeper blackness filled the screen. Light filtered into the blackness, as when daylight brings dawn. An image took form. The motionless, gelatinous mass of the village's *Tohu*-like sea took up most of the screen; a ribbon of shore ran down the left side. On this thin shore a lanky female form lay on her back, arms and feet held taut by four shadowy figures. The female was small-breasted and long-bodied, much taller than the shapes that pinned her to the sand. More light, seeping in, lent her skin an ebony glow. The head cocked backward. Frightened eyes jumped among those that held her, then out at Jacob. They begged for rescue, these eyes. Utter fear consumed a face whose high nose and narrow cheeks added final confirmation of an identity Jacob already suspected.

"I'm sorry, Sybil! I'm sorry we left you behind!"
"Sshhh!"
"Quiet!"

"You wanna spoil the fun!?"

Jacob scrunched down in his seat. His initial urge to see a blood-and-thunder horror movie—a horror movie to beat all horror movies, one whose pretend violence thrilled him as much as a pretend monster could tickle his imagination—had curdled to revulsion. Never had he seen a face like Sybil's in any movie. She was terrified. For real. All the acting had been torn away, and what was left was knowledge that her life was about to be snuffed out. *I don't want anybody actually to be hurt!* He wanted to cry this out. He wanted to crawl up into the screen and stop them. But even if he could? Four against one, and him with no weapon?

On the screen, a hooded figure limped down the shore to where Sybil lay. He was short and stocky, but why he limped, Jacob couldn't tell. A purple robe covered his whole body, a conical hood hid his face and head. Only his hands were visible out of his flowing sleeves. One hand gripped a knife. He held it high, to display its blade to the audience. It was narrow and curved, meant to probe carefully. *But not Sybil. Please, not Sybil. I will never watch another movie with this kind of violence ever again.*

Kneeling, the hooded figure went about his task. He lifted out Sybil's insides, organ by organ, then arranged them neatly on the sandy shore beside her. Tears poured from Jacob. He had never realized that the kinds of movie deaths he loved to watch were clouded in actual agony, in anguish for the loss of what it was to live. Sybil's writhing became all the more awful for her muteness. As she expired, there poured into the theater the tutelary stink of her entrails, the stench of waste exiting her body in that moment. *This is what such death means,* Jacob was being told. And he cried more.

On the screen, the figure who had done the slaughtering now yanked off his hood. His wide cheeks and curly hair and ruddy skin lent him the rugged good looks of some actor playing the hero in one of Jacob's jungle films. The man studied Sybil's insides as if trying to decipher some message they held. He rearranged the organs with his hands as if to fit together pieces of a jigsaw puzzle. Finally, he lifted one dripping organ and examined it. It was a gleaming reddish brown, divided into two sections. The left one, a large mass, crowded the right one to a mere strip, as the Sea of *Tohu* crowded the strip of shore. The robed figure shifted his focus from one section to the other. Shaking his head, he sank in defeat onto his haunches. Then his gaze came out of the screen. Out to Jacob. He pushed the two-lobed body part down towards Jacob.

And Jacob saw.

The massive left lobe stirred. Something moved beneath it, as in monster movies when a creature rises from ocean depths to destroy cities. Here, only a ripple cut through the surface. Nothing emerged. His attention shifted to the much narrower right lobe. Here, there was something. Arms that were not Sybil's were reaching out to him, as they had to his closed vision in that Ogville bedroom. Those same sad eyes, pleading and desperate, reached inside Jacob and pulled him to stand up.

"Hey! You! Sit down!" Cries of resentment pelted Jacob from the Yellow Shirts behind.

Gadreel stood too. Facing the audience, he growled a warning at them: "You all better shut up! If you know what's good for you, you won't get on this fellow's wrong side!" Then he turned to Jacob. "You saw something," he said. "What was it? Well? What was it!?"

####

"Asmodeus: the demon of impurity... in Hell, the controller of gambling houses... the inventor of carousels... and all the new French fashions."
—A Dictionary of Angels, Gustav Davidson

"...in the Book of Tobit... a demon characterized by carnal desire... in the Talmud...a good-natured and humorous fellow... would seem to come into direct comparison with a Greek satyr..."
—Jewish Encyclopedia, 1906 edition

With surprising abruptness, the Black Shirts abandoned the sidewalk in front of Gadreel's Weapons Emporium and rushed down the street. What could have drawn them so quickly? Debbie risked peering outside. One block down, they now gathered on a street corner. Beyond them, two figures marched at the head of a legion of Yellow Shirts that filled the center of the street. Gadreel and Jacob? Despite the distance, Debbie saw that her brother was not being restrained. To the contrary. He was being followed, as if he were their leader.

I can run to them, she thought. *Jacob will probably ignore me. But Gadreel had offered protection, had he not? If he sees me, I will be safe. Will I not?*

The parade veered right, down a side street, towards the sea. The gang of Black Shirts still crowded their corner. She could not get past them now. Not on her own. Which left her only one choice: Tubal-Cain. She went to knock on his door. A sorry-to-disturb-you knock. The keyboard clacked to an impatient halt. She took that as invitation enough to enter.

"My brother's outside. But he's too far down the street for me to go to him alone. Will you escort me?"

"Escort? What kind of talk is that?"

"I only thought—"

"Yeah, yeah. You only thought."

"Please. Something important is happening. And Jacob—my brother—is at the head of it."

On an exasperated sigh, Tubal-Cain shut off his computer and brushed past Debbie. Staying close, she followed him out the front door and down the sidewalk. Jacob was no longer in sight. All she saw was the last of the Yellow-Shirted throng turning down that side street. When Tubal-Cain and Debbie reached the gang of Black Shirts, they tightened to block the progress of this human female and her Blue-Shirt companion.

Okay, Tubby. Hand her over."

"It's been a long time since we had meat this sweet."

Tubal-Cain shrugged. Debbie tried stepping back, but the Black Shirt behind her shoved her to her knees. Eyes shut, she waited for their collective grasp to initiate her violation. None did. There came a scrape, a limp, a presence at her side. She opened her eyes to a man in a flowing purple robe, like a priest's vestments. He was short, like Tubal-Cain. His stockiness echoed that of Tubal-Cain, but his physique seemed more solid. He looked anything but slovenly. Not, what word had that Black-Shirt fallen angel used, tubby. His face was far more refined, even handsome. The cheekbones were wide, the full lips sensitively curled. His hair was drawn back in a neat ponytail. His mix of robustness and delicacy reminded her of a movie star hero in some action film she had let Jacob watch. A purple hood dangled from one hand. His face bore traces of make-up, as if he had just left some theatrical production.

"This is no way to treat a lady." The charm in his voice was aimed at her. It was too smooth, too obvious, but before she could think of a way to reject him without losing his protection, Tubal-Cain mashed one meaty hand to this new arrival's chest and thrust him to the pavement.

"Get out of here, Asmodeus. Go on back to your fruitcake world."

"Sorry for existing," Asmodeus called up to Tubal-Cain—adding, with a defiant spin to the word: "Daddy."

"You're no son of mine!" Tubal-Cain spat his retort. Asmodeus rolled onto his side, back turned to his father.

The Black Shirts laughed as if watching a comedy.

"Go run to your mommy, Asmodee," one cried. "Tell her Daddy's treating you bad again."

"Mommy Naamah will protect you, sonny," another called.

All the Black Shirts now took up a mocking chant.

"Shoulda been a blacksmith, shoulda been a blacksmith!" From the practiced rhythm in their conjoined voices, it was clearly something they had sung before. "Isn't that right, Tubal-Cain?"

"Damn right," Tubal-Cain muttered.

"Instead he runs a movie theater. And a merry-go-round. Whoo whoo. Round and round."

"Mr. Entertainment," a Black-Shirted fallen angel threw in. "Puts himself in his own movies too. Probably likes having make-up on. Probably lets Mama Naamah smear it on him before she lets him have his fun. Did you know what was going between your sister and the baby boy you made with her, Big Daddy?"

Tubal-Cain seethed.

"All right, dearie." The Black Shirts addressed Debbie now. "It's your time."

One Black Shirt's hand clutched her forearm. Another hand, banded in work-hardened tendons, yanked that grip away. The crowd of Black Shirts loosened, fell back.

"Come on." Gadreel squinted down hard at Debbie. "Your brother wants you to watch."

She clambered up from the sidewalk. On a vanquished snort, Tubal-Cain headed back to the weapons store. The Black Shirts disbanded, leaving Asmodeus curled on his side.

Gadreel led Debbie away. She knew to stay behind, in his trail.

"Where are we going?" she asked.
"*Tohu* Sea."
"*Tohu*. I know that word."
"Who cares what you know."
Debbie followed in silence.

####

"Everything and every person has its own purpose or task, and this does not make anyone any more or less important, for everyone is important in the totality of things, just as every limb or organ of a body is important. If one person would wish to change his or her function, it would not only disturb his or her own personal harmony, but would also disturb the total harmony."
—Torah: the Five Books of Moses, "Spiritual Vitamin", reflections by Rabbi Chaim Miller

Jacob gazed down upon the crowd of Yellow Shirts spread below him. He stood on a boardwalk-like expanse of elevated planks that ran behind *Chitzonim*ville, between the village and the body of pale, motionless liquid at his back. Sea of *Tohu*, Gadreel said it was called. *Tohu*: a Debbie word. Like Tofu, which his sister sometimes made for Jacob to eat when she decided they both needed healthier food.

Not anymore.

He was glad she hadn't been with him when he had gone in to see *Shriek of the Haruspex*. She probably would have tried to stop him from watching a movie he had ended up not wanting to finish anyway. He wouldn't have wanted her to see his horrified reaction to what was being done to Sybil. He'd just wanted to get out of that theater, fast as he could. Debbie would have gotten all flustered and dragged him out. She might have been able to explain, better than Gadreel had, that word *haruspex*: something about reading the future from the entrails of the slaughtered. Jacob didn't know entrails and barely knew slaughtered. Debbie could explain. But first she would beat him down hard. She would blame his idiot side if he told her about seeing those same arms from that Ogville bedroom reaching out to him, those same sad eyes pleading from within the wet reddish-brown of a body organ that Gadreel had identified as a liver.

But this honoring, he wanted her to see. Everything had changed when Gadreel saw that Jacob had discovered some meaning in *Shriek of the Haruspex*. He had led Jacob out of the theater in such a way that the Yellow Shirts had followed like servants. Never had Jacob's world shown him praise like this. But the world of Shemhazai's game was different.

Gadreel returned with Debbie. She shrank behind him as they mounted the steps to this boardwalk platform. She stumbled as she crossed the planks to where Jacob stood. Never had Jacob seen her so messy. Her black skirt twisted on her hip. Edges of her white blouse plumped out at her waist and stomach. Her short black hair needed to be combed, her face washed. Not that it was dirty. It was more that her skin looked drained, puffy, like from being in water for too long.

"Do you want her down on her knees?" Gadreel asked Jacob.

"No. She's gotta see what I can do."

"You're running things. You mind if I bring the other Black Shirts up here?"

"Okay."

Gadreel motioned the gang of Black Shirts to join them on the platform. As soon as they had, Jacob faced the Sea of *Tohu*. He waited for it to do something, but it just lay there, flat and gel-like. He didn't know what else to try. Then he remembered the bag. Should he open it and waste a letter? No. Not yet. He had played enough video games to know the need to store up tools with a limited number of Escapes. For no better reason than that he had seen the gesture in that extra-long Moses movie Debbie had made him watch, he raised his arms towards the Sea of *Tohu* and opened them. Still nothing. All he knew was that, when the time came, the surface would churn, as if stirred by something cruising beneath, as had the larger-massed left lobe of Sybil's liver.

"It gonna happen here." Jacob spoke absently, a stranger to himself. "It comes outta there and does bad things on the shore."

"What kind of bad things?" one Black-Shirted fallen angel demanded to know.

"I don't know. I can't see that." He thought a moment. His savant side brightened. "You get me that Plasma Wand, maybe I can see better."

"Don't believe him," warned another Black Shirt. "It's not true. Ogville's coming at us either on the ground or from the sky.

How can they sneak their great weapon into our sea when we're watching it all the time?"

"Maybe he's a spy."

"Maybe Ogville sent him."

"No. He saw something. Isn't that what oracles are for?"

"When does it happen?" another Black Shirt asked Jacob.

"I don't know. I didn't see."

"Somebody go ask Lil what's going on."

"She wouldn't tell us. Even if she knew."

"What are we supposed to do, then? Trust this human?"

"We have to ask Azazel."

"You go ask him."

"Not me."

"Not me either. I'm not going into the Desert Wasteland. The Mountain of Darkness, the Great Abyss—those landscapes aren't for us anyway. We don't have the power."

"He does." One Black Shirt pointed to Jacob's bag.

"He has to go. He has to be the one."

"Do I gotta?" Jacob asked.

"If you want that Plasma Wand." Gadreel answered.

"He can't have it. Not without a—"

"Azazel can fix that." Gadreel cut him short. "Azazel can fix anything. Down here."

All fell silent. Then a Black Shirt eyed Debbie. "What about this one?"

"We bring her along," Gadreel answered. "Azazel might be... interested."

"I'm not taking her there," a Black Shirt protested, fear in his voice.

"Not me."

"Me neither."

Gadreel crossed his arms. "I'll get one of the Blue Shirts. I already know which one." His muscles bulged, his eyes glinted. "And I won't ask him. I'll tell him."

####

"*I form the light, and create darkness; I make peace, and create evil; I am the Lord, that doeth all these things.*"

—Isaiah 45:7

> "The Lord hath made everything for His own purpose. Yea, even the wicked for the day of evil."
>
> —*Proverbs, 16, 4*

"Oh, I'm a bad boy, all right."

Debbie ignored Asmodeus' wink as he limped beside her, across a waste place dim and barren, upon an endless stretch of sand that did not yield beneath their tread. His initial chafing at Gadreel's fierce imperative had evaporated the moment he learned that Debbie would be with Jacob in their journey to Azazel's Great Abyss. He had changed from the purple robe he had worn for his role in *Shriek of the Haruspex* to a natty sky-blue sport coat and silk vest of a deeper blue. His pants, also sky-blue, were of the bell-bottom variety for which Debbie had always felt such aversion, symbolizing as they had a too-facile, knee-jerk defiance of convention in the 1960's that had evolved into eccentric self-expression in the seventies. Or so went the case that Debbie had mentally prepared against such fashion.

Jacob walked ahead of them in this new landscape. He seemed to know where they were headed... or did he? Mountains loomed in the vast night before them. The Mountains of Darkness, these must be. Past them lay the Great Abyss. And Azazel. By whom Jacob would be measured for his worthiness to receive his cherished Plasma Wand. While Debbie stayed behind, with this Asmodeus. Who at least had tried to save her from the Black Shirts.

"So you make movies?" she asked him.

"Oh yes. The worst kind, filled with those devil's brew intoxicants, sex and violence." He blinked comically, confessionally, as if to block any justification to which she might expect him to proceed. Debbie smiled at his left-handed honesty. She thought him not unhandsome, this son of tubby, boorish Tubal-Cain. Asmodeus must have inherited his looks—also his smooth charm—from his mother Naamah, whose flowing blonde tresses and overtly ripe form Debbie had observed in the camera eye of Tubal-Cain's computer. With the make-up off, Asmodeus' skin glowed a vibrant olive. His eyebrows, black-thick and bushy, lent an accent of perpetual readiness to his broad-boned face. His ice-blue eyes played upon the blues of his outfit. They positively twinkled when he spoke.

"I write songs too. I create dances. You've heard of the Twist? That was mine. Opened all kinds of doors. Bedroom doors." He shrugged, good-natured in his guilt. "But you wouldn't want to hear about that. Or would you?"

"Not really."

"You sound like my father." A smile, saddened yet defiant, curled his lips. "Tubal-Cain didn't want me splashing around in any pools of pleasure. Like acting, songwriting. Unless they were his pleasures. Practical inventions. Like better knife sharpeners. Or lathes to make gun barrels. That kind of thing. Of course, Mother Naamah steered me in entirely the opposite direction. I'm all they ever fight over. Otherwise, they get along fine. Sometimes too fine. If you know what I mean."

"I think I do. Now."

"It's like that story from your world of the coal miner's son who wants to play the violin."

"So you act in movies and write songs for a living?"

"A living? Oh yes. I see what you mean. I run a movie theater, too. Among other things. Want to hear more about what I do?"

"Not really."

"Hey, let's speed up. Your brother's getting too far ahead of us." He placed a hand in the small of Debbie's back. She twisted out of his touch.

"Why do you limp?" she asked. It was one thing that seemed to work down here: changing the subject.

"Aha! Showtime, the lady wants. Curtain up!" Stopping, he pulled the blue fabric above his left thigh. The voluminous bell-bottom cuff lifted to reveal a three-taloned rooster's claw. "Isn't it a beauty? Observe the color! Pure cartilage! See how each talon is serrated, like a worm's body, before it tapers to the claw! Well? What do you think?"

"I've seen worse." She didn't know why she said it.

"So have I. But not by much." Asmodeus lowered his pant leg. Openly, his eyes roamed her figure. "Such promise you have. But you know that, enough to deny it. Otherwise, you wouldn't stay dressed the way you are. To speak to a woman like you of liberation would be a waste of breath. If I had breath." He laughed gently. "Then again, liberation takes many forms."

"What would be mine?"

"A lover, I could say. My own part-human, part-demon self, I could say. But then you would become suspicious of me and pull away even farther. On the other hand, maybe it's not too late."

"For what?"

"For you to be liberated."

"Are you trying..."

"Yes and no, Devorah. Do you mind if I call you Devorah? It's so much more regal than Debbie. And there is a touch of... the regal about you."

"Please." She smelled Trojan horse.

"All right. You can't blame a half-demon for trying, can you? Tell me, has Shemhazai tried?"

"Of course not." Never mind that he had, in his way.

"And what if he did? Shemhazai and Azazel provided the start-up impulse for every store in *Chitzonim*ville. Metalwork and cosmetics, arts and sciences, astrology and enchantments—these secrets existed in the Seven Heavens. Why not bring them down to Earth and spread them among humankind? Are there not myths in your world of one called Prometheus who gave the secrets of fire to mortals impoverished in all ways except their scrabbling to survive? Was Prometheus not chained, like Azazel, for his sin of wanting to give? Is human progress a sin? If a weapon is hurled at you, must you not take action with a stronger weapon? And passion—aah, passion! Is it truly a sin? If so, why is it so omnipresent? Have not the residents of your Earth learned, throughout the millennia, to channel the constant throb of their desires into stories and games, music and theater? Are these not ways to play out, without always having to perform, impulses to plunder females and obliterate one's adversaries? Have not these twin impulses reinvented themselves from the time of Creation to this day? Sex and violence, you call them! Old wine in new bottles, are they not?"

"I don't believe anything that you're saying."

Asmodeus laughed, gently tolerant. "Well then. Would you believe me if I told you that your God willed there to be *Chitzonim* like us? Without outsiders, could there be insiders? It is our duty to spawn demons, as many as we can. We replenish Earth with them. Without us, there is no tension between light and darkness. Good and evil. Right path and left path. Choose life or choose death. Free will: isn't that the term of favor up there, where you're from? Down here, the Dark Other works like a well-oiled machine. Sin gets recycled. New demons are formed by the minute. Some are sent off to your world. Some stay as our army. You'll see how it works. When you meet Azazel. At least he is honest. Not like Shemhazai, with his infernal smokescreen."

"I don't want to meet Azazel."

"Of course you don't. But he will want to meet you. He tires of the female demons that descend to him. And you have some of Lilith, his first wife, in you. You are rent through with *Gevurah*, as is Lilith. Severity, I believe is your English word. But you are... complete, shall we say, from your long white throat through the flow of your loins, however hard you try to hide them. Also, you are a Daughter of Man. Do you realize how long it has been since Azazel has beheld a female of Earth? His eyes are weak. But he will want to admire you. Don't worry, though. You'll be safe. He can't touch you."

"And why is that?"

"You'll know. Soon enough." He pointed ahead to the looming wall of mountain range. "The Mountains of Darkness are close."

"Do we have to climb them?"

"Of course not! That would be impossible. One throw of Jacob's letters, and we are past them. It's the only way. I'll ask him."

"They're so black. Even blacker than this desert."

"The Great Abyss is blacker yet. But don't be afraid, Devorah. I'm here. Would you like to hold hands?"

CHAPTER 12

"Aaron shall place lots upon the two he-goats: one lot for Hashem, and one lot for Azazel. Aaron shall bring near the he-goat designated by lot for Hashem, and make it a sin-offering. And the he-goat designated by lot for Azazel shall be stood alive before Hashem, to provide atonement through it, to send it to Azazel to the Wilderness."
—Leviticus 16, 8-10 (Yom Kippur service described)

"And... the Lord said to Raphael: 'Bind Azazel hand and foot and throw him into the darkness.' And he made a hole in the desert which was in Duda'el and cast him there; he threw on top of him rugged and sharp rocks. And he covered his face in order that he may not see light."
—I Enoch 10: 4-6

Only too readily, Jacob had loosed the second letter of God's name. *It will bring you closer to Azazel*, Asmodeus had explained. Which meant closer to Jacob getting the Plasma Wand.

The Mountains of Darkness were behind them now, a hooded blackness that separated them from the dim glow of the desert. Ahead lay a narrow plateau ending at a cliff, beyond whose edge the plain yawned to vast nothingness. The Great Abyss, Asmodeus had called it. Here was greater blackness. Yet it was no landscape of silence, as the desert had been. Elfin giggles animated the space where this blackness merged with the dome of sky. Jacob made out spheres plummeting into the Great Abyss from all parts of the sky. In the ones that passed closest, he recognized the slimy, cuticle-crusted objects that had accumulated in his closet. *Kelipot*, these were called. Made by the sins of the people of the realm above. Including, he now was beginning to figure, his own.

The cackles showered from demons that rode the *Kelipot*. He knew they must be demons; they had the same blackened forms, the same white-point eyes and white-slit mouths, of many of the creatures in Lilith's Orphanage. Yet these were gleeful sounds, each *Kelipah*'s demon rider happy as a child on a hobby horse.

Asmodeus limped to the edge of the cliff. Jacob followed; his scared-of-everything sister stayed behind. Asmodeus bent over the lip of the cliff. He murmured some information that Jacob couldn't hear. He cocked his ear to listen. From deep in the pit, there came a voice.

"You have done well, Asmodeus. You will have your reward." Asmodeus smiled and withdrew. "Your turn," he told Jacob.

Jacob neared the cliff edge. Kneeling, he rocked forward onto his palms and looked down. A jagged crevice plunged far beneath him. Hundreds of *Kelipot* piled up on all sides where the demons dropped them before zipping off like fairy lights. A faint glow radiated from far down at the very base of the pit. Specks of whiteness, Jacob saw. A clanking as of chains, Jacob heard; a sloshing, as of some imprisoned entity stirring in a water-filled pit. As his vision adjusted, Jacob determined that the points of white were eyes, a dozen perhaps, peering up at him from upon a single motionless cataract, as from one being.

"Azazel?"

"Yes. I am Azazel. And you are He-Who-Is-Known-As-Jacob." The voice crackled—soft, even a bit weak, but also smart-sounding. Wise, was the word. A bit like Yoda.

"That's me, sir," Jacob answered.

"Come closer. Bend over the edge. Let my meager eyes take you in."

Jacob hesitated.

"Do not worry. I cannot grab you. Besides, I have no reason to do so. You come to me. Not me to you. Asmodeus tells me of the weapon you want, the woman you seek. He speaks of your power to see what others cannot. And of your bag of letters. Shemhazai gives it to you?"

"Yes sir. Well, not exactly. But kind of. He put it in this game. Sir."

"There is no need to call me sir. Does Shemhazai impose on you such a requirement?"

"No sir. No. Nope."

"Shemhazai." An aged chuckle emerged from Azazel. "He claims to repent. He does not repent. Do you believe all that he says?"

"I like him well enough."

"But do you believe him? Do you believe... in him?"

"Like he was God?"

"If you wish."

Jacob fell silent.

"Why do you not speak?"

"My brain's got two sides, Mr. Azazel. There's a high wall in between. That's what they tell me. Sometimes the savant side shuts down, and the idiot side opens. That's what just happened."

"They are wrong. I see your mind. No wall divides it. Think of your savantness as an island. Very small, but full of light. A vast ocean of dark surrounds it. Very wide, but very shallow."

"Shemp once said it was the other way around. I didn't really understand."

Laughter floated out of the pit. "Up to his old tricks again, eh? Shemhazai used them on the Daughters of Men. He fed sweets to their primitive little minds, as a kidnapper might lure a child with candy. So he tells you that your idiot side is an island in a sea of savant genius? And you lap up his encouragement? It is the opposite, Jacob. Do you understand?"

"No."

"Of course you don't. You are an incomplete being, like the demons left unfinished at the first Sabbath's twilight. They are incomplete, defective, dross of Creation's gold. As you will never be complete in your world. Dross you will remain, in Earth's gold. When you return there. If you return."

So I can be trapped here? Jacob dared not express the thought.

"Trapped is not the right word," Azazel commented, as if he had heard. "Consider how high you may rise in this place. Think what it means, truly to see, as you saw what no others have seen in the movie that was shown to you in Asmodeus' theater. On Earth, your gift survives on a tiny island. Here, in *Chitzonim*ville, it is your only island. No sea of ignorance will surround you. Only the adulation others show for your vaunted position. Do you know these words?"

"Some of them."

"You will be worshiped, Jacob. You will be complete. And you will have anything you want."

"Including the Plasma Wand?"

"I will arrange that. As well as any movie you wish to see."

"I don't want to see any more like *Shriek of the...* what was that word?"

"*Haruspex.* Reading future events in creatures' entrails. Thus were such diviners called, in the language of your world's ancients. That is you, Jacob. One-Who-Is-Gifted. Earth sees the idiot. We see the savant. Up there, the savant remains enslaved. Here it is freed. Here, you will rule as the Oracle of *Chitzonim*ville. That door stands wide open. Do you wish to walk through it?"

I don't know.

"You do know." Again, Azazel knew Jacob's thought. "When you return to *Chitzonim*ville, you will accept your high rank, your completeness. Go with Asmodeus. You will have your Plasma Wand. And you will find the woman you are to rescue. I will send word to Gadreel. Through the letters. Please leave that bag with me."

"I can't do that."

"Aah. You do not trust me yet. I cannot blame you. Go, then."

"Can't Asmodeus tell them what you said? About giving Gadreel permission and all?"

"Asmodeus is of the Blue-Shirted ones. He will not be believed. But a letter that floats the message of my consent in the sky...."

"I can't."

"All right, then. Leave the bag with your sister. It will not stray from her hands. You have my promise. Return to *Chitzonim*ville with Asmodeus. Together you will inform the other Watchers of my decision. Gadreel will return to me as the spokesman of the Fallen Ones. He will bring to me a secret word that you will have told your sister. This word will signal to her your assent to give me the sack. When the letter flies to the sky, all of *Chitzonim*ville will know of my decision. But you must be there to receive your cherished Plasma Wand in that very moment. There will be a ceremony, a celebration. You will be complete."

"What about—"

"The one who is to be rescued? She will be waiting."

"No. I mean her." He jabbed a thumb over his shoulder at Debbie.

"We have things to discuss as well. Besides, have you not thought often that she does not matter? What do you call her in your silence? Your No-Good High-Horse-Stink-Queen-Sister?"

Please stay out of my head, he longed to cry. *It's like you put me in a prison.*

"Jacob," Azazel called. "I too know what it is like to be imprisoned."

####

"... on the Day of Atonement, Israel's sins are heaped on the annual scapegoat; it is then thrown over a cliff to Azazel.... This goat was believed to take away Israel's sins and transfer them to their instigator, the fallen angel Azazel, who lay imprisoned under a pile of rocks at the cliff-foot."
—Hebrew Myths, Robert Graves and Raphael Patai

"Azazel is a term of considerable controversy, referring to (a) an evil power, or (b) a location... it is not clear if the word refers to an entity or a place... a barren, rocky zone in the desert.... Some claim Azazel is an alternate name for... Samael."
—The Encyclopedia of Jewish Myth, Magic, and Mysticism, Geoffrey W. Dennis

"Come closer," Debbie heard from the pit.

At first, she backed away. Then she halted, gladdened to hear a voice, any voice, to lighten the crush of her solitude. She had been alone since Jacob and Asmodeus had used the third letter of God's name to vanish through the Mountains of Darkness. It pained her as never before, this solitude that ate away at the whole of her like some deadly corrosive. Jacob had not even looked back. He had shown no concern for her safety, here by herself in the bleak wilderness of the Great Abyss. Obviously, he thought nothing of her. Nothing at all.

Demons continued riding the *Kelipot* into Azazel's pit. Their cackles wormed without cease into her mind as if aimed at her, a pointed cacophony that ridiculed every aspect of the life she had lived. None fell at her feet; still, she imagined them doing so, each bearing the imprint of her every sin, every failing—the accusing glares of Derek and Josh, joined in other *Kelipot* by the faces of men of sincere intentions that she rejected; by every person, male or female, to whom she denied access to her island of isolation; by Jacob, framed as Abel, she as Cain, driven to murder by her rebuffed offerings to her father, the godly Dr. Forman, who had always chosen Jacob.

Am I my brother's keeper? Her silent retort to herself scarcely lightened Debbie's mood.

"No you are not," came the voice from the pit. "Nor is Jacob his sister's keeper. Have you not yet found that out?"

"You hear my thoughts?"

"Of course. I roam inside you, as you fear. But I do not violate you. I only examine the rotted fruit that is the produce of your life. And I see that your time has come."

"For what?"

"For you to join us."

"Never."

"Who then will you join? Who is there for you to call companion?"

"Jacob," she blurted, having no other answer.

"Aah. Jacob. Who bequeaths you this ache of solitude that gnaws within you. Tell me, has Jacob ever shown you even a glimmer of appreciation, much less affection?"

"Why do you say bequeath?" she asked, to avoid his question.

"Because he will not be back. He will arrive in *Chitzonim*-ville, and he will forget you. Think of his face when he left you. Was that the face of one who will remember someone who has imprisoned him for all of his life? Do you think he will choose you over his cherished Plasma Wand, a lover to awaken the pleasure of his loins?"

"He left me this password." One hand tapped the side of her head. The other clasped the blue bag with its remaining letter. "Gadreel will have to know that word when he comes here. Nothing can happen until the letter is released to the sky. That was the rule you told Jacob. You said so."

"There will be no Gadreel. No letter in the sky. Asmodeus will inform the legion of fallen angels of what has happened here. They will believe him."

"But you promised."

"Yes, I promised. I needed for them to go away, for you to stay."

"Why?"

"Come closer. Allow me to explain."

Slowly, Debbie approached. At the edge of the pit she kneeled to await Azazel's next command. If commands these were. It would have been better had he blistered her with imperatives. But that was not so. His aged and fragile voice all but pleaded from the depths of an isolation far greater than her own.

"Bend over the edge so that my pathetic array of eyes may behold you. Do not fear. I am chained here." There came a clanking of iron, the shifting of a being intent upon proving itself imprisoned. "And do not be shocked by what you glimpse. It is part of the punishment that has been imposed upon me. I am no longer a beautiful Seraph. My form is now so hideous that any Daughter of Man who happens upon me will flee in horror."

Debbie leaned forward. Many eyes were indeed peering up at her, easily a dozen, scattered across the surface of a disc that floated, indistinct, edges blurred, upon a bed of liquid that shared the same shade, opaque and colorless, of the Sea of *Tohu*.

"You do not flee."

"I have no choice."

"You do have a choice." Azazel paused. "I do not see well. But I do see why Shemhazai desires you as he does."

Debbie rocked back on her heels, out of Azazel's sight.

"No. Please. It has been so long since I have beheld a Daughter of Man."

"I owe you nothing."

"We will speak. We will trade stories. Perhaps you will see otherwise."

"I already know your story."

"What is it that you know of me? Surely Shemhazai has painted me as Creation's worst villain, the Serpent and Satan, Samael the Soul Stealer and the Angel of Death, combined into one? I am blamed for every ill to befall your Earth. But why do you trust Shemhazai so readily? He was my equal in the first days of the Watchers' descent. He specialized in the use of magic spells to entice the Daughters of Men. Did he try any such on you?"

She thought of Shemhazai's eyes, how his gaze had been capable of enfolding her in their embrace from the very first moment of their having met. But she said nothing.

"Tell me, has he tried to lure you with his Istahar story? How one Daughter of Man would not succumb to his advances—

how he loved her for this, how he loves you for the same purity he had found in Istahar?"

Debbie nodded, though Azazel could not see.

"Do you think you are his first Istahar? There have been many through the centuries. He courts them. He professes to make them special. Then he has them and abandons them. There have been many, Debbie. You are far from the first. He would make you feel that you were the center of his world. Until he possessed you. Then you would be nowhere in his world. Except on the trash pile of his consummated desire. Istahar suspected this of him. She remained out of his reach. A virgin to the end. I assume that you are a virgin? You have that glow about you. Even my poor eyes are able to discern as much."

Curious, still cautious, Debbie peeked into the Abyss.

"Your shell is hard on the outside, soft as the tissue of mollusks within. You have lived to keep men from breaking through to that softness. You know they will not honor it. They will trample upon it and leave tracks of your soul's very blood as they depart. So you hate men. This you know. What you do not know is that all women share this same hatred, to one degree or another. The distrust comes down from the Beginning Times, well before Shemhazai and myself and our Watcher followers insinuated our divine seed into the wombs of mortal females. It finds its genesis in the Eden story, the punishments that preceded expulsion. *You will have your legs cut off,* the serpent is told. *You shall slide on your belly.* Does not a snake erect itself before it strikes, like a man's member? *Enmity shall forever reign between you and womankind,* the serpent is then told. Enmity. Do you not hear, Devorah? If you hear, you do not see. Other women let their virgin selves die from the venomous strike of men's desires. They resurrect without maidenheads and go on in life. You shut yourself off. To live. So goes your life's assumption. But it is wrong. You shut yourself off to die. Look inside yourself. Consider your core. Has it not always been one of isolation and dread? If you return to your life of before, it will be no life. It will be more death in life. Until the day comes when you realize that men no longer yearn to possess you. You will have grown too old, and there will be nothing to fill the vacuum of their withdrawn desire. There will only be the meting out of the rest of your days. With or without Jacob. Who will always hate how you imprison him. Is that what you want?"

"I don't believe you."

"Would you believe me if I told you that Shemhazai has fashioned this game not for your brother Jacob, but for you? Every angel has a single mission. Even Fallen Ones. Shemhazai comes to your world to prepare you for your death. That is his mission. You are diminished here in *Chitzonim*ville, are you not? No doubt, similar humiliation greeted you in Ogville as well. That is part of the game. You are to be brought to a point where you choose to let death take you into its arms. I am to take you. Then you win."

"I don't believe you," she repeated, more weakly.

"The End of All Flesh, I am also called. Of your flesh, of which you grow so weary. But you must decide. Until you do, you will be sealed in the bleak irrelevance that curses you. So it was in your Earth, so will it ever be if you return there. Is that the life that you want? Or would you prefer to accept the tender cradling of the death that I promise? "

"How is it to happen? How will I... die, as you say?"

"It is to be the gentlest of deaths. A mere kiss, feather-soft, like that by which Moses was taken out of this world and into the next. Tell me, have you ever been kissed? Truly kissed? A kiss that you desired?"

"I want to go back to *Chitzonim*ville."

"All right, then. Throw down to me the bag of letters."

"I can't do that."

"Of course you can. Why do you hesitate? Do you fear betraying Jacob? Has he not already betrayed you? How many letters remain?"

"Just one."

"Good! I will use it to be present when you make your choice. I will come for you. Tomorrow at noon. I will stand before you, not in this form. If you desire my embrace at that time, step forward. If not, hold your ground. And I will retreat."

"Can't I be the one to release the letter?"

"It will not heed you. The letters were placed in Jacob's charge."

"Can't Jacob release it, then?"

"Think, Debbie. Use your logic. Do you really believe that Jacob will return here? Do you still think that he cares? Throw the bag down to me. Enough of the divine remains in me to wield the final letter as the tool that you will need. More than any tool. Ever again."

"How will I get back to *Chitzonim*ville, Azazel? Jacob used the third letter to leave here. I need that fourth letter. I can't, I just can't...."

"I will open the way for you. Through the Mountains of Darkness."

"But isn't it wrong," she gasped, "to use the name of God for purposes that are... selfish?" She avoided using the word 'evil' with Azazel. Someone had told her that improper hands have endeavored throughout history to manipulate the letters of God's name for baneful reasons. Saul perhaps. Or Rabbi Seth. Or Shemhazai himself.

"Am I being selfish in wishing to help you? Then again, if you do not see my offer as help...."

With the speed of a twig already primed to snap, Debbie let the bag drop.

####

"Our world is an alma d'shikra, a place of concealment and deception. Things reach us, but we have only a distorted perception of their cause."

—Yanki Tauber, chabad.org

The Mountains of Darkness proved as thin as the image on a movie screen. Debbie passed right through them in her return to the same isolated stretch of nocturnal desert of their approach. Why had Jacob let himself be persuaded to use up two of the letters to surpass what had only seemed a daunting obstacle? Did the *Chitzonim* seek to take the power from his hands? That would be the answer, would it not? Or would it?

She sighed, her mind fogged by confusion, her heart dragged down by sorrow. *All because of Azazel.* No. She could not blame him for the gloom. Only, at most, for the confounding tangle of logic he had embedded in her mind. She had until tomorrow at noon to make her decision. Whatever tomorrow meant. Or noon, for that matter. How long would this night last in Shemhazai's game? Would its duration be as spare as the scrim of mountains behind her?

*Chitzonim*ville's lights blazed in the distance. They reminded her of a beachfront boardwalk at night, the artificial light shining in festive arrogance against the expanse of ocean, trumpeting the supremacy of civilization over nature, of artifice over reality. Music she heard, a familiar tune, not recorded but live, as from a band. "Dr. Feelgood": one of Jacob's favorites, here without lyrics, only the melody, carrying the good-time randy mood of this song to whatever crowd was enjoying it.

Surely Jacob danced among them. Bare-chested perhaps, as he had that afternoon with Shemhazai to that awful song, "Louie Louie". Now might not be the best time to confess that she had given the Escape Tool bag containing the final letter to Azazel. What would he say? Would he speak to her at all? He was with the *Chitzonim* now. The likes of Gadreel and Tubal-Cain were his guides. His tutelary presences. Azazel and Asmodeus had poured their truths into her as well. *Male truths.* Should she have believed any of them? Had she not encountered such men (always men) on the other side of the courtroom during her days as a public defender? They had specialized in twisting logic to their advantage. Too often, she had tripped over their stumbling blocks. But not always.

Now it's my turn to cross-examine: so Debbie tried to bolster herself, as she walked through the night. What about God's side of the story? Looking down, what had God seen? Metallurgy leading to warfare, female adornment to deception, astrology and divination to the dark manipulations of witchcraft. If the fallen angels had endowed humankind with writing, to say nothing of machinery and the sciences, who could say that these gifts had not been far more blemished by the overriding taint of misuse? The Watchers had spoon-fed the evil inclination to an infant humanity, for whom knowledge became more a route to gratifying passions, less a path to advancing progress, spiritually or materially. If a path at all. Asmodeus had compared the Watchers to Prometheus. Yet were the motives of these fallen angels nearly so altruistic as those of that disgraced Titan? Had the Watchers shared heavenly secrets out of compassion for an ignorant and suffering humankind, or to gain sufficient power to gratify themselves, at their whim, through the flesh of the Daughters of Men? Was it not like all the men who had tried to buy their way past Debbie's defenses with expensive dinners, rides in fancy cars? Wasn't there a better route for mortals to have chosen? Could not that be the path for which God had hoped and was still hoping?

Yet who is more rightly condemned, you or your brother? Debbie's own internal accuser hurled rebukes right back at her. *You erect a labyrinth of denials through which your handicapped brother finds it impossible to navigate. You blacken his world with condemnations that twist down murky corridors to back aisles at Walmart. You keep him so shut off from female contact that he frightens even waitresses in pancake houses. You profess to abhor violence, yet you flee from assaults on children by children at Lowery School. And you dare question the landscapes of Shemhazai's game? Here in Chitzonimville your Jacob thrives among presences, male and female. Here you are as alone as you were upon Earth. Hiding your hypocrisy, your dread of life, under the thin guise of self-righteousness. Not a guardian protecting the cave of proper living from vile intrusions. But a Cyclops, preventing her brother from exiting that cave and entering life. You dwell alone, guilty as charged. Of negating human existence. Of smothering the breath of life from all around you. While your brother finds life in these liberations of Shemhazai's game. Surely such is the message. Of Shemhazai's game.*

Debbie fell to her knees on this desert waste's hard sand. She shook her head then lowered it in shame. *I do exist in the wrong*—this much she now acknowledged. *But I may not be wrong about these Chitzonim.* If only she could persuade Jacob to consider that possibility. If only she could spell out to his savant side what his idiot side had rejected. *You have good cause not to trust me,* she would say. *But don't be so quick to trust them. They are as smooth-tongued and cunning as Eden's own Serpent. What they want from you, I do not know. But do not let them sway you with their animal enticements.* It was a long shot, but she had to try.

First, though, she had to find him. Somehow she would pass through his phalanx of Black Shirts and Blue Shirts and Yellow Shirts and plant herself before him. If he listened, so be it. If not, so be it as well. She will have tried. Then she will go to her meeting with Azazel.

Ahead of where she knelt, someone limped towards her from the direction of *Chitzonim*ville. Someone short, stocky, well built. Dressed in blue. Asmodeus. Rising, she went forward to meet him.

CHAPTER 13

> "Everyone has his share of sparks that he has to extricate and disencumber."
>
> —Jacob Immanuel Schochet, *Mystical Concepts in Chassidism*

"I leave you in good hands."

Good hands.

Funny, Jacob thought, how Asmodeus had twirled these last two words into something kind of sexy when he introduced Mama Naamah to Jacob. Then Asmodeus had left them alone. Well, not really alone. Jacob and Naamah were together, side by side, high over the denizens of *Chitzonim*ville, up on the same boardwalk platform where Gadreel had taken him this afternoon. It glowed as part of a Nightscape now, not pitch-black but bathed in the glare of lights strung above the stage and out over the throng of Yellow Shirts and Black Shirts and Blue Shirts that had come together to celebrate in Jacob's honor.

Beyond the crowd, carnival rides now occupied Main Street. Jacob made out the spinning good-time shapes of a merry-go-round and a Ferris wheel. He heard the happy grind of calliope music, the pops and pings of what may have been a shooting gallery. How many times had he longed to go to carnivals and fairs whose ads had appeared in Atlanta newspapers? How many excuses had his sister found not to take him?

Naamah took his hand. Its unexpected coldness alarmed him. Reading his reaction, Naamah smiled encouragement. Jacob went ahead and grinned back. This Naamah was so different, as Lilith was, from the way she was drawn in *Sisters of Nightfall*. This Naamah's blonde hair spilled past the straps of her sky-blue dress and down her back, teasing him to see what he couldn't see, knowing he wanted to see. And she was alive, breathing, wanting him. Moist red lipstick widened her smile. False lashes enlarged her eyes to blue pools that invited him to come on in, swim, enjoy.

Microphone in hand, she began to croon one of his favorite oldies, "Splish Splash", a record he had played, over and over, with Shemp. Except Naamah slowed it down. She turned it into a love call, with "I was taking a bath" sounding like it was her bath, and she was asking him to join her. "Love Is Strange", she next sang, a soft moan of polished desire.

"How do I call my Lover Boy...," went the words. "Come here, Lover Boy... baby, oh baby, my sweet baby, you're the one."

Back to the audience, she bent close over him and began "Angel Baby", a girl song whined by the original singer, milked for desire by Naamah.

"It's just like heaven... being here with you...."

She sang every song directly to Jacob. Finally, when his eyes held to her without letting go, she backed away, coquettish, smile deepening, her own gaze never leaving Jacob as her crooning gave way to her dance. She pranced back and forth on the stage, microphone tight against her lips, close enough to be kissing it. The music molded her body into serpentine wriggles. The overhead lights sprinkled yet more illumination onto the diamonds on her fingers, the sequins that blanketed the blue of her dress. The blood-red stilettos of her glittering high heels jutted firmness into her calves. She didn't mind his clumsy gawks and stares the way most girls and women did. Just the opposite. She almost seemed to welcome them.

So why didn't he feel any better?

In truth, Jacob felt more alone than ever—assailed by shadow forms that leapt fast at him then vanished, thoughts that would not complete themselves, abstractions that always had tormented the idiot side of his savant syndrome. Naamah was beautiful, with the kind of ripe figure and accepting smile he had always hoped some woman would grant him. She let him take sips of her attractiveness. It was how he had always dreamed women would act. But was she the one he was meant to find? How could someone so carefree and playful need any kind of rescue?

If I can only get my Plasma Wand. Then I won't be so confused. It was supposed to be his. Both Gadreel and Asmodeus had said so. There would be no secret password to be brought to Debbie. No letter from God's name would blaze its signal across the sky. He was to get the Plasma Wand anyway. But when?

This adoring crowd, now swarming in gleeful dance below Jacob, also puzzled him. He was to lead them to victory through his savantness. But how? And what if he failed? Where was his sister, with his Escape Tools bag? "She will bring it back to you," Azazel had promised. "Later."

But when was later? And why had she kept following him down here, when up there it had always been the other way around?

"What's bothering you?!" Naamah, leaning close, whispered cold breath against his ear.

"I want my weapon. My Plasma Wand."

"It's all arranged, my love! No one has to go back to that dirty old Abyss! Enjoy the bright lights, the life! We are celebrating! And you are the guest of honor!"

"I want my weapon," Jacob repeated.

"Let's not delay, then! Asmodeus should be over with the rides. Let's go find him!" From her ever-smiling lips, the words flowed as sweet enthusiasms. "Our cherished Jacob wishes to enjoy the rides!" she announced to the crowd, which parted as she led him down the steps.

The festive atmosphere of the carnival area matched that of the boardwalk platform by the sea. It was alive with strolling Yellow Shirts, their faces lit by celebration. Only Lilith, by the merry-go-round, scowled. Lilith—distinct in her sullen gloom, garbed in the same loose-fitting brown garment draping where her feet would have been. Her severity lightened when she saw Jacob. She fought against showing it by nodding curtly, arms folded beneath the swell of her bosom. Again he hoped she wasn't the woman he was supposed to rescue.

Behind Lilith, demons from her orphanage jostled in restive eagerness to board the merry-go-round. It was a bewildering contraption, like none Jacob had ever seen pictured. Snaky shapes with happy grins took the place of horses. Some were long, others compact and worm-like, all pinks and greens and purples. All wore smiles, placid and benign, glad to be ridden as demon after demon fluttered up from the platform and seated itself, talons clutching poles, unfinished mouths and eyes slit in glee as their slimy steeds bobbed to the melody of a wordless "Louie Louie". Among them, Jacob spotted the ebony creature that had been torn from inside Sybil the Fana Giantess. This demon now joined the others in manifesting its joy.

"Wait here, Lover Boy." On a teasing wink, Naamah went to Lilith. They exchanged murmurs and nods, with occasional glances at Jacob. Naamah returned to him. "Do you want to ride the merry-go-round?" she asked. "Don't worry, my love. We can clear off its riders!"

Sharp pops to Jacob's left drew his attention to what did turn out to be a shooting gallery. Yellow Shirts, several deep, were lined up at six firing stations. Their targets were two-dimensional representations of giants, like from Ogville. When they were hit in the right places, they fell over, screeching in recorded agony as red liquid spurted from their forms. When all lay flat, a giant resembling Little Og rose from the base of the gallery. As one, the Yellow Shirts blew its head off.

"Do you want to take a few shots? You won't have to wait in line. That's a promise!"

"Where's Asmodeus?" Jacob asked.

"Let's ride the Ferris wheel! We can spot him from up there!"

They climbed into an empty carriage seat. With aid from no apparent operator, the Ferris wheel jerked into motion. It swept them high over the carnival to the top, where it stopped. Naamah settled her head against Jacob's shoulder. Her white hand opened against his chest.

Jacob scanned Main Street.

"There he is!" He pointed down to two isolated figures far beyond the edge of the crowd. Jacob recognized Asmodeus by the cut of his pale blue suit. He could not make out the female's face, though she was dressed in Debbie's black skirt and rumpled white blouse, with Debbie's soup-bowl haircut. But it could not be Debbie. His sister never would have let Asmodeus snake his hand around her waist.

"Her again." The smile left Naamah's lips. Her hand, withdrawn, gave a slap to the side of their carriage. As if obeying, the Ferris wheel commenced its downward swoop.

"I know." Lilith, waiting at the bottom, scowled at Naamah's words. "She's back."

"Who is she?" Jacob asked her. If *she* was back, then it couldn't be Debbie. Or could it?

"A pest. A wet blanket. Always trying to cramp our good times."

Jacob swung his stare from Lilith to Naamah. It was as if they were talking about his sister and somebody else, both at the same time.

"Never mind." Naamah smiled her answer to him. "It doesn't matter."

"At least she's not wearing her damn sackcloth this time," Lilith commented.

"What she has on isn't much better." Naamah shook her head. "I'll see what I can do."

"It's him she's following." Lilith threw a sidelong glare at Jacob. "She'll try to get near him. She always does when one of her kind gets in trouble. Then she will try to pull him away from us. It always happens."

"What do we do?" Naamah asked.

"Get him his weapon. You want your sword, don't you?" Lilith asked Jacob.

"It's a Plasma Wand."

"Call it what you will."

"Come with us!" Naamah gave Jacob's arm a cheerful tug.

"And my... the rescue... is she...?"

"That one? Are you serious?" The blaze in Lilith's eyes cooled as she spoke. "You will have your woman, Jacob. Later. When it is time."

Naamah and Lilith turned him, one on each arm. The three of them marched down Main Street. To Gadreel's Weapons Emporium.

####

"In general, it was an accepted article of faith that wherever their exile took the people of Israel, whether to Egypt, to Babylonia, or to Edom (Rome), the Shekhinah went along with them, and that she would remain with them until the time of their redemption."
—The Hebrew Goddess, Raphael Patai

"Asmodeus, please. Keep your hands off me."

"Have it your way." With a self-incriminating shrug and grin, Asmodeus withdrew his hand from Debbie's waist. From the back of the crowd, she strained to spot where her brother and his two female companions had vanished into the crowd of Yellow Shirts.

"I have to find Jacob."

"Now might not be the right time," Asmodeus cautioned.

"Let me try. Won't you at least help me to try?"

"What is so important?"

"Do I have to tell you?"

"No. I guess you don't."

"Listen. You're the only one down here that I half-trust. If that makes any difference."

"It does make a difference. To me. And I hope it makes a difference to you." His voice leveled off to that too-smooth glide which only meant one thing. But at least Asmodeus admitted it.

"Let's go, then." She started forward then halted, waiting for Asmodeus to lead. Fallen Ones and Yellow Shirts alike now eyed her as she followed him through the throng of celebrants. Instead of desiring her, they twisted their gazes away. Did their lusts flow elsewhere? Had her encounter with Azazel sucked away the remnant of her womanhood, whatever that had been? It did not matter. She had to reach Jacob. She had to explain about the bag, with its final letter—how, mistaken or not, she had thrown it down to Azazel; how there had come from the maw of the Abyss a clanking as of chains falling away, a sloshing as of some creature moving along subterranean channels.

He is coming this way, she would tell him, whether as warning or not, she did not know. But she did know that, with the four letters of God's name used up, he had no more protections. Maybe this didn't matter either. Maybe Jacob had found his intended home here. Perhaps, as Azazel had told her, Shemhazai had devised his game to bring an end to her flesh and a beginning to Jacob's own fullness. But what words could she use? How might they best be delivered? Could she muster the strength to address Jacob as if she weren't speaking down to him? Would he ever see her as anything but his jailer?

She spotted him up ahead. Arm in arm he walked, between two females, the one draped in a loose-fitting mud-brown garment, the other in the figure-flattering blue dress she had seen in the camera eye of Tubal-Cain's computer. This same one she had just been watching, at a distance, strutting her womanliness on the stage, all for Jacob. Naamah, this was. But who was the other?

Upon seeing Debbie and Asmodeus, this other one left Jacob and Naamah. She glided straight to Debbie, her scowl settling on Debbie, chilling her. The face was like that of some merciless bird of prey, an owl perhaps: rounded in contour, centered with a downward-hooking nose, above which peered gold eyes with onyx slits for irises. Her red-orange hair pulsed like sheathed flames. Her hands ended in talons. Her frown seemed eternal, her stare implacable, threatening, as if she might eviscerate anyone who dared to defy her.

"You're not welcome here," Lilith said. "You know that. You have never been welcome here."

"What do you mean?"

"You trail those who are lost. You are like a camp follower. A woman who soothes the flesh of war-torn soldiers with her worn-out body. A war whore for the lost. Has it never occurred to you that instead of being lost, they are found? That what you see as their defeat is actually their victory? That you block their joy with your grief-sodden ways?" Sparks jumped from her words. Debbie felt actual heat in this female's breath.

"I don't understand—"

"Now get out of here! Go back to Azazel! Let him have his way with you! Nobody needs you around here. Do you hear?!" The redness of her deepened. Talons cocked, she loomed forward.

"Back off, Lilith!" Limping, Asmodeus placed himself between Debbie and her assailant. Lilith brushed him aside, the sweep of her arm so powerful that Asmodeus again crashed to the pavement.

"Your gloom pollutes everything," Lilith continued, eyes pinned to Debbie. "Don't you know that yet? Or is it that you do know but revel in the blackness you bring, everywhere you go?"

"Heyyy." The soothing voice came out of Naamah, who had joined them. The singer placed a hand on her companion's forearm to stay her. "Let me handle this one. You go on back to Jacob. He needs a strong hand. To protect him. That's you. Not me. Besides, this... female, this woman, she needs me." Naamah's rouged smile deepened. Her blue eyes widened in sympathy.

Lilith unlocked her glare from Debbie. She slid back to Jacob, who had watched at a distance. Why hadn't he come forward? Why hadn't he tried to help? Debbie longed to ask him. To speak with her brother, to make some contact. But Lilith had pushed her hand past Jacob's elbow, her touch settling on his forearm. Together, backs turned, this couple headed down the sidewalk, towards the stores of *Chitzonim*ville's Main Street.

Naamah now kneeled before her fallen son. She cooed assurances to which Asmodeus nodded, a smile breaking through the clouds of his humiliation.

"There now. Don't you feel better? And didn't Azazel promise that you would have your reward?"

"Yes, Mommy."

"My dear son. My lover boy. Wait for me in your theater. I'll come to you soon."

"Yes! Oh please! You don't know how much I need...."

"Of course you do. As does this tormented lady with us. For too long she has been in exile. It's time for her to return."

To where? Debbie could not ask. Already Naamah was turning her, the press of her palm cold through the fabric of her disheveled blouse.

"Please don't touch me."

Nodding good-naturedly, Naamah pulled her hand away.

"Listen. What I really need is, what I need...."

"Whatever you need is fine." Naamah's voice carried solace, as it had with her son. "But first, let me offer help of a different kind."

"How?"

"By showing you what I have in my store."

"No."

Naamah answered with one of her tolerating smiles. "If you see anything that you like, it's yours. Anything at all! It's up to you, whatever you feel like! If you see nothing, that's fine too. At the very least, you'll have a chance to pull yourself together. You know, straighten up! Tuck in your blouse, comb your hair. Catch your breath, rest for a bit. Prepare yourself, that's all! Then I'll escort you wherever you want. Even to your Jacob!"

Prepare myself. For what? Does Naamah know of the choice Azazel has given me? She slumped now, oblivious to the failings of her posture. *I'll prepare myself all right,* she told herself. But not for her brother. Who had spurned her as never before, his rejection scalding in its finality. *Prepare myself indeed.* What self remained of Debbie Forman anyway? Debbie Forman—abandoned by all, even in Shemhazai's game. Except for pathetic, half-trustworthy Asmodeus. And his mother, the ever-consoling female creature called Naamah.

I am your last chance, Naamah's constant grin said. *Your only hope. So come with me. Now.*

####

"...*the further I am separated from God, and the more contemptible and loathsome, the deeper in exile is my divine soul, and the more greatly is she to be pitied; therefore, I shall make it my whole aim and desire to extricate her and liberate her from this exile, in order to restore her to her Father's house as in her youth... that she may attach herself to Him, blessed be He.*"
—*Tanya, Ch. 31; from Understanding the Tanya, Yaacov Shulman trans., Adin Steinsaltz commentary*

Half a dozen Black Shirts marched ahead of Jacob, the legion of Yellow Shirts massed behind. Gadreel led the way, his waxen blonde locks bouncing in cadence to the swing of his muscled arms. Lilith walked beside Jacob, her hand iron-hot atop his forearm. Whenever she caught him trying to look behind to where his sister had been, her talons curled to prick his attention back to Gadreel's Weapons Emporium, now no more than half a block ahead of them.

He hadn't noticed the Escape Tools bag in Debbie's hands. All he had really seen were her eyes, peering out at him, sad and small and as darkened in their sorrow as that female figure's had been in the *Haruspex* movie, in King Og's bedroom. Why hadn't he gone to Debbie? Was it Lilith's insistence? Or the promise of the Plasma Wand? Was he scared that the offer would be cancelled if he didn't take it right away? Or did he still want to show Debbie who was boss now?

"Are you going in or not?" Lilith's taloned hand shoved him forward to where Gadreel waited. He brought Jacob inside, then down the Future Alcove corridor. Without so much as a spasm of ceremony, Gadreel removed the Plasma Wand from its wall mount and handed it to Jacob.

"It's yours. Fully loaded. Never runs out of ammo, for that matter. You just aim it and pull the trigger. The charges have homing devices. They know how to find their targets. It dissolves everything. Solid, liquid, gas."

"I know that." Jacob didn't have to look up at the explanatory plaque to remember what it said. *Shaped charge explodes within victim.... Sends killing in all directions.... Defies all matter....*

"You want to try it out on one of the Yellow Shirts? How about three of 'em? One solid, one liquid, one gas?"

Jacob shook his head no.

"What color scabbard you want? Black or gold?"

"Black."

"Anything else you need?"

"I want to see my sister."

"You want to see your sister." Gadreel snorted a derisive laugh. "Well, I don't know where your sister is. We can try to find her. We can walk and walk, and you can keep on acting like a sniveling little mama's boy. Or sister's boy. Is that what you want?"

"I guess not." An involuntary yawn bent Jacob's words.

"You tired? That's another thing. Go on up to the room we got ready for you. Get some sleep. Been a long night. Tomorrow's another day. A big day, your first in your new life. A red-letter day. Isn't that what they say, up where you came from?"

"I guess so."

Gadreel took Jacob next door. *Soothsayer Wanted,* read a sign on the door. Gadreel yanked it down and tore it in half. Unlocking the door, he pushed it open for Jacob to enter.

####

"Exile is a state of spiritual dormancy...it is an eclipse of G-d."
—*Rabbi Menaheim Nahum Twersky (18th century),*
paraphrased by Rabbi Chaim Miller,
Torah: The Five Books of Moses

Naamah escorted Debbie up the street. Her hand now rested, cool on Debbie's forearm, its consoling reassurance like that of one nurse at the hospital where, years ago, her father had lain dying. That nurse had intended her touch to serve as a gentle flame amidst the consuming blackness of impending death. Yet Debbie had needed no such beacon. After a lifetime of seeing Jacob put first, she had felt her father's passing with more relief than sorrow. It had been more like the removal of a splinter than the loss of one dearly beloved.

The splinter now in her from Jacob's repudiation was not so easily extracted. It dug at her as they walked. Did he really hate her sheer presence? Is that what Shemhazai's game had been intended to reveal? Or was it something more? Azazel had dismissed Shemhazai as a lust-minded Seraphim whose sophisticated deceptions must be seen through. If he couldn't have Istahar, then he would take a shot at Debbie Forman. A virgin is a virgin, was this not so? But her wall was too rigid. Her gate wouldn't open, so why not be rid of her and have some fun while he was at it? Get in touch with your old pal Azazel. Devise a game to draw a fly named Debbie Forman down into a honey pot where she was doomed to drown. In which case, Debbie Forman was indeed nothing. *Nothing*: that was the true lesson of Shemhazai's game.

They reached Naamah's Cosmetics Boutique. Stepping back, Naamah waited for Debbie to absorb the glitter of this salon. And it did glow for Debbie: not with promise of transformation, but to illumine the ever-darkening avenue down which she now knew she must travel.

"Come on in." Naamah's voice rang soft and good-natured, like a light breeze through chimes. "Take your time. Browse around. There's no hurry. The important thing is that you feel comfortable with what you choose."

"I have no idea where to begin."

"What's the occasion? A wedding, maybe?"

"In a manner of speaking."

"Do you want a gown that shows off the richness of your skin?"

"Not really."

"A woman's complexion is an adornment too. The simplest, maybe the most powerful. But if you aren't comfortable...." Naamah eyed Debbie analytically. "Say, has anyone ever commented on your figure?"

"No." She hated to lie. But she had no desire to air the false compliments with which various males had tried to slip past the gates of her reserve. Her willowy height was often a starting point.

"You're... lithe, is the word. There is natural grace in the way you move. The most delicate sensuality comes out of you. It's mysterious, but not threatening. It must drive men crazy! I envy you those qualities, so different from my own. Try to see me as males do. Right away my curvaceous surface beckons to them, and right away they want to storm me. So I let them." She shrugged and smiled. "But you're different. For you they must reach. And it's always for the wrong things. Not for who you are. But for the hot core beneath your cold face. That's what they think. Listen, I'm clumsy with my words. But maybe I'm a little close to being correct?"

"You are. Yes, you are."

"Hey, I know just the dress for you!" Naamah led her to a single rack of wedding gowns in her store's back area. Compared to the ostentatious plentitude of the rest of the displays, this rack felt solitary, neglected, like Debbie herself. "We don't have much demand for wedding gowns down here. Every once in a while, a demon and demoness want to pretend they're husband and wife. It helps their enjoyment of each other, if you know what I mean. Aside from that...."

Naamah pulled from the rack a maroon gown. She held it against her own blue dress for Debbie to examine. "It's dark purple, but with an underlying brightness that burns with passion. That's you, isn't it?"

"Where is the top?" Debbie asked.

"I thought we might try to leave it bare. Your shoulders are one of your best features. You have a deliberate posture that many men would find delicious. Rounded yet firm, they show off how independent you are, but how clinging you can be! Men like that too. We can try something different, if you wish."

Debbie studied the garment. The sleeves would cover her arms past the elbows. Beneath its open top, the body fell as a tube, even below the waist, where most wedding dresses bloomed outward in sprays of chiffon.

"Why don't you try it on?"

The dressing room had no mirrors. Debbie had to come back out to look at herself. She did not recognize the woman staring back at her from the three-way mirror. Yes, baring her shoulders did lend them a certain appeal. The tubular flow of the gown accented the contours of her shape without vulgarizing them. It showed her off as slender without being harshly so; of being, what was Naamah's word, delicate. Her dark eyes were accented by the nocturnal richness of the purple fabric. Spanish eyes, some man had once called them. Blueness so deep in the black—

Debbie stopped herself. She had begun to think of her physical presence in metaphors. And women do not belong in metaphor. That path leads to the deceptions of the fallen angels, the corruptions of the ten generations. And she had no wish to transform herself into a lie.

"Let me work on your hair." Naamah pulled a bench to face the mirrors. Debbie hesitated but briefly before seating herself. Naamah ran her fingers through Debbie's short black locks, combing and shaping Debbie's "sheepdog chic" hairdo into something different. Naamah swept the flopping front into bangs. Each stroke added more luster to the black until it took on sheen. She sculpted the hair at the nape of Debbie's neck to points that curled forward below Debbie's earlobes and along the line of her jaw. It was a style that even Debbie knew to be called "pageboy".

Stepping back, Naamah placed her hands on her hips. "How do you feel now?"

"I'm tired."

"Of course you are. Let's go find you a place to rest. For your big day!"

CHAPTER 14

> "God said: 'Thou [Moses] shalt die the death that thou didst wish, as peacefully and with as little pain as thy brother Aaron... cross thy feet... fold thy hands and lay them upon thy breast....' Then God spake to Moses' soul: 'My daughter, one hundred and twenty years had I decreed that thou shouldst dwell in this righteous man's body, but hesitate not now to leave it, for thy time is run....' God thereupon took Moses' soul by kissing him...."
> —*The Legends of the Jews, volume III*, Louis Ginzberg

Debbie's bedroom was upstairs in Naamah's Cosmetics Boutique—in back, a second floor as austere as the first floor was florid. The room itself had only two pieces of furniture. One was a bed covered by a thin blanket as antiseptic as that of hospital linens. Across the room stood a dressing table with a mirror in whose reflection she saw herself, dressed once more in her black skirt and white blouse.

With great care she draped her wedding gown across the end of the bed. Seating herself, she opened the bag of accessories Naamah had let her have: "Yours to use if you choose them."

The bag's hot pinkness antagonized her. The color emblemized all that she had ever resented about women's cosmetics, its falsifying barrage of lipsticks and eye rouge, perfume vials and nail polish.

She lay down on the bed. Propped on her back, she studied herself in the mirror across from her. She had changed into her old clothes to keep the wedding gown from becoming wrinkled. Azazel would want her to look nice. Of that she felt certain. Closing her eyes, she tried to imagine Azazel at the foot of her bed, this six-winged fallen Seraph, handsome and Heaven-shaped, this prince of seducers. That was before. What of now? She had barely glimpsed him in his pit. Many eyes she had seen, scattered across a flat disc of a grayness not unlike her own pallor when too much solitude sucked all color from her. It might be better if his appearance was monstrous. She might more readily accept him that way. Beauty to his Beast, she might be. Yet she would not transform him into a handsome prince. To the contrary. He would transform her, mold her sorrowing self to a shape more vital. Through death's embrace he would free her from a life already as emptied and withered as death itself.

It will be soft as a feather's kiss, Azazel had promised. *I will open my arms to you, and you may decide to let them close around you or not. I will not touch you. Unless you so choose.*

But what would be the manner of her choosing? Would she wait demurely or join him right away? Smiling like a young girl courted, she opened her eyes and let them drift across the room to the mirror. Once more she would inspect her form. What words had Naamah used? Lithe and graceful, delicate yet sensual—

Someone was there. In the mirror. Now emerging from the mirror. A man. In a blue leisure suit. Limping towards her.

"I like what you've done to your hair." The voice, mellow and smooth, assailed her in silken persuasion. "It gives you the look of a high-priced courtesan, don't you think?"

"I think no such thing, Asmodeus. Please leave here."

"But you are my reward. Azazel has promised."

"I am nothing to you."

"You are nothing to anyone, my sour one. You need to be sweetened." He hobbled closer. "Have we not been destined to couple since our eyes first met?"

"Keep away from me!" She tried to answer with authority, but no force animated her words.

"Remove your garments. Free your darkened shape to the light of my desire. Say nothing more! Only breathe. Let me hear the language of excitement that your body speaks. Words cheapen you. They drain the woman out of you. Let your flesh speak for you. Your human flesh, so sweet, so succulent. Let me devour you, Devorah. My Devorah."

His words were meant to titillate her. They did not. They were like what she imagined cheap erotic fiction to be. He was an actor, after all. So she would react. She raised her knees to block his view of her still-clothed body. She turned her face away, her silence voicing rejection.

Asmodeus chuckled. "Let me say it differently, then. I will plow you as virgin land is plowed. How does that sound? I will make fertile your arid passion. Now peel off those fragile protections. Slowly. Like a curtain being drawn."

"Please, Asmodeus. I won't let you."

"Yes!" He hovered now at the foot of her bed. "Beg more! Protest more! The louder the outcry, the greater the reward!"

"No." Her protest shrank to a quiver.

"She is not your reward."

This voice—a distant echo, a shimmering gurgle, as from the bowels of a water-filled cavern—came from behind Asmodeus. From within the mirror.

"You said I did well," Asmodeus stammered.

"She is not your reward," the voice repeated.

"I want her. I earned her. You promised—"

Suddenly, Asmodeus was wrenched backward from the bed and sucked up into the mirror. There his form diffused, as if pulled apart from every direction. It burst into particles which, evaporating, allowed Debbie to behold her rescuer—a figure submerged, as if the mirror were a clear pond, the gray pulsing disc of many eyes just beneath its surface.

"Thank you." It was all Debbie could think to say.

Azazel did not answer. His shape bobbed gently within the mirror. The plane of eyes held to Debbie. Instead of showing desire, as had the eyes of Asmodeus, they drooped, seeming weary, saddened.

At a loss for how to continue, Debbie searched around herself for a way to shift the moment away from what had just happened. Naamah's cosmetics bag—she lifted it for Azazel to see.

"Do you want me to use these tomorrow?"

"It is for you—"

"I know. For me to choose. But I don't know how to choose, Azazel. Are these adornments not meant to trick men's eyes? Hasn't there always been enmity between the serpent of men's loins and all female descendants of Eve? Wasn't that what you told me?"

A sigh wheezed out of the disc that was Azazel. He had wearied of speech. Yet speak he did. One last time.

"The beauty of females is a fact of Creation. 'Fair to look upon'—do not these words appear throughout the books of your Earth's Bible? Are not the wives of Abraham and Isaac, of Jacob and Moses, described as women of beauty? Do not the women of the wandering tribe of Israel donate their mirrors to line the wash basin for God's Tabernacle? The beauty of women may decorate the world. It may also poison the world. Consider the Watchers' gift of metallurgy to mankind. It has been used to construct the most helpful of machines, the deadliest of weapons. Have you heard enough now?"

"So it is for me to choose, not only the instruments, but also their purpose—"

"Tomorrow I will stand before you. At Noonday. If you desire my embrace, step forward. If not...."

Azazel sank back into the depths of the mirror.

####

"What role can we play in this effort to reunite the Shekinah with Her Divine Mate? This union can only happen with our involvement, because She is in us. By purifying, making whole, and mastering our own soul, we help to heal the shattering of the World Soul."
—Theresa Ibis, Universal Kabbalah website

"RESCUE US."

The words were emblazoned, in alternating letters of fiery yellow and oozing red, beneath the familiar *Sisters of Nightfall* logo on the comic book's cover. It lay on the night table next to the bed where Jacob was to sleep, in the upstairs room to which Gadreel had taken him.

Jacob did not want to sleep. Not right away. The night table was filled with Jacob things. It had a spindle record player, just like the one at home, its stack of 45's ready to drop. The top one was "Sleepwalk", his favorite instrumental. A DVD box lay next to it. *Massacre in Space,* the front advertised. Above that title, a star-clogged night sky swarmed with comets and asteroids. Below, an army of Yellow Shirts used weapons sheathed in the militant blacks and golds of Jacob's cherished Plasma Wand to explode enemy giants to blotches of red. At their head was a figure, small yet strong—Jacob himself, robed like Yoda, his own Plasma Wand raised high in leadership.

A flatscreen TV like the ones at Walmart took up much of the wall opposite the bed. A remote control lay beside the DVD case on the night table. Lying down, he picked up the remote; immediately, he set it right back down. He no longer wanted to watch movies like this one. He'd had enough of seeing bodies blown apart, giants dying with screeches of true agony, adversaries of solid forms or liquid fire or smoke-like gas writhing as if incinerated from within. He had no wish to be asked to read the future in torn-out entrails, to fish more predictions out of pooled blood. The idea exhausted him, beyond the fatigue he already felt.

The comic book was safer. It was about rescue, was it not? It was why he was here. Right? He laid his Plasma Wand on the bed, close beside him. Into the softness of the mattress, he sank. It was all he could do to stay awake. But first—

This issue looked brand new. The Sisters' faces peered out in the exaggerated close-up that only comic books can provide. They were not the savior faces of his two *Sisters of Nightfall* comic-book heroines. They looked more like the Lilith and Naamah of *Chitzonim*ville. Except the artist had drawn them scared. Fear thinned the severity from Lilith's mouth. Naamah's wide red lips no longer smiled but implored. All levity had drained from her blue eyes, as had the predatory fix of Lilith's avian gaze. Both pleaded to Jacob from the cover:

RESCUE US.

He opened the comic to the first panel. It showed not the Sisters but a male figure identified in the introductory narrative as Savant Savior. He stands, legs parted, before the Sea of *Tohu*. He is waiting, staring at the sea, eyes hardened as if in challenge. He is small yet strong, cloaked in a Yoda-like robe. He is Jacob himself, Plasma Wand gripped at his side.

"SHOW YOURSELF!" he demands, in a big bold dialogue balloon.

The next few panels alternate. The two Sisters race to Savant Savior along the shore. The sea stirs, an underwater track paralleling their flight. Some submerged creature stalks them. Shark-like it cuts a line of water on the surface. The Sisters reach Savant Savior and cower behind him. He aims his Plasma Wand at the sea. The waters part. A form emerges—female, he knows this. A giantess, but not Sybil. A white blouse bunches her shoulders to muscles. Her black skirt tightens over legs bulging with strength.

"STEP AWAY FROM THOSE SISTERS," the giantess orders, in letters dripping blood. The body is sinewy, the black hair sheepdog short. She looms over Savant Savior, eyes darkening. Debbie's eyes.

The comic sagged to Jacob's lap. He forced himself to resume reading.

"STEP AWAY FROM THOSE TWO!!! I DO NOT PERMIT IT!!!!"

The letters spray across the one-panel page. The exclamation points descend at Savant Savior like spears. With expert strokes of his Plasma Wand, he explodes them. But the Debbie giantess elongates. Her spindle arms grow fast to tentacles. They grasp Savant Savior and lift him close to her face. Her eyes fill with flame to incinerate him. Her mouth widens to speak.

"YOU ARE NO HERO. YOU ARE—" the Plasma Wand plunges through her open mouth and exits the back of her neck.

"AAAIIEEEEE!!!" The squeal is cut off. The head collapses to a mass of slime that melts downwards until the whole of her dissolves like a salt-drenched slug.

Her demise did not gladden Jacob. Just the opposite. It confused him. Saddened him. More weariness descended. He yawned hard, fighting sleep. Only half the story was done. He had to know how it ended. Yet he had no wish to know. Never had he encountered such phantoms of puzzlement. It was like they were dancing back and forth on opposite sides of a bridge, with real at one end and not-real at the other. The comic slid from his hands to the floor.

Jacob slept. He dreamed. Of a bridge. *That bridge.* Debbie stands at the far end. Short hair, wasted body, dressed in the sackcloth of mourning. She calls to him. He does not hear. Cannot hear. Desires, so very badly, to hear. He starts across. He must see her. He must know what she is trying to say. A blast of sudden lust intercepts him. It roars like storm winds across his dream consciousness. It drowns out the voice. It sweeps down through his loins.

He awakened to blonde Naamah. Naamah, unclothed. Settled upon his knees. Bending forward towards him. Her smile no longer encouraged; now it demanded. Lilith hovered near his night table—naked also, her lower half that pillar of fire. He remembered her words, *if you ever need*—a lie, he now realized. Lilith smiled. It was the smile of one whose trickery had succeeded. The smile deepened. Her taloned claws opened a sack to receive the demon they will draw from him. After they gather his seed. After they split him open.

And Debbie? Alone she will wander *Chitzonim*ville's night streets. Like a woman awaiting her murder in one of the slasher-type movies Mrs. Benederet had smuggled in for him.

No.

"Get off me!" He bucked at Naamah's cold weight. "Right now! I gotta see, I gotta find—"

Naamah threw back her head. He expected it to nod forward on a peel of laughter; instead, it continued to roll back until the head tore from her body. Both parts sank to the floor in pools of white-gray liquid.

Lilith's smile ceased. She rotated on her fiery base to face the wall TV. A disc now filled the screen. Its dozen eyes aimed dagger glares at Lilith.

"You are no husband to me!" No true defiance rode her voice. Her shoulders heaved, the charred wings sagged. A sob broke out of her. She nodded once in final acquiescence. On one defeated screech-owl cry, she melted upon her pillar of fire, like candle wax touched by flame from below. Steam rose from her, as when water strikes a hot pan.

And Jacob was left in the company of Azazel.

"Stay in this room. Until we are finished."

We? Jacob did not ask. He already knew. "For how long?" he asked instead.

"Until Noonday passes. And we are done. If you come, your sister will send you away."

The disc of eyes receded. The TV screen emptied to its former darkness. Beneath Jacob the floor rumbled, as if Azazel were surging through a subterranean passage. It faded to silence.

####

"Angel of Death: Malach ha-Mavet... the most dreaded of numinous beings... he can alter appearance... Some traditions fuse Satan and the Yetzer ha-Ra with the Angel. Others give the Angel the name Samael ('the gall of God') or Suriel [also called Azael, who is also called Azazel]... some claim Azazel is an alternate name for... Samael."

—*The Encyclopedia of Jewish Myth, Magic, and Mysticism,*
Geoffrey W. Dennis

> "Satan, the evil impulse, and the Angel of Death are one and the same."
>
> —*Babylonian Talmud Bava Batra 16a, from the Zohar Pritzker edition, translation and commentary by Daniel C. Matt*

From her bedroom, Debbie descended into the scalding heat of Noonday. The warmth of the day blazed upon shoulders bared by her maroon wedding gown. For Azazel, Debbie had put on the dress that Naamah had chosen for her. For him, she had combed her hair to the raven points that favored the line of her jaw. Naamah's lipsticks and powders, perfume vials and nail polish, eye shadow and ear hoops—with these, she had not adorned herself. *The beauty of women is a fact of Creation.* Azazel himself had told her as much. But the line between beauty and manipulation—that was her choice. Surely Azazel would understand.

The heat came from no sun. The sky above Main Street remained a copper-like dome, its reddish-brown pulsing down without cease upon this Noonday landscape. Yellow Shirts filled Main Street below it. As soon as she appeared, they began to close around her. Sealed in Azazel's protections, she marched straight into their mass. Parting, they followed her towards the Sea of *Tohu*, where Azazel would await her decision. Its waters heaved, an agitated tossing, as if churned by forces beneath its whitish-gray surface.

I will not come forward, he had promised. *It will be up to you.* That death itself might be her first and last lover—rather than slow her, the thought propelled her onwards. The side street led straight to the Sea of *Tohu*'s narrow strip of shore. There she halted. The waters surged higher, as if to acknowledge her arrival. She drew in a breath. There entered her nostrils a rotting sweetness: the stench of death, perhaps heralding Azazel's arrival. The roiling intensified. And Azazel emerged. At first, he lay motionless upon the surface, his shape that of a large sand dollar, floating softly on the sea. The multitude of eyes, the grayness of the disc she had glimpsed deep in the Abyss, again in last night's mirror—these she recognized. The restless waters swept him towards her. Then, at the edge of the surf, Azazel rose.

The disc was not the whole of him. It topped a being much taller, of Shemhazai's height. Azazel stood on legs that looked human. Three pairs of leathery wings folded across the loins, the chest, the face. Slowly, the wings parted. Human-like arms spread, palms outward, as if inviting her to gaze close upon the true Azazel. The disc was the face. It had no nose, only a space above a mouth that had no lips but was a rounded opening, as to a pipe. The dozen eyes were embedded in scalloped ruts, glistening, possessed of the horny translucence of the *Kelipot* she had seen in Jacob's closet, her own dresser drawer. They clung to her, these baleful eyes. They were begging her to accept him.

"What is your decision?" Azazel asked, his voice made meek by the fact of his ugliness, the melancholy of his Heaven-sent punishment. Pity filled Debbie. Compassion for this Beast, exposed before his Beauty. She stepped forward to him. His dozen eyes scanned her. Briefly, but scanned her. In that instant, this fallen angel's gaze held something else. A flicker, a murmur, of something false. Some fundamental contradiction lay tucked within Azazel's burdened façade. She recognized it in the quick downshift of those eyes, his furtive devouring of the contours of her figure.

Debbie edged away.

"Accept my embrace."

"No."

"Aah."

Azazel pounced. Both arms encircled her waist and jerked her hard against him. *The ultimate Trojan horse act,* Debbie Forman's spiraling mind realized, as Azazel bent her back, the tube-like orifice of his mouth lowering towards hers.

####

"When we do the right thing... then sometimes, in some way, almost without our realizing it, we may actually experience moments of awareness and recognition. The Shabbat or festival table, the birth of a baby, a... wedding—moments of recognition of the Divine. Gentle, almost imperceptible. But real."

—Tali Loewenthal, paraphrased from the Lubavitcher Rebbe's teaching on Leviticus Shemini, www.chabad.org

In that day the Lord will punish, with His great, cruel, mighty sword Leviathan the Elusive Serpent—Leviathan the Twisting Serpent; He will slay the Dragon of the Sea.

—Isaiah 27:1

A blazing luminosity clicked on in the sky beyond Jacob's bedroom window, its brightness so powerful that Jacob had to shield his eyes. With its coming, the churning of the *Tohu* Sea intensified as well. He rushed to the window. A legion of Yellow Shirts milled about Main Street below, facing the direction of the sea. A narrow strip of shore divided *Chitzonim*ville from the sea. On this strip stood one lone figure. A woman, tall and slender, her short black hair combed to pointed curls at the jaw. Her shoulders were bare. Every contour of her spare figure gained accent from the purple flow of her gown.

Debbie?

Plasma Wand in hand, Jacob raced down onto Main Street. He tried to push through the crowd of Yellow Shirts; when they refused to part for him, he retreated to the edge of this Noonday landscape, ran up an empty side street, and reached the shore. He charged up the strip of sand. A Seraph-sized figure loomed over Debbie. Three pairs of wings unfolded from its muscled torso. Arms shot out. Hands took hold of Debbie and bent her back, so far that Jacob feared her spine would snap.

"Let her go!" Jacob warned, planting himself beside them. "Or else!" With both hands he raised high his Plasma Wand.

The face now turned towards him was that of the disc of the Abyss: shiny and viscous, with pitted dents couching many eyes. Mocking Jacob's challenge, those eyes simply observed him.

"You ain't taking her, Azazel." Jacob's voice shrank. The Plasma Wand wavered.

"Oh, but I will." The mouth was a round cavity, motionless when Azazel spoke. "She knows that no other embrace will gladden her. Except death's embrace. Isn't that true, my darling?"

Suspended in Azazel's arms, Debbie rotated her head to her brother. Her eyes found his. Her lips, as yet unkissed by Azazel, moved as they had when she had called to him across that bridge in Jacob's dream. This time he heard.

"Help me, Jacob. Tell me what to do."

Azazel's grip tightened around her waist. He lifted her towards him, his maw now drooling yellowed rot. Jacob's heart sped. His stomach heaved. He swept the Plasma Wand down onto Azazel's wrist. The hand, severed, dropped into the sea. Debbie, rolling free, fell to her knees on the sand.

Azazel spread his arms to Jacob. He showed neither pain nor rage but only stood there, arms parted, death gore oozing from the stump. The multitude of eyes fixed on Jacob, inviting him to witness his next action. Before Jacob could react, Azazel's remaining hand stole the Plasma Wand from Jacob's grasp and flung it into the *Tohu* Sea. There it was absorbed into the grayish fluid. Just as quickly, Azazel's stump-ended arm knocked Jacob to the sand. By the time he righted himself, Azazel had once more lifted Debbie with his one good hand. His mouth clamped hard upon her lips. There came a streaming sound that lingered, not a kiss but a transfer. Debbie went limp in his grasp. Azazel removed the hand from the small of her back. Dropping her, he straightened. From his mouth there leaked a remnant of the pus-yellow slime he had poured into her.

His deed finished, Azazel lifted from the sand. On great leathery wings he mounted towards the sky. His form elongated as he ascended. It became much larger, much longer—not a Seraph with wings, but a huge winged dragon. Shemhazai had tricked them after all. He had told Jacob stories of the great sea beast Leviathan that becomes God's enemy. But he had said nothing about Azazel becoming Leviathan in Shemhazai's game. Nothing about Azazel as Leviathan triumphing in Shemhazai's game. Above where Jacob sprawled, Leviathan's serpent shape rippled and twisted, almost playful in victory, as it winged towards escape in *Chitzonim*ville's copper sky.

Debbie curled where she lay. Her deadened gaze sought no one. Righting himself, Jacob scrambled to her. He took hold of her. He raised her, clasped her, saying nothing, wishing life. For his sister. Debbie's enfeebled arms reached up for her brother. Meekly, she drew him to herself. Jacob's own grip tightened her against him. In this posture, they blended.

Halfway up the sky, the winged serpent split apart in a shower of pixels. And Azazel was no more.

Jacob should have felt triumph; had not Azazel just been obliterated, like the deadliest adversary in one of his video games? But he had discovered a new sight. A wonder, like none he had ever seen: Debbie's eyes. Beautiful, as never before. Gazing, as never before, into Jacob. Loving Jacob. Appreciating him. As he appreciated her.

Jacob hugged her tighter yet.

####

> "A light that emerges from the darkness and that is generated by means of the darkness is superior to light that comes from light."
>
> —*Learning from the Tanya*, Rabbi Adin Steinsaltz

High above them, the copper dome over *Chitzonim*ville opens to a sliver of light. It is not golden, not distant blue sky, but a faded mauve that both Jacob and Debbie recognize as the living room walls of their apartment.

A six-winged figure descends from it towards them. Shemhazai. He curls his hands around their waists and lifts them. Midway up the Noonday landscape, he nods for them to bear witness to the fruits of their embrace down below. Yellow Shirts and Black Shirts and Blue Shirts alike jerk in spasmodic writhing. It is not pain that fuels their motion but robotic contortions as all fluidity exits their shapes. At the end they freeze, their forms momentarily transmigrated to tiny spots, as when an animated form in a video game is dispatched. Then they crumble. Fast upon their dissolving, the Noonday landscape itself convulses. Main Street, its buildings, the Sea of *Tohu* itself—all break apart and are nothing.

The final remnants of Shemhazai's game evaporate. Debbie and Jacob are returned to the living room of their apartment. Shemhazai sets them down on the floor. He kneels with them. He continues to hold them as when he had carried them. They resume their embrace. They are together. Still united. In harmony. Only now does Shemhazai retreat from where they cling to each other. As he withdraws, his hand slips down from the small of Debbie's back to the curve of her spine.

"Shemhazai!" She initiates a protest but stops herself with a playful frown of disapproval.

"Mission accomplished." The fallen Seraph nods. A smile of completion crowns his face.

And he is gone.

Part III

"Rabbi Yaakov says: 'This World is like a corridor before the World to Come; prepare yourself in the Corridor so that you may enter the banquet hall.'"
—*Perkei Avos, Chapter 4*

"In the future, the Holy One, Blessed be He, will make a feast for the righteous from the flesh of the leviathan."
—*Babylonian Talmud, tractate Baba Batra 74*

CHAPTER 15

My first funeral.

One way of looking at it would be to say that I did everything right. I quoted from Psalm 144, altering the potential gender slight from "man is like a breath, his days are like a fleeting shadow" to "we are like a breath, our days are like a fleeing shadow." The thought always gave me pause when I'd heard it expressed at funerals during my secular days. The same somber ring of this verbal death knell deepened the silence of this morning's small group.

We met at grave-side. Saul, Rebecca, myself. And Jacob. Of course, Jacob. A couple of women from the school that had been her last place of work. Seven males I had contacted so that an Orthodox *Kaddish* might be said. The eulogy was the hardest part. *Yekara d'schichba*—honoring the deceased, expressing sorrow over the loss. Though I don't think sorrow and loss are the right words to describe Devorah's passing. In truth I don't know what those words might be. Not after all that has happened.

I spoke of her in the most positive terms I could muster. I characterized her as a seeker who had shown up at services one day then began stopping by during the week with her questions about traditional Judaism—koshering a kitchen, proper welcoming of the Sabbath. I referred to her throughout as Devorah, not Debbie. She would have liked that. In her first days of visiting Rebecca and myself, she was always asking how to "ascend" to Devorah from "what I am." And what is that? I would ask. To which she would give no answer. She harbored so low an image of herself; that was my own private assessment, one at which I never so much as hinted in today's remarks. I spoke of her years of having served the less privileged of Atlanta as a public defender. I made much of her lifelong dedication to caring for her dear brother Jacob.

Dear indeed. The word slipped out of me, a mask that more or less fit over the public face of the eulogy. Jacob himself provided more exact context for those who had never encountered a person with savant syndrome. Throughout the brief service, he neither spoke to nor looked at anyone. He kept his eyes on the coffin, not in bereavement but with unbroken focus, as if expecting instructions to emit from it. He never joined the others in the chairs under the tent canopy. Instead he kneeled, back to them, between the coffin and the hole in the earth that would soon receive it.

How Debbie had resented Jacob in the days of our first knowing her! She had never said as much, but I knew she had seen him as a lifelong parasite, sucking her dry. All that had changed in the weeks before her passing. I should have recognized the signs sooner. It began before she knew she was sick—well before the morphine hijacked her mind and ran with it, down trails of raving fancies about this "game" she and Jacob had played, at whose origins I have at best only begun to speculate.

If it was the morphine. In truth I don't know what it was. Nor would I have been surprised had Jacob spoken of his sister as "Dear Debbie" during today's service. Nothing would surprise me. Not after all that I have seen. In the past two days alone.

####

Her final weeks had been ones of a happiness I had never witnessed in her. Except for medical appointments, these were weeks spent at home, in the sanctuary of her bedroom. Devorah needed no hospice. The four of us—Jacob, Rebecca, Saul, and myself—we were the hospice. At least one of us was there, around the clock. With her nursing assistant certification, it fell to Rebecca to handle the changing and bathing chores. The training no doubt helped, but it was Rebecca's very size that allowed her to lift and rotate a cancer-shrunken Devorah as if she weighed no more than a rag doll. Always Devorah would smile up at Rebecca while in her massive arms. "My *Almaot*," she would call Rebecca. It was a term I knew. From *Zohar*. It refers to the female angels of night who attend the *Shekhinah*.

When Rebecca wasn't tending her, Jacob stationed himself in a chair by his sister's bed—never taking his eyes off her, keeping vigil. At times they shared muted interchanges. She would be gazing up at the ceiling, scanning it then smiling, as if it was performing for her. I have seen similar looks on the faces of people watching fireworks displays. Then she would speak to him, and he would murmur back to her. They might have been comparing impressions of some distant tapestry whose description needed to be more sharply articulated.

Once, from the living room, I observed a series of actions involving some hidden possession. Devorah, sitting forward, was motioning for Jacob to feel under her pillow. There was an imploring quality to her gaze, relieved only when Jacob withdrew his hand and nodded, yes, what she hoped was there was indeed still there. Later, when I asked Rebecca if she knew anything, she simply shrugged and shook her head. "She tells me not to disturb it, whatever it is. Even when I change the sheets, she has Jacob put it away."

At one point Devorah asked Rebecca to purchase for her a *sheitel*. One would suspect the usual reason: she wished to keep her bald head covered. The weeks of chemotherapy had not been kind to her; in addition to the loss of hair, there had been the bouts of nausea, the broken sleep pattern, the skin infections, the dwindling of weight. Yet not for this reason had she demanded the very object of Orthodox Jewish female adornment at which she had expressed such tacit disapproval in her first visits to us. Rebecca chose one with a silken black sheen that amplified a similar quality in Devorah's vanished hair; reaching past her shoulders, its long curls framed her face in a way that accented the spare beauty of her drawn features.

Devorah wore the wig only for *Shabbat*. Our few weeks of sharing Friday evening observances together were always preceded by closed-door sessions during which Rebecca readied Devorah to meet the Sabbath. She not only combed out the *sheitel*'s dark flowing tresses but also applied touches of rouge to Devorah's sun-deprived cheeks and pale blue shadow to the sunken cavities beneath her eyes. We would then come into her room and seat ourselves in folding chairs around her bedside. Once, Saul complimented her on how "fetching" she looked. It was his nature, I suppose, this mild tease of a flirt; no sooner had he floated his words than his face flinched in instant regret.

"A woman's beauty is a fact of Creation," she had responded. It was something the old Debbie never would have said. "The enhancement of that beauty doesn't need to be a negative," she went on, "any more than nuclear energy needs only to power bombs." She had spoken robotically, as if having learned her lines by rote. Her face had momentarily clouded; a smile soon banished that cloud as we launched into singing *Lekhah Dodi* to welcome the Sabbath Queen.

"I am that Queen," she had beamed. "I am the *Shekhinah*, returned from my exile." She had rambled on, adding that the *Shekhinah* is in all women, that with the lighting of the *Shabbat* candles the *Shekhinah* is united with her male counterpart, her spiritual other half. And her gaze had fallen on Jacob.

From what wellspring of mystical thought was she drawing such knowledge? I was always thrown off-balance when she sprang such notions at me, seemingly out of nowhere. Most of the time, if I thought carefully, I could come up with some tangible precedent for her source. Perhaps a morphine imbalance had indeed freed some concept that Kabbalah had implanted in her mind. I myself may have quoted the writings of Adin Steinsaltz, who has written of three manifestations of the exile of the *Shekhinah*: Jews among the nations, Jews among their collective selves, then, ultimately, each Jewish soul within its own self. And where there is exile, there is a chance for reunification—in Kabbalistic terms, the return from exile of the *Shekhinah*, God's feminine aspect, to God, Her Husband. It is why Judaism encourages husbands and wives to make love on Friday night. Of course, Jacob and Devorah were not married, nor could any spark hinting incest have ever ignited between them. Somehow—in this Hansel and Gretel video game in which she claimed both of them had triumphed—they had made their way back, from whatever witch's gingerbread house had threatened to gobble them up, and found each other.

Jacob now fostered this unity. I say now because things had been so maddeningly opposite before. If one denominator linked what I understood of the old Jacob and what I saw of the new one, it was the one-track nature of his insistence. How changed he was from the rampaging imp who, Debbie had told us, would not even sit at her Sabbath table unless he could have one of his comic books there and watch one of his "DVD barbarisms" (her words) afterwards! No longer was he that screeching wild monkey who tore the spirit of the evening to shreds. His insistence now ran in an entirely opposite direction. The welcoming of the Sabbath had to unfold correctly. Jacob set the candlesticks and challah plate and wine cup on Devorah's night table. Jacob made sure that Saul's *yarmulke* was positioned properly before putting on his own. The oven had to be turned off, the twin challah loaves already properly warmed. Everything had to be right.

I knew enough of savant syndrome to understand that the specifics of welcoming the Sabbath had to be as exact as ball scores recalled, from a certain day in a certain year, decades ago. But I had never witnessed Jacob's savantness in action. Never had I seen any human face settle in such consummate focus on each moment. The *Kiddush* prayers recited (in my Hebrew) and the wine shared (Devorah sipped last), we would eat with her. Seated at our small TV tables, we would surround her bed. Together, we would elevate the simple act of taking in food into something worthy of thanks and blessing for what ultimately must be seen as having come from God. Devorah would smile out at us, propped as she was on her pillows. Our Sabbath Queen. Our *Shekhinah*.

What lingers most with me from those days is that precise moment of each *Shabbat*'s Friday night arrival. The image remains emblazoned in my mind—Jacob steadying Devorah's hand as she lit the candles, the glow spreading, Devorah's bedroom bathed in his insistence, her joy. I would feel the change in the very air. We all would. A different spirit would enter the room.

Before, I had always thought the shift of energy at *Shabbat*'s arrival to be psychological, the door closing on the week and opening on the day of rest. Now I know otherwise.

CHAPTER 16

A different door indeed opened. It is one that, for me, may never close.

It began a little more than a week ago. Last Wednesday, to be exact. The afternoon had been quiet. Jacob was napping. As sometimes happens when too many emergencies flood her nursing station, Rebecca had been called in on short notice to a parttime shift. I was sitting with Devorah. From me, she liked to hear Psalms. Actually, one in particular. Psalm 148. It's not one of the pretty Psalms, not one rich in bracing or comforting thoughts. But she loved certain phrases in this one. "Celestial heights"... "the highest heavens"... "the waters above the heavens"—she nodded even more vigorously at praise for God from "all His hosts... the sun and the moon... all bright stars." It was as if she had seen them all firsthand. She mined nuggets of a more profound reality from language I had always read as little more than catch phrases to fill the spaces between key ideas in the Psalms. To Devorah, they were the key ideas. At the mention of the subjugation of the "sea monsters of the depths," she positively beamed in triumph.

Saul came in around that time. He had his own key; we all did. I was glad to see him. I wanted him to spell me so that I could return to Devorah's kitchen and whatever source book I had brought along. It still disturbed me whenever Devorah sailed one of her metaphysical curve balls past me; sometimes it kept me up at night, trying to figure out where she might have gotten such thoughts. I was determined to ground every supra-rational notion she floated in some rationally explicable context. That afternoon, off in her kitchen, I had no sooner started reading when my search was interrupted by Devorah's extended groan from her bedroom—not in exasperation at a given day's struggles, as all people sometimes do; not in weariness, as when we long for sleep. But a groan that erupted out of separation from the world, the solitary province of the very ill.

When I came to her door, Saul was standing with his back to me. He had removed his sandals; without so much as an instant of hesitation, he crawled into bed with her. Carefully avoiding the IV tubes that entered one arm, he positioned himself next to where she lay and hugged her from the side. I would never have been so bold. Saul was not so circumspect. It was not in him to stand back. Had he not always played the *satan*—in Judaism, the accuser, the stumbling block—to the insights I shared in my *Shabbat* morning talks? What better way to describe a man who, in his professional life, had been a prosecuting attorney? That day, he simply lay with her. Some impulse from his hippy past had reawakened, and he cradled her, not in any lustful way but to send love to her. To hold her, to comfort her. To reinsert human contact into her world, now so isolated from touch. It was the sort of impulse he would have obeyed in his younger days when the tutelary spirit of the counterculture would have counseled him to heed the voice of spontaneous action. And it worked. Devorah's smile returned. She began whispering to Saul, and he began nodding. So I left them.

Fifteen minutes or so later, he joined me. The Saul that sat across from me at the kitchen table that day was not the same Saul that had joined Devorah in her bed. Nor do I suspect he will ever be the same. Gone was the arrogance, the insouciance. He plopped down, pale and defeated, in the chair opposite me. He sat with his shoulders slumped, his bony, vein-ridden hands dangling between the thighs of his khaki hiker shorts. Never had I seen him look so mauled by bafflement. Never had his eyes been so tired, so old, so drained of combat. He reported to me what she had whispered to him while they lay together. Confided in me, would be the better phrase. In our shared mystification over all that came out of Devorah Forman, Saul and I became allies.

"It's that game she keeps saying they had played. Shemhazai's game. Shemhazai. Leader of the fallen angels, along with his buddy Azazel. They're all over the Kabbalah. Stick a finger into the *Zohar* or the *Book of Enoch* and you're liable to pull out one of these Watchers. And who do they end up watching? Earth chicks, of course. They're supposed to be keeping an eye on mankind; instead they eye the gals. Wow. Load those 'sons of God' lines from Genesis 6 into the Jewish imagination and watch it blast off in a hundred different directions. But for Devorah to keep insisting that Shemhazai would visit them in her apartment? That's reefer madness, Jewish-style. Big time. You couldn't invent a woman more straight-arrow in her thinking than Debbie Forman. So why does she rave on about Shemhazai himself appearing at her door in suburban Atlanta, Georgia? Why does she insist that this angel who tumbled from grace on the day after the day after Creation created this game for her and her brother to play then took them down into it?

"Giants, they see! Amorites! Some descendent of King Og, the Super Giant himself! I mean, she's pumping on all cylinders! She's hanging out with *Nephilim* and fallen angels and offspring of Cain. She's throwing out names like Gadreel and Naamah and Asmodeus—'who almost had me but didn't,' she adds, with that little grin of triumph we all keep seeing. She puts spin on each name. It isn't like she's just dreaming them up. It's more like she's had some sort of interaction with each one. Even that feminist favorite, Lilith. Creation's first liberated female. But the feminism isn't the issue. Lilith's having to be under Adam, her killing babies to punish male dominance, all those other myths that Aquarian Judaism weaves around her. No. 'Lilith loathed me,' Debbie says. Lilith called her a killjoy, always trailing lost Jews when they've strayed from the proverbial path. She was out to do in Debbie, in that cockeyed Never Never Land to which she keeps saying she and her brother went in that game she keeps saying they played. Then she got on this jag about Azazel. Yeah, the one from Yom Kippur. But not the cliff, the demon. 'The slickest Trojan of them all,' she called him. I don't know if she was referring to Greek history or prophylactics. 'He kept changing shapes,' she said. From this disc thing covered with pits of eyes to this hideous Seraph that 'poured the slime of death into me' to 'some kind of giant half-dragon, half-worm that came apart when Jacob hugged me.' That was exactly how she put it," Saul recounted.

"She could have been making it all up," I answered, though it was the last thing Saul wanted to hear. "You know. Morphine latching onto what she had read and lifting it sky high. It's all in the literature, Saul. That has to be where she's getting it. Even that business of her following lost Jews in their cursed wanderings. It's the *Shekhinah*-in-exile thing. It's in *Bahir* and Talmud and Luria, from hundreds of years ago. It's in Heschel and Steinsaltz and Patai, from today. It's the sex side of Kabbalah. It's female *Malchut*, the lowest of the ten *Sephirot* emanations, longing for union with the maleness of the higher realms."

"That's where she says they went, Seth. Down through *Malchut*. Into the game."

"That might explain her *Shekhinah* rants. Somewhere along the line she picks up the notion that she herself is the *Shekhinah* in exile. That's how some Kabbalists view *Malchut*. As the lowest Sephirah, it opens into our world from the supernal heights. Into our imperfect world. A world of chaos yearning for order, for reunification with the holy. Until that happens, the *Shekhinah* wanders with the Jews in their compromised state. She can't give up on them despite their alienation from oneness with God. But for Devorah, there wouldn't be a whole tribe of lost Jews to which she would attach herself. Just one lost Jew. And you know who."

"Sure I know. Our friend Jacob. But that wasn't all! She went on. And on. Then she really took off."

"Where to?"

"To what she sees. Up there. Beyond the ceiling of her bedroom."

"And what is that?"

Instead of answering, he pulled from the breast pocket of his shirt several sheets of folded notepad paper. He gave them to me then stared. I unfolded the pack and scanned the first page.

"*Chutes and Ladders.*" I grinned. "Interesting title."

"It's what she sees!" Saul insisted, working himself up again.

"It's probably all in the literature, Saul," I repeated.

"Okay. You win, rabbi. But you lose."

"What do you mean?"

"I mean, please tell me which website can explain the Ladder."

"Which ladder? Jacob's ladder?"

"No." Saul thought a moment. "You ever been at the beach? Maybe when you were a kid, you wanted to stick your hand down some hole in the sand to see if something with tentacles wriggled back? That's more or less what happened. While she was talking, I managed to push my hand under her pillow. That was when I felt it: something soft on the outside, hard *and* soft on the inside. Alive. Pulsing, if that's the right word. I pulled it out. Devorah tried to stop me. Too late. Out it sprang. For the quickest of moments, it hovered in the air before me. Then it vanished, fast as it had appeared. But it had been there long enough for me to see."

"See what?"

"The Ladder of Ascents. That's what she calls it. Me, I don't want to call it anything." Saul shook his head hard.

"You're tired." I hated myself for backing off from probing his confusion. It affirmed my own hypocrisy—me, the self-styled mystic, the sensitive searcher, clinging as tightly as I could to rational explanations. I tried to hand back the papers. Saul wouldn't take them.

"You keep it. I've read it. I know what it says. I know what she thinks, what she feels. I love her. In every way there is to love a woman. At least, ways that I know. Even though I never, we never—" he stopped. Again he shook his head, more slowly, causing tears that had gathered to spill from his eyes. With the old Saul's brusqueness, he wiped them away. "Anyway, I unwound myself from where I had cradled her. She thanked me. For holding her? For having offered to help out with Jacob after she's gone? I don't know. Her words were flat, her tone distant, as if she had already left me before turning her shoulder to me and drifting into sleep. Which is what I need now, Seth. Sleep."

"We can continue this later."

"No. Listen. You read what she wrote. You're stronger than I am. You're 29 against my 71. So maybe you have more natural power. More *chi*, as the Buddhists would say. Me, I'm all *chi*'d out. I gotta be home. I have to turn on the television and watch commercials for anti-depressant drugs with happy people bouncing through clover while some announcer tolls out the jump-out-the-window side effects. I need to watch reruns of *You Bet Your Life* with Groucho quipping his contestants defenseless and old episodes of *The Honeymooners* with Ralph failing at his get-rich-quick schemes and threatening to send Alice to the moon. I need to be grounded in the mundanities that keep most of us anchored to this earth. All right?"

And I was left alone. With Devorah's account of what she saw. Beyond the ceiling.

####

"Chutes and Ladders"
For My Sweet Menfolk

Surely you know that game, Rabbi Seth. From your secular days. The Ladder of Ascents is like that game. Except it takes more than a lucky throw to rise on that Ladder. You find a way to link. To connect with God, of course. But just as vitally, with others. With the world. Sounds simplistic, does it not? Almost corny. But human-imposed obstacles cripple this world. It takes more than an unlucky roll of the dice to fall down a chute. It takes a willful act of ego. Of murdering a connection. Which all of us do—in our choice of words and actions, the slightest roll of the eyes—every day of our lives. As I murdered Jacob. Over and over. As he has murdered me.

For all your New Judaism, you never believed in angels, did you, Saul? I didn't either. Then one appeared at my door—a living embodiment of all that I would refute in Jacob's world of pulp entertainments, in the Judaism of the mystics. I doubted him at first. He hid in a shape that would make Jacob more comfortable. He spoke to Jacob in the vernacular of low Brooklyn comedy. He tried sneaking his hands onto my body. He is crafty, Shemhazai, yet he is fallible. For he has fallen from the grace of Heaven. But he had a mission to fulfill. Every angel is given just one. Even Seraphim, the highest order of angel, which Shemhazai is. I was his mission. Even more than Jacob. I know that now.

He carried us into the game we would play, win or lose. He brought us down through Malchut, the arena of human endeavor, the battlefield of human discord, at the very base of the Ladder. He set us down in the first screen. Then he left us alone. From there, we wandered among the game's different landscapes. That was how Shemhazai designed it—like one of Jacob's video games, each new screen laden with hidden challenges, fresh dangers, unexpected hurts. We did suffer. We were lost to each other, much as we had been lost up here in the world of Atlanta. The game, however, reversed our positions. I became the one beneath, Jacob above. Until we found our way, in the final landscape, to our embrace.

What did it mean, that embrace? Again, I risk inviting accusations of blind optimism, of sounding like the most bathos-ridden Hollywood movie: life as Prince Charming waking Sleeping Beauty with the joining of their lips. Jacob and I do not kiss, of course. And to say we were reunited, then stop there, would be too profound a simplification. We are all fallen from Creation. All imperfect, as we grope our way through the foggy mists of Malchut. But sparks of goodness, of Godliness, have fallen among us as well. They give us hope, these sparks. They feed us strength. But we have to find them. We have to rescue them from their exile, restore them to their rightful place, high on the Ladder. Chaos to order, Saul. Discord to unity. Isn't that what you, Rabbi Seth, have articulated in your Kabbalah lectures? Even the wind and the leaf it blows manifest Divine harmony. If I prevent the wind from blowing that leaf, I disrupt the harmony. If I cut off Jacob from all that is vital in himself, I cause his unity with all that is good within himself to wither. Some of it, Jacob causes. He is human, after all. But year after year, we slay each other's oneness. With the blade of our ego. Our misunderstanding. Our fallibility.

"Hear O Israel," we are taught. "The Lord our God, the Lord is One." Where oneness is absent in the chaos of Malchut, we must fashion it. We must embrace our opposite. As I did, with Jacob, in that final Noonday landscape. And bingo. In that instant, the infernal traps of Shemhazai's game began to disintegrate. Shemhazai came down to us. He gathered both Jacob and myself in his arms. He carried us back through every landscape that had tested us. One by one, these landscapes collapsed, their order reversed, from last to first. We had won, Jacob and I. Above us, the Seven Heavens opened. And I saw them, Saul. From far below, but I saw them.

Then I am in this bed. I am sick, I am dying, because of the slime Azazel poured into me in that final landscape. Yet never have I been more free. When no one sits with me, I free the Ladder, Shemhazai's final gift to me. I climb as high as I am allowed to climb. I look up and observe the Heavens, one atop the next. Oh, how can I describe it?! Is it right to perceive physical design in metaphysical space? Do crystal palaces truly house the most righteous? Are the colors of saintly robes really of a whiteness so pure that it dazzles human eyes? Yes. To me, yes. I see mountains of precious stones, garnet and emerald and sapphire. I see the Garden of Eden's Tree of Life itself, crimson and gold, alive with healing fire, its springs of milk and wine flowing into Eden. I see hundreds of angels, all aflame, their never-ceasing songs of praise so intense as to change their sound into something to be seen. Angels bathe in fire there! Good fire! Rivers of fire that carry the scent of roses, of wine! I smell their fragrance! It banishes the stink that fills me from Azazel's death kiss! Sweetness pours from a Cave of Vapors, would you believe that? Would you believe that storehouses hold the winds, the rains, the snow that God sends to us? There is even a Storehouse of Souls, where male and female interlock but separate as they are released to descend to Earth!

Jacob cannot see the Seven Heavens at all. It's not his time yet. He grows frustrated when I describe to him what I am permitted to see. It saddens him so, to imagine us apart. He blames the walls that separate the two parts of his savant self for separating us once more. Yet no walls separate Jacob from himself, as too many of his well-meaning, if ineffectual, counselors have told him. Understand that, Saul, when you are caring for him after I am gone. Think of him more as a small island of utmost clarity surrounded by a sea of bewildering fog. So Azazel explains it; even Azazel, who contains a spark of truth. Jacob understands better now. Sometimes he ventures forth on that sea. But not too far. Not without a hand to navigate for him. A hand he trusts not to sink him, drown the clarity.

"We will be together again," I reassure him. "Just you wait." Tell him the same thing, Saul. When he grows irrational or impatient or quivers in agitation, send that thought to him. It will settle him. It will give him strength.

Speak to him too of the banquet. Make it a riddle. Ask him to guess who he will see in this feast of the Seventh Heaven. With me. When he joins me. When we look up together, from a lower rung on the Ladder of Ascents. Because we have not yet earned the right of ascent to that Heaven. Not yet. Not in the life just past. Perhaps in the next one. Perhaps. So I am told. Ask him to imagine, then. High above us stretches a table as long, from end to end, as the Seventh Heaven itself. The guests are seated. Hundreds of them! Beings of all kinds. Humans in suits, in gowns, in Biblical robes. Angels with wings, two and four and six. Beings of a strangeness I cannot describe. Four-faced creatures: infant and man, lion and eagle. Others shaped like wheels, the rims coated in eyes. All wait eagerly to feast upon the gargantuan carcass spread on the table before them. It is Azazel in his sea-monster guise! Worm or leviathan or dragon, I don't know how best to describe him. I can only relate the deep joy we both will feel upon seeing Azazel, in final defeat, strung out and sectioned, for this Banquet of the Righteous. Azazel. The one who tricks you, Jacob. The one who kills me. Here, it is he who has been killed. I know, Jacob! Thanks to our embrace in the Noonday landscape, my eyes have been opened! It is as if cataracts have been peeled away! I see serpentine Azazel slither up towards the game dome after kissing his poison into me! I see not Azazel's escape but the downward swoop of a great sword that slits Azazel lengthways down the middle! Together, Jacob, we will peer up at Azazel's end!

We will see the divisiveness of Azazel, itself divided, served up at this Banquet of the Righteous! The entire Heavenly Host digs in!

Even the six-winged Seraph at the very end of the banquet table. But first he looks down at us. He smiles, and he winks. And who do you think that is, Jacob? Your Shemp, of course!

Our Shemhazai!

CHAPTER 17

The funeral done, I can now look back upon Devorah Forman and begin by commenting that she was nothing if not intelligent. This was her light, I suppose, the gleam that Jacob once denied. She was too rational for him. As he, what shall I say, was too irrational for her. Then through Shemhazai's game the two opposites are reconciled. The chaos of their personal relationship resolves in the oneness of their embrace. Chaos finds unity. Such is the purpose of this world. According to Kabbalists. And Debbie Forman as well.

She was no Kabbalist. Yet what she described reflects with uncanny accuracy so much of what I have read in my own groping for alternate truths along the varied paths of Judaism. I could trace most of what she had written back to one source or another. The Seven Heavens? All in the *Zohar*, the *Apocrypha*. The Messianic Banquet at which Leviathan is served? Pure Talmud. Wheels with eyes? These are Ezekiel's *Ophanim* angels, side by side with the four-faced *Cherubim* of that book's confoundingly mystical opening chapter. The Storehouse of Winds, the Cave of Vapors? Check out the *Pseudepigrapha*, the *Book of Enoch* in particular. Reincarnation? *Zohar* again, or Chaim Vital's sixteenth-century *Sefer ha Gilgulim*. The Fallen Sparks, the *Tohu* to *Tikkun* concept? Start with Isaac Luria. The harmony of leaf and wind? From the Baal Shem Tov. The angels' songs of praise, sound seeping into vision? Synesthesia is the medical term. The blurring of the senses. It happens at Sinai when the people "see the sounds" as the Ten Commandments are given. It happens to some savants as well. So I have read.

Permeating all is her obsession with that hug-your-opposite idea. If you've got too much *Gevurah*/Severity, hug its *Chesed*/Kindness antithesis. Or vice-versa. Instead of hating your brother, give him a squeeze like you mean it. He'll squeeze you back. It's the unity that God wants to see on this earth plane. Not Hitler and Mussolini unity. But conservatives and liberals unity. Husbands and wives unity. Jews and Christians and Muslims and all the rest.

How Devorah found her way to these ideas, I'll never know. Had she secretly read such literature? Had notions been planted in her mind which, watered by the morphine, bloomed into full realities? Had Saul tutored her in such matters? I doubt it. If he had, he would have told me so. He would not have been pushed against the wall of his own bewilderment by what he told me last Wednesday. He would not have handed me Devorah's papers then staggered out the door of that apartment. Saul may have tormented me in many ways during our adversarial contacts. But he never lied.

Before Devorah's passing, I could have tried to refute her. I could have used every intellectual muscle in my supposedly anti-intellectual mind to show her that everything she had said, every idea she had expressed, could be found in existing Judaic sources. Gently but conclusively, I could have tried to find a way to dismiss her visions as so much metaphysical hyperbole.

Then tonight happened.

####

Actually, it began last night, the coloring of my life by the cryptic shades of the non-ordinary. I borrow the term from Carlos Castaneda, whose books on Yaqui shamanism had pointed my secular self down many an arcane path before I found my way back, along many of the same, surprisingly congruent paths, into Judaism. I had chased theories concerning the non-ordinary down every alley I could find, as long as they were safely lit by writers' words. Then, with Devorah's passing, the non-ordinary came out of an alley and chased me.

It is Jewish custom that, before a burial, someone must sit with the deceased. *Shemira*, the custom is called. The word translates most accurately to watching or guarding. But what is to be watched or guarded? Through my readings I have come to a sufficiently delineated, if limited, acceptance of the existence of a spiritual afterlife; more than one Jewish text speaks of the disorientation of a recently deceased soul when it exits the flesh. *Hibbut Ha-Kever*, is one such explanation. Pangs of the Grave. *Olam Ha-Tohu*, World of Confusion, is another. The use of the word *Tohu* in this context is of special interest. Chaos has many faces, I suppose.

In any case, I volunteered to sit with the coffin for the overnight shift. It was a small room at the funeral home, with the simple pine coffin set in a softly lit alcove, separate from the seating area for the living. No sooner had I entered that room than I felt a change in the air. I was no longer in the company of the living. The very silence became the voice of the dead. *You are in my land now*, it told me. *I do not threaten you, nor do I impose my power upon you. I only ask that you set aside your mental safeguards for this brief span of hours and anchor my temporary impermanence with the temporary permanence of your flesh until mine is placed in the earth.*

    Yet I was not alone. Jacob was in the room with me. He had not left Devorah's side since her passing. He had been with her in that moment of separation. He had come out to us from her bedroom and nodded, and we had known. He had accompanied her to the *Chevra Kadeesha*, where the body was cleansed and dressed in white linen. He had stayed at the funeral home. I do not think he had slept a moment. Now when I entered the chamber of *Shemira*, I found him dozing on the floor beside her coffin.

    A book of Psalms is available in all rooms for *Shemira*; the reading of them is said to console the wandering spirit, stranded as it is between one world and the next. I picked up the copy on the table beside me. I started at the beginning, more or less, knowing that I had many hours to fill. To myself I read the first few lines of each Psalm, and if it seemed an appropriate chapter with which I, as a *Shomer*, might soothe the passage of one so recently deceased, I would continue. I read softly, so as not to disturb Jacob. All the while, he lay motionless on the floor, below his sister's coffin.

    I anticipated reaching Psalm 23 with the eagerness of a mountain climber nearing his first rest cabin. I felt certain that its lines of comfort—of God as our Shepherd, of fearing no evil as we pass through the valley of the shadow of death—would settle Devorah's spirit, if her spirit was indeed listening. No sooner had I spoken that verse than Jacob roused himself from the floor. Or was aroused, it might be better to say, for he blinked in surprise, as if awakened by an urging hand. I expected his gaze to settle upon me, perhaps question my presence. Instead he stared at the coffin. He stood and placed his hands upon the lid. Leaning forward, he cocked one ear towards it.

    "It's okay," I heard him say. "It's okay. Don't cry. Everything's gonna be fine, wasn't you the one always tellin' me that?" Again he inclined his head, as if to listen. This time, he began to nod. He came to me. He took the book of Psalms from me, placed it atop the pine box, and waited. Within moments a whir of pages tested the silence. It ceased as quickly as it had begun. How could that have been? Had a faint breeze stirred the coffin's alcove? I doubted it. Yet what else might I believe? Jacob brought the book back to me. Handing it to me, he pointed down to where it had opened. At Psalm 148. Devorah's favorite.

"That's all she wants to hear." He walked back to her coffin and lay down beside her once more.

I began to read Psalm 148. Over and over, lending special emphasis to the lines which had pleased her most. Simple words animated concepts we had shared; phrases bore pictures.

"Praise Him, all His angels" brought with it images of six-winged Seraphim and four-faced *Cherubim* and wheel-shaped *Ophanim*. "Praise Him, the Highest Heavens" now came freighted with visions of palaces in the sky, sweet-scented rivers of fire, mountains of color-rich jewels. "His splendor covers Heaven and Earth"—and in that splendor, Earth joins Heaven, as the *Shekhinah* joins God in His symbolic bed chamber.

"Praise the Lord... all sea monsters." On this line, the heavy silence that had filled the room lifted. There came in its place a laugh, soft, triumphal, not quite human.

The hold of the non-ordinary loosened at daybreak. No light entered this small cloistered room, but we knew. Jacob now sat cross-legged, staring up at the coffin, only occasionally glancing back at me, as if I were some harmless insect whose progress up a wall he was checking. I heard sounds of the funeral home staff circulating upon their arrival. A man looked into the *Shemira* room and pointed to his watch. It was 7:00. The concretizing of time in my mind elicited a cavernous yawn from my body. In a few hours, I had to lead Devorah's funeral. I needed to be sharp. I left the funeral home, drove home, and tried to nap. I could not. I kept seeing the pages of that Psalms book whir.

####

Several of my congregants were good enough to return to Jacob's apartment after the funeral so that the *Kaddish* Prayer for the Dead might be said. He seemed to understand the function of the prayer—to be joined by others in mourning a loss, to acknowledge one's acceptance of God's will. But I did not broach the topic of sitting a week or even a day of *Shiva* mourning with him. Few would have come, nor would Jacob have wanted it. So I left Jacob alone in his apartment. It was late Friday afternoon, with dusk not too far off. Rebecca was preparing for *Shabbat*. Again I tried to nap. Again, I could not. Rebecca and I shared our candle lighting, our blessings, our meal. "Is something wrong?" she kept asking. She knew me well enough to doubt all my shrugs and denials. When I announced my intention to walk over to Jacob's apartment to see how he was doing, she was already nodding.

In all honesty, Jacob's well-being wasn't my sole motivation. I kept thinking of what Saul had found under Devorah's pillow. I burned to know what it was. I could hardly say that to Jacob, of course. He would see through me right away. It would be at least somewhat more honest to explain that I was worried about him and wanted to check in on him.

The door was unlocked. The living room was dark. Beyond, in the kitchen, I made out the faint glow of two candlesticks, already lit. Jacob wasn't in there. Quietly I peeked into Devorah's bedroom. I expected to find Jacob seated by her vacant bedside, where he had been when I left this afternoon. He wasn't there either. Rather than search for him, I went in. Her bed was freshly made—by Jacob? No matter. Careful not to disturb its punctilious savant tidiness, I slid one hand under the pillow. My fingertips brushed against an object that seemed, as Saul had described, at once spongy and solid. I squeezed it. What lay inside responded with charges, at once scorching and frigid, in apparent defiance of all physical laws of this earth. Was it giving off a warning, as Saul had feared? Would it chase me down if I released it? I started to pull my hand away. Then I changed my mind.

What came out was a small bag, black yet sparkling. It felt not like fabric but the outer sac of some living organism. It tingled in my palm. But it no longer threatened to singe or freeze my skin. In this way it seemed, if not to welcome me, then at least to acquiesce to my presence. Tentatively, I flattened my hand upon it. Its shape was animated by faint undulations within, like the settling and resetting of some sea creature, edged with rounded knobs. I thought of Saul's analogy: *have you ever wanted to stick your hand down a hole in beach sand to see if anything wriggles back?* I pressed lightly. It collapsed to nothing under my fingertips then reclaimed substance. I carried it into the living room.

Jacob was there.

"We gotta finish bringing in *Shabbat*," he told me. "Bring that bag with you."

"You already lit the candles, Jacob. What do you need me for?" It was a stupid thing to say.

"The blessings. They gotta be said. You know the Hebrew. I dunno how. I don't know...."

"Yes. Of course. Sorry, Jacob."

"Everything's gotta be right or she won't come." He led me into the kitchen. *An Oasis in Time* lay next to the candlesticks. I had forgotten that Rebecca and I had given Devorah a copy of this pamphlet. The wine cup from our Sabbath kit sat next to the bottle of kosher wine. I took the two rolls that Rebecca had baked from the pockets of my robe, set them on the challah plate, and covered them with a paper towel. It was all we had.

I opened the booklet to the page with the blessing over the candles.

"It ain't too late to say them Hebrew words? You ain't gonna mind? You bein' Orthodox and all?"

"Not with the candles already lit, I don't think. Not... under the circumstances."

"Well, it's gotta be right, rabbi." Jacob's face sagged, as if every ounce of his savant side had drained from it. He looked lost to the moment, an abrupt vacancy of expression I had seen before on him. Absolutes still ran Jacob. That hadn't changed.

I started to speak.

"Wait a minute. Open the bag first."

"Are you sure?" I remembered the dread, the perplexity, that had depleted Saul; his longing to go home and soothe himself in the palliatives of the mundane. Ralph Kramden, Groucho Marx—

"She's waiting."

"Where?"

"Open the bag," he repeated.

I teased the edges apart. The object that flew out took on an instantly recognizable shape in the air over the kitchen table. The Ten *Sephirot*. The Kabbalists' Tree of Life. I had read so much of it. Dozens of illustrations I had studied; now here it was, suspended above me. The framework was indeed the familiar three vertical columns down which ten spheres were embedded, linked by a mesh of spokes, 22 in all, had I wanted to count them—paths they are called, channels, zig-zagging downwards among these ten globes. From *Keter* at the top. The Crown. The supernal heights, where *Ein Sof*, the Hidden Infinite, exists. Down through eight more Sephirotic emanations to where the *Shekhinah* resides, in self-chosen exile, in the *Malchut* sphere at the base. They pulsed with watery flames, these spheres—heat and cold, impossibly melded, as I had felt under the pillow. Each threw off its own color, so vivid as to have been that of red or green, white or blue, at its first articulation in Creation itself. Their blazing luminescence was that of stars beheld up close, without the filter of a telescope—throbbing with divine energy, pouring from the eternal to the earthly.

I blinked, I squinted, stealing what glimpses I could. Part of me wanted this image to vanish, as Saul had wished. A greater part longed to examine it. All the while, palpitations sped my heart. I could not calm them. What would the attending physicians in a hospital's emergency room think when they asked what had brought on my heart attack, and I told them this?

"Now say the blessing, rabbi. Do that thing with covering your eyes."

I did as Jacob asked. In truth I was glad to reach the part of the ceremony where I used my palms to block out all vision. It was what I needed just then. The only private prayer I threw to the Heavens was that I come out of this experience with my health intact.

When I brought my hands down, the central *Sephirah* sphere was stirring. A whitish paleness began streaming from within what would be *Tiferet*—*Tiferet*, the sphere of truth, of beauty, positioned at the level of what would be a human heart. From that sphere, Devorah emerged.

She drifted to the chair across from me and settled. The white linen of her burial garb still draped her. It faded towards transparence then reclaimed discernibility. I am hard put to describe her facial expression, though. Like the rest of her, it too faded to near nothing then filled in with features approximating those of the flesh she had left behind. And when it was that way, it reflected not tranquility but confusion. Not peace, not enlightenment, but the ebb and flow of her longing to be here one moment, gone the next. Her eyes, soft and large against her greater translucence, held not to me but to Jacob, pleading with him, though for what I had no idea.

"Read the prayers, rabbi," Jacob hastened to tell me.

I was surprised by the trembling, involuntary, all but subliminal, that had taken over my body. Still, I managed to flip to one of the Psalms with which the Sabbath is initially welcomed. Jacob smiled as I read, but Devorah's presence diminished. So I stopped. I jumped ahead to the *Woman of Valor* prayer. It did not release the agitation from her spirit. I paged back to *Lecha Dodi*, the sixteenth-century hymn with which the Sabbath even now is so passionately welcomed.

"Come meet the Bride... God will rejoice like a groom for His Bride the *Shekhinah*, the Sabbath Queen...." I half-spoke, half-sang these words. Alone. For Jacob would not sing, and Devorah perhaps could not. They were looking at each other. Their eyes were speaking to each other. I might as well not have been there.

"Okay." Jacob all but whispered his consent. To Devorah.

A faint smile—of affection, of sorrow—played briefly at her lips. Then the whole of her shrank back and absorbed, upwards, into the Tree of Life—what Devorah had called the Ladder of Ascents.

"She wants to sit at the banquet table," Jacob murmured as we watched. "But Shemp tells her it ain't time. She ain't ready yet to climb that high. Just like it ain't time for her to be back down here. With me. That's why she's all confused."

Above us, the Ladder vanished. As did the bag from my hands. The game was done.

"Let's finish up, rabbi. Let's do the *Kiddush* thing. Then you can go home."

Somehow I managed to begin. "And it was evening, and it was morning, the sixth day...." We recited the blessing over the wine. We washed our hands, then blessed the challah, then sat at the kitchen table and ate it.

"Good stuff," Jacob said, through a bite of one of Rebecca's fresh-baked rolls. "Can you bring some next week?"

"Sure."

We sat together for a few more minutes. Then my fatigue took the better of me. I yawned deeply. I could not stifle it.

"You oughta go home. Yer *Shekhinah's* waitin', ain't she?"

"My—" I didn't need to finish. I had forgotten. Sometimes savants stumble far behind us. On occasion, though, they skip many steps ahead.

"You sure you're okay here? By yourself?"

"I ain't by myself. Not really. Just kinda. And that's okay."

"Saul will be along tomorrow. Just to check in."

"Does he like old movies? Like gorillas and monsters?"

"Probably."

"How about video games. Can he play 'em?"

"You can teach him."

"How about you?"

"Well...."

"Maybe Rebecca then. When she ain't workin'. She's a sport."

"I guess she is."

"But only the clean ones, rabbi. *Space Invaders. Galaxia.* That kind of stuff."

I didn't know what those were. Video games hadn't so much as grazed me during my years of navigating the secular universe. "That's fine," I answered anyway.

Jacob walked me halfway to the front door. In the retreating light of the Sabbath candles, I saw his face—his savant gift of understanding struggling with his vacancy of expression. Without so much as a word of farewell, he turned aside and entered Devorah's bedroom. He started to sit in the chair by her bedside; pausing, he picked up the chair and moved it back to the doorway. There he sat. Already he had forgotten me. His attention was split between Devorah's empty bed and the two candles in the kitchen. He would stare into the near-darkness of his sister's former bedroom. Then he would shift his gaze to the candles.

CHAPTER 18

Yer Shekhinah's waitin'.

I cannot put into words the ache that grew inside me as I walked home through Buckhead Atlanta's Friday night. It was as if some metaphysical microbe had infected me in that apartment. Yet of all that I had witnessed—all that had been said—that one statement of Jacob's gnawed at me most patently. Why had I never thought of Rebecca in that way? Yes, we have performed the *mitzvah* of Friday-night lovemaking. We have abstained during the two-week *Niddah* period of Rebecca's menstruation. She has immersed herself in the flowing waters of the *Mikveh* pool at the end of her time.

We have dwelt within these strictures. We have allowed them to dictate the timing and frequency of our sexual contact. But we have not procreated. We have not, as the *mitzvah* instructs, been fruitful and multiplied. Once we sought the counsel of a reproductive endocrinologist. My sperm count is borderline low. Rebecca's excess weight may have affected her ovulation. I believe none of that. I believe that the reason lies within the letters of the Hebrew word for to know. Yod-Dalet-Ayin. *Yawdah*. As in, "And Adam knew his wife Eve."

Rebecca and I have never known each other. Not in that sense. She has been everything else to me—a sport, as Jacob had also said. She is always finding ways to join with people. She becomes a blank tablet on which others inscribe their questions, their hopes, their torments. But she has never been a lover to me, nor I to her. Our essences have never blended, as had Jacob's and Devorah's in the final landscape of Shemhazai's game. Even without the actual lovemaking.

Yer Shekhinah's waitin'.

I could have found back streets through Buckhead by which to walk home. Instead I chose Peachtree Street's main drag. The bars and clubs and restaurants were still clogged at this late hour, Peachtree jammed with stop-and-go traffic. I no more belonged here than I did in the world I had just left in Jacob's apartment. Such Friday nights now seemed foreign to me, though I had once tried to be a part of them. I had been no good at it. Now it all seemed so much static emitting from a radio station to which I no longer listened—the rock music thundering out of the clubs; the fluctuating laughter fueled by aimlessness or nervousness or alcohol, at least so I judged; the random cry of outrage from a driver betrayed by some sinful road hog, some cell phone-absorbed pedestrian. I beheld all manner of couplings, at all manner of stages, on this Friday night. A Lexus at a red light encapsulated a middle-aged man and woman seated in equally stiff primness, parted on the front seat, the space between them as high as the walls of Jericho. Two strapping young men of apparent college age peered without apology at the half-exposed bosom of a somewhat older woman in a thigh-high red dress with a bare spot that made a diamond of her belly.

There seemed no ground rules. Or was I fashioning this Sodom-and-Gomorrah scenario to shield myself within my own acquired Judaism? How many Friday nights had I spent, in my former wanderings through what I saw as the wilderness of secularism, sitting at a bar then skulking home along streets full of males about to score and women about to put out to everyone but me? In this way, among others, Judaism had rescued me. Its very strictures had liberated me to wonder, in my own self-righteous way, just how unmoored from valid moral context these Buckhead relations had become. I tried to convince myself that the myriad restrictions of Orthodox Judaism may have been a human construct, but one preferable to the mine-filled no-man's land through which the Buckhead crowd so blithely and blindly wandered. I knew I had no right to condemn. Even tonight, my favorite words of Jesus demanded to be heard: *judge not lest you shall be judged.*

I paused not far from one very young couple that had separated themselves from Buckhead's throngs. They faced each other, down an empty passageway, between a bar and a night club. The young man stood as I might once have, shoulders hunched, hands jammed in pockets. He was dressed more conservatively than most. A well-pressed gray shirt, its sleeve wrists buttoned, tucked hard into simple black slacks. His short hair was too well combed; his too-large glass frames caught the gleam of the overhead string of lights. She was taller than he was, though her height was augmented by high heels. She had a long waist and narrow hips that barely filled the lower part of a midnight blue dress that stopped at her knees. The top hem scooped not far down her chest, well above the faint swell of her breasts. The sleeves dipped over the white flesh of her upper arms. Her profile indicated a face long and angular, above a slender throat. Her blonde hair, freshly washed, angelically puffed, seemed to bounce against her shoulders even when she wasn't moving.

Something was happening between them that I could not decipher. Despite the intimacy that accompanied their solitude, the young man made no move to embrace his companion. He stared as if entranced; she simply smiled, though with occasional girlish tremors, as if she knew his stare was gently peeling away whatever layers of female artifice may have adorned her. It struck me that he was honoring her. He would behold the girl she had been before there were curves and menstrual periods and males peeling at her in other ways in the halls of the high school to which she no doubt went. He did not budge from his hands-jammed-in-pockets, bent-forward posture. But she did. Those tremors were a form of communication—shy in their receding, animated by a natural female slink in their returning. It was no mean or false slink, no taunting salvo. She rolled her knobby shoulders and smiled, and in the half-light of that walkway, something eternal passed to him, some great and profound female power, as though she knew without fully realizing that she bore within herself some secret he longed to know; that, with his knowledge of that secret, he might possess her, be possessed by her. She would not share that secret. *Not until you have earned it,* she was telling him. *Then I will be your Shekhinah. I will follow you into every exile your life imposes on you. Our exiles, they will be. If you truly honor me. If you reach across the chasm of opposites that separates us and join me to you. Without wounding me. Without stealing from me what I give to you and fleeing with it.*

All this I perhaps imagined. After the brigade of unknowns that had assailed me over the past 24 hours, my mind lay in shambles, a demolished ruin. Gone were the rational paths that guided me through my days, my urge to explore arcane side paths, if only through what I read. Perhaps I was imposing a fallacious construct upon this couple in a moment of nothing more than awkward silence when their chit-chat fell through the cracks. He might have been wondering whether or not to try to kiss her, she whether to have another drink if he offered to buy her one.

Then, out of nowhere, the girl turned her attention to me. Her gaze absorbed me; instead of the instant of being taken aback with which most people react when they spot a black-robed Jewish figure among them, she nodded and spoke.

"*Shabbat Shalom*," she said. Her eyes, of the same midnight blueness of her dress, caught the artificial luminosity surrounding her. I brought my own eyes down. She had intended no seductive signal. To the contrary. Appreciation had ridden her words. She had known what to say to an individual practicing Jewish observance. Instead of answering, I turned on my heel and scurried away. I found the nearest more or less deserted side street and finished my walk home.

Rebecca was already in bed. She lay on her side, her back to me, her head a shaven crown in the darkness of the back room we shared in our strip mall *shul*. I did not know if she slept or not. As quietly as I could, I said my evening prayers, took off my clothes, and slipped into bed beside her. *There is still the mitzvah to perform,* an inner voice reminded. *Yer Shekhinah's waitin'—*

"Is Jacob all right?" Rebecca asked.

"I think so." I swallowed then continued. I knew she was waiting to hear more. "He wanted me to recite the Sabbath blessings with him. He was sitting in his sister's bedroom when I left him." I couldn't say anything about all the rest. The black bag and Ladder of Ascents, Devorah's presence—

"And you, Seth? What about you? You don't sound right."

"I'm tired, I suppose."

"Try to sleep. Everything will be okay."

It was what she always said when flames of worry consumed my logic. I put a hand on her raised shoulder. Beneath the sheet, she turned onto her back and grinned up at me. It was her usual Friday-night grin, self-conscious, a little ashamed, the one that said, *I know you don't want me, but thank you for doing this anyway.* I slid one hand under the covers and began caressing those parts of her that I knew most aroused her. Her eyes closed. Her breath raced. My heart blackened. My desire imploded. I withdrew my hand and turned away. For the first time ever in Rebecca's presence, I broke down and cried.

"It's all right," she whispered behind me.

"No. You don't understand. You have no idea what I saw. What I heard. I can't begin to tell you."

"Then don't." Her grip tightened on my shoulder. Gently, she rotated me and brought me to rest against her body, my head upon the pillow of her bosom. It was a pose we had assumed many times before: familiar, theatrical, false. We lay that way for quite a while, the sound of our breaths, the points of congruence of our flesh our only contact. My cheek inclined. My lips found hers. Dreaming of the blonde girl in Buckhead, I roused myself for her.

No sooner had we finished than the sadness once more filled me. It filled Rebecca as well. I knew by the depth of her sigh, its true nature in this context, that of her receiving the contagion of my own despair. She inhaled through her nose, the wet sound of one who has wept but tried to hide it. Surely she could not have known of my waking dream. Unless she had the power to see the images men cast on the screens of their most private sexual narratives, as I have always suspected of women. To think of another woman while making love to one's own wife—some law exists, somewhere in Judaism, prohibiting such fancies. Even into so obscure a corner of human awareness, Judaism casts its light. I had read it. In Talmud. In *Zohar*. Somewhere—

Rebecca trembled, then shuddered.

Stop thinking, I scolded myself. *Don't you see? It doesn't matter. Right now, Rebecca alone matters.* I rolled her to me. Now it was I who held her—I, on my back, Rebecca curled against me, her face nestled into my chest. The enveloping warmth of her flesh, the sweet scent of her body, her large eyes reaching up to me—I saw her naked as never before. Stripped naked by her sorrow. I beheld her: Rebecca, my own liquid shadow, taking the shape of whatever mood I brought to our door. My own personal *Shekhinah*, all mysteries of the female encased within her, a being exiled for my sake, one who had followed me into the exile of my own *Bemidbar*, my own wilderness that Rebecca had braved, retrieving me from it, then as now, again and again. As I now, for the first time, retrieved her. I caressed her face. She smiled and brightened. I drew her more tightly against myself. As she now, more tightly, embraced me. As Jacob and Debbie had embraced each other. To begin their new journey together. But not to end it.

Eventually, from the soft rise and fall of her chest, I knew that she slept. I lay awake, trying to make sense of everything, chastising myself for trying to make sense of any of it at all. I silenced the yawn trying to fight its way out of me. I did not want to awaken Rebecca. I lay there, her head upon the crook of my arm. In a matter of hours, our front room would begin to fill for services.

How many would come? Two or twenty? We never knew. Rebecca prepared the *Kiddush* platters anyway. And I prepared my talk. What was it this week? *Be-Shalach.* The portion containing God's parting of the waters for the people of the Exodus to pass through. After the pillar of cloud containing God's Presence separates pursuer from pursued. After God has enforced the tenth plague, the deaths of the first born. Except in Jewish homes whose doorposts are marked by blood spread by a plant called hyssop. Long after Aaron's rod has turned into a snake then changed back again. Right before the Nile turns to blood. Then back again. Lay that sequence before any rationalist from any century, and he or she will point you to the nearest mental hospital. But it is there. The unreal, the unexplainable, permeating the real, the rational, in Judaism.

My mind swarmed, as it often does in those hours of wakefulness before I have to get up. But not as it usually swarmed, with details of what challenges had to be faced for the day, which ones might prove gargantuan, whether I would confront them adequately. This time I felt it being torn apart then reassembled then torn apart once more as if it were a toy with which the natural and supra-natural forces of the Judaic universe were playing. I tried to avoid the hidden presences that nipped at me as I flailed through my jungle of perplexities. They pounced out of nowhere—four-faced angels, wheel-shaped angels, pages of a Psalms book whirred by unseen fingers, the feel of an otherworldly black bag, a pulsing Ladder of *Sephirot*, Azazel-who-is-the-Angel-of-Death-who-is Leviathan cut open on a banquet table in the Seventh Heaven, Devorah's World of Confusion in that kitchen chair, Devorah's Pangs of the Grave, the Throne she cannot yet see, the feast she cannot yet eat, Shemhazai telling her so, denying her, not now, not yet, as her ultimate unity with Jacob is not for now, not yet, but someday, as the permanent unity of God with His *Shekhinah* is not for now, not yet, not until we have finished our job of unifying down here. Someday.

Our bed faced the sole window of our back room. It looked out onto the sea of concrete that ran behind the strip mall. I watched as the first fingers of dawn wove their way into the darkness. I welcomed the light. Yet I was also sorry to see the night go. There came that special moment when the darkness released itself to the day. As, later, the day would give way to night. Twice in the span of 24 hours, night and day embrace each other. They go their own way before joining once more in the moments of dawn, of twilight.

Both moments hold magic. Both instruct us, if we listen. Both matter.

GLOSSARY

Adam Kadmon – the "first man", a blueprint for Creation. The Kabbalists picture the ten *Sephirotic* spheres (see below) as embedded throughout this figure.

Amorites – one of the Canaanite tribes from whom the Promised Land was wrested by the Jewish people. The Amorites are often described as particularly crude in their manners and practices.

Asmodeus – a demon of Jewish legend; depicted variously, from spoiling humankind with lustful impulses to aiding the forces of good when properly yoked.

Azazel – either a remote place to which the "scapegoat" Yom Kippur sacrifice of Biblical times was sent or an entity meant to receive this goat. Azazel is treated more as a personage in the *Pseudepigrapha* (see below) and the *Zohar* (see below); often described as a Seraph (see below).

Chesed – among the highest of the 10 *Sephirot* (see below); literally, translates to "kindness". It balances *Gevurah* (see below) in the flow of God's emanations from the hidden world of His essence to *Malchut* (our world, see below).

Chitzonim – literally, "outsiders". Often depicted in Kabbalah as inhabiting a dark mirror world that is an antithesis to the brightness of good; theirs is a world glutted with *Kelipot* (see below) and characterized by willful separation from all that is Godly.

Gehenna – in Talmud and Jewish legend, a place of punishment for the wicked in the afterlife. Some traditions characterize *Gehenna* as a temporary realm, similar to purgatory, where the soul undergoes a process of repentance and is cleansed of sins committed on Earth before moving on.

Gerushin – a term of Jewish meditation; the separating of one's mind from distracting thoughts through visualization of a word, an image, etc.

Gevurah – among the highest of the 10 *Sephirot* (see below); literally, translates to "severity". Though intended to balance *Chesed*, it is pointed out in the writings of many Kabbalists that an excess of *Gevurah* led to the destruction of worlds God had created before this one and continues, in its excess, to be a negative force in ongoing Creation.

Kabbalah – literally translated, "receiving". It is not one book but an umbrella term to include many works of Jewish mysticism.

Kelipah/Kelipot – to the Kabbalists, these are negative husks, created not only from the time of the original Creation but on an ongoing basis, as a result of each individual's negative actions. They are often described as shells that litter our world. *Kelipah* is the singular form.

Lilith – one of the "superstars" of Kabbalah, about whom legends abound. In early Kabbalistic literature, she is depicted as Adam's first wife, who left Adam when she refused to submit to his dominance; in other legends, she spawns Creation's first demons. Among Jewish feminists Lilith has been championed as the first liberated female within the patriarchal world of traditional Judaism.

Malchut – the lowest of the 10 *Sephirotic* spheres (see below), it is our world, the *Sephirah* where God's creative force enters the active realm of humanity, where we are challenged daily to decide, in our thoughts and actions, between pursuing a path of right or the ways of the *Chitzonim* (see above). *Malchut* is often characterized as female in manifestation, the abode of the *Shekhinah* (see below), who compassionately follows the Jewish people in their exile.

Mitzvah/Mitzvot – 613 (248 positive, 365 proscriptive) statutes and directives looked upon within traditional Judaism as Divinely communicated patterns of behavior. *Mitzvah* is the singular form.

Naamah – in the *Zohar* and other Kabbalistic writings, a descendant of Cain, sister of Tubal-Cain, and mother of Asmodeus (see above). Of exceeding beauty, she is often depicted as "teaming" with Lilith to seduce men and breed demons. Separately, also the name of Noah's wife.

Nephilim – first mentioned in Genesis 6, these are giants, the half-human, half-divine offspring of the union of fallen angels and earthly females.

Og – the last of the primordial giants.

Pseudepigrapha – written (it is thought) in the centuries before and after the beginning of the Common Era, these books were presented as "authored" by such prominent figures in the Bible as Moses, Abraham, Enoch, and others.

Sephirah/Sephirot – often visualized in Kabbalah as spheres, these are the ten emanations of God's attributes as they flow down from the highest *Sephirah* (*Keter*, Crown, the dwelling place of God's *Ein Sof*, His Hidden Essence) to the lowest (*Malchut*, see above). *Sephirah* is the singular form, *Sephirotic* the adjective.

Seraphim – among the highest of God's angelic host; often depicted as having six wings. Seraph is the singular form.

Shekhinah – many legends exist throughout Kabbalah, the most common of which is that the *Shekhinah* is the manifestation of God's divine energy in Creation, more specifically in *Malchut* (see above). This manifestation is often characterized as female, with God's Hidden Presence as male.

Shemhazai – one of the two leaders of the fallen angels, as mentioned in the *Book of Enoch* and other Kabbalistic texts; often described as a Seraph (see above).

Sheol – Originally, a subterranean domain to which all human souls, evil or good, went upon death. Later myths viewed *Sheol* as more like *Gehenna* (see above) as a realm for the wicked. The Hebrew Bible mentions *Sheol* but says little about it. In much of Jewish faith, the existence of an afterlife is acknowledged but not emphasized; one's behavior and deeds on Earth take priority.

Tikkun Olam – "repairing the world" by restoring the fallen shards of Creation to God through prayer and *Mitzvot* (see above). The concept has evolved to include all ethical behavior and social actions as contributing to the healing of an imperfect world and returning it to its original state of perfection.

Tohu – the primal "chaos" from which God shaped the unorganized matter of existence into the order of Creation. The term first appears linked with *Bohu* in the second verse of Genesis' first chapter.

Torah – commonly translated as "instruction" or "teaching"; the first five books of the Bible (Genesis, Exodus, Leviticus, Numbers, Deuteronomy); embraced by traditional Judaism as having come from the Divine hand of God, thereby becoming, from the time of the giving of the Ten Commandments at Mt. Sinai until today, the most vital element in Jewish faith among those who look upon Torah as containing the directly revealed wisdom, teachings, and laws of God.

Tree of Life – another visualization of the *Sephirot* (see above). Here, the 10 spheres are spread as upon a tree and/or connected by 22 interlinking paths.

Watchers – according to Kabbalistic legend, the 200 archangels who accompanied Shemhazai and Azazel (see above) to the newly formed Earth. Their purpose, to watch over humankind and report to God, was derailed by their attraction to human females.

Yesod – one of the ten *Sephirotic* spheres (see above). On *Adam Kadmon* (see above), it appears in the area of the genitals; in Kabbalistic thought, the "flow" of God's attributes exits "male" *Yesod* and enters "female" *Malchut*, bringing about the actual act of Creation.

Zohar – a multi-volume foundation text of Jewish mysticism. Its date of authorship, possibly the second or thirteenth century, remains a mystery.

ACKNOWLEDGMENTS

Richard Bank's knowledge, from a writer's perspective, of the realities of the publishing field has proven invaluable to me. He possesses a gift of being able to "tell it like it is" while offering guidance and encouragement that are never false. Rich's initial feedback on *Shemhazai's Game* set me on the right course for shaping the manuscript for Auctus Publishing to read. He has, in short, been a godsend. He never lets me express my gratitude for all his aid. So let me break your rule once more, Rich. Thank you.

My dear wife Thuong Ringel has drawn on her talents, her instincts, and her considerable intelligence to help me move forward in *Shemhazai's Game*. The tenacity with which she went about exploring options for the cover design often led me simply to sit back and admire her efforts. She was always by my side as *Shemhazai's Game* progressed towards publication. She has always been just that—by my side, in our 30 years-plus of marriage. I cherish her.

How fortunate I have been to know and to learn from Rabbi Shaya Deitsch of Pennsylvania's Lubavitch of Montgomery County! He opened my awareness to possibilities within *Shemhazai's Game*—not only its Judaism, but its secular aspects as well. He suggested additional sources for me to check. He saw possible avenues to readership that I had not envisioned. Rabbi Deitsch helped *Shemhazai's Game* ascend to a higher level of quality. I am honored that he has lent his name to this manuscript.

Copy editor Alexa Flood not only proofread the manuscript; she enhanced its readability. Page after page, I was impressed by the level of attention she poured into her efforts. She evaluated not just every line, but every word in every line. Her uncanny accuracy was matched by her sensitivity to my goals as the author. Through her edits, the power of the book was amplified. Thank you, Alexa!

Auctus publisher Dr. Shrikrishna (Krish) Singh is that rare individual in the field: a person of both genuine human warmth and professional expertise, one whose primary wish is to help an author find a publication platform from which his or her voice may be heard. Somehow Krish manages to balance his needs as a publisher with his desire to honor a manuscript's purpose. To say that I feel lucky to have found Krish Singh and Auctus would be a profound understatement indeed.

Thanks also to Sarah Eldridge for her creativity and commitment in designing the interior layout of the book as well as its cover. Her precision in readying the document for its emergence from the chrysalis of manuscript to the beauty of book form was special indeed. It was such an exciting moment for me to gaze upon the galleys she had prepared! Sarah has been an indispensable member of the *Shemhazai's Game* team.

Finally, special heartfelt thanks to my cousin Harry Sears. Harry has taught me what it is to rise above oneself; sometimes I think he is so far behind me when, in reality, he is so far ahead. Harry has given much to *Shemhazai's Game*. His courage and spirit permeate this novel.

www.ingramcontent.com/pod-product-compliance
Lightning Source LLC
Chambersburg PA
CBHW071233080526
44587CB00013BA/1589